STAN MUSIAL

Edited by Bill Nowlin and Glen Sparks

Associate editors Len Levin and Carl Riechers

Society for American Baseball Research, Inc.
Phoenix, AZ

Stan Musial
Edited by Bill Nowlin and Glen Sparks
Associate editors Len Levin and Carl Riechers

Cover and interior design: Gilly Rosenthol

Front and cover photographs are from: SABR/The Rucker Archive.
Unless otherwise noted, all photographs are from SABR/The Rucker Archive.

978-1-960819-47-5 (paperback)
978-1-960819-46-8 (ebook)
Library of Congress Control Number: 2025908659

Copyright © 2025 Society for American Baseball Research, Inc.
All rights reserved. Reproduction in whole or in part without permission is prohibited.

Cronkite School at ASU
555 N. Central Ave. #416
Phoenix, AZ 85004
Phone: (602) 496-1460
Web: www.sabr.org
Facebook: Society for American Baseball Research
Twitter/X: @SABR

STAN MUSIAL

CONTENTS

7 ..... Stan Musial
BY JAN FINKEL

19 ..... Stan Musial, Pitcher
BY BILL PRUDEN

24 ..... Musial Picks Up the Nickname "Stan the Man"
BY RICK ZUCKER

27 ..... Stan Musial MVP Years (1943, 1946, 1948)
BY JEREMY GIBBS

32 ..... Musial and the World Series
BY PAUL HOFMANN

39 ..... Musial Arranged a Masterpiece in 1948
BY MIKE EISENBATH

43 ..... 1949: After His Greatest Season, The Man Faces Challenges
BY JOE SCHUSTER

46 ..... Stan Musial, Jackie Robinson, and the Strike Heard 'Round the League
BY NICK MALIAN

48 ..... Stan the Man and Trader Lane: How Musial Almost Ended Up in Philadelphia
BY VINCE GUERRIERI

51 ..... Examining Stan Musial's Batting: Consistently Uncoiling 'An Explosion of Power'
BY MIKE HUBER

53 ..... Of (A)symmetry and (In)consistency: Stan Musial's Home/Away Splits
BY CLEM HAMILTON

56 ..... Stan Musial, John F. Kennedy, and the President's Council on Physical Fitness
BY BILL PRUDEN

61 ..... Stan and St. Louis
BY DANNY SPEWAK

65 ..... Baseball, the Pope, and Politics: Stan Musial and Poland
BY JOSH CHETWYND

68 ..... Musial Breathes Joy into a Somber Night
BY MIKE EISENBATH

69 ..... When Heroes Become Friends
BY EVERETT "EV" COPE

SELECTED GAMES

74 ..... Stan Musial Debuts
BY JOE SCHUSTER

77 ..... Musial Enjoys One of His "Finest Days" in September 1941 Call-Up
BY RICHARD CUICCHI

79 ..... Stan Musial Smashes First Career Major League Home Run
BY ANDREW HECKROTH

82 ..... Stan Musial's First Career Multihomer Game
BY ANDREW HECKROTH

84 ..... Five Hits, the First Time for The Man
BY KEVIN LARKIN

86 ..... Musial Hits Two Home Runs, Has Five RBIs against Dodgers
BY GLEN SPARKS

89 ..... Musial's Four Hits Over the First Four Innings Help Cruising Cards Crush Braves
BY MARK S. STERNMAN

91 ..... Musial's Blast Helps Cardinals Level the Trolley Car Series at Two Games Each
BY KEN CARRANO

94 ..... Third Straight Four-Hit Game Raises Musial's Batting Average to .375
BY TOM SCHOTT

97 ..... Stan Musial Finds Motivation in Attaining 1,000-Hit Milestone
BY CHAD MOODY

100 .... Stan Musial Solidifies "The Man" Moniker with Second Five-Hit Game of Season
BY MIKE EISENBATH

102 .... Stan Musial Dominates the Dodgers Again as Cardinals Complete Sweep
BY ANDREW HECKROTH

104 .... Stan Musial Wows St. Louis Crowd with Home Run in All-Star Game
BY C. PAUL ROGERS III

107 .... Stan the Man Swings Five Times, Gets Five Hits
BY GLEN SPARKS

109 .... **Musial Drives in Both Cardinals' Runs and Ends Game with Throw to Plate**
BY RICK ZUCKER

111 ...... **Musial Hits for Cycle to Lead Cardinals Rout at Ebbets Field**
BY MIKE HUBER

113 ..... **Musial Slugs Two Homers on Final Day of Season but Just Misses Capturing NL Batting Crown**
BY MIKE HUBER

116 ..... **Musial Returns to Mound, Clinches Sixth Batting Title**
BY BILL PRUDEN

119 ..... **Stan Musial Sets Major-League Record with Five Home Runs in Doubleheader**
BY RUSSELL LAKE

123 .... **Stan Musial Powers Cardinals to Win Where He Was Known as "Stan the Man"**
BY ALAN COHEN

126 .... **Stan Musial Seals Milwaukee's First Baseball All-Star Celebration**
BY NELSON "CHIP" GREENE

129 .... **Musial's Perfect Opening Day**
BY DANNY SPEWAK

132 .... **Stan Musial's Eighth Career Grand Slam Not Good Enough**
BY BRUCE DUNCAN

134 .... **Musial Delivers in the Pinch for Number 3,000**
BY GREGORY H. WOLF

136 .... **Stan Musial Knocks in Seven Runs**
BY TOM HAWTHORN

138 .... **Musial Homers in Four Consecutive At-Bats vs. Mets**
BY PAUL HOFMANN

141 ..... **Stan Musial's Five Hits Highlight Day as Cardinals Defeat Giants**
BY ALAN COHEN

143 .... **New Grandfather Stan Musial Makes Home-Run History with Surging Cardinals**
BY ANDREW HARNER

146 .... **Musial Equals Ty Cobb; Spahn Takes an Early Shower**
BY JEFF FINDLEY

148 .... **Stan Musial Hits His Final Home Run**
BY CHRIS BETSCH

150 .... **Stan Musial's Final Game**
BY JOE SCHUSTER

153 .... **Contributors**

STAN MUSIAL

BY JAN FINKEL

How good was Stan Musial? He was good enough to take your breath away.

– Vin Scully[1]

Twenty-eight miles south of Pittsburgh, roughly along the Monongahela River (Western Pennsylvanians call it the Mon and the Mon Valley) lies the town of Donora. Donora and the surrounding communities were once a fairly thriving multi-ethnic area made up of Eastern Europeans, Slavs, Italians, and Blacks that turned out steel, zinc, and world-class athletes. The Great Depression and management chicanery took care of the steel industry. A thermal inversion brought about a deadly smog that finished off zinc. Because of the overall poverty of the area, many young people left before having children, athletic or otherwise.

It was glorious while it lasted, though. "Deacon Dan" Lee Towler went to nearby Washington and Jefferson College and then to the old Los Angeles Rams, where he led the National Football League in rushing in 1952 and finished in the top four three other times. All-American quarterback Arnold Galiffa piloted Red Blaik's undefeated 1948 and 1949 teams at Army, leading to election to the College Football Hall of Fame. Buddy Griffey didn't make it to the top, but his son (Ken) and grandson (Ken Jr.) did well. And Stan Musial stood out above them all.

According to Musial biographer James N. Giglio, Lukasz Musial, age 19, left "the [Polish] village of Mojstava in the province of Galicia, at that time part of Austria-Hungary"[2] in January 1910 on the *President Grant* out of Hamburg, landing at Ellis Island six days later. Claiming to be 5-feet-7 and 150 pounds, deemed much smaller by people who knew him, but physically strong, Lukasz went straight from New York to Donora, where he worked at a variety of unskilled jobs. Among other things, he was what was called a "machine helper" and a porter at the Public Hotel. Early on he met Mary Lancos, 14 years old and the daughter of Czech immigrants (who had a Hungarian surname) from the Austro-Hungarian Empire. One of 10 children, Mary, born in New York City, was close to 6 feet tall, big-boned, and although untrained, a good runner and probably athletic. Not unusual for the time and place, she had become a housekeeper when she was 8.

Mary and Lukasz married in Donora on April 14, 1913; he was almost 23, she 16. The marriage certificate said she was 21, suggesting that she hadn't received her parents' permission to marry, as was the law in Pennsylvania for people under 21. They had four daughters (Ida, Victoria, Helen, and Rose or Rosella as she is listed in the 1920 census) in six years, and then Stanislaw Franciszek (named by his father) came along on November 21, 1920. In addition, Lukasz gave the little fellow the nickname Stashu, which was quickly shortened to Stash, usually pronounced "Stush," as in "push." Once he entered public school, Stash's name was anglicized to Stanley (or Stan) Francis (or Frank). Family and Donora locals pronounced the family name "MU-shill" as opposed to "MU-si-al," as Stan came to be known. Edward John (presumably named by Mary) was born two years after Stan, completing the family.

Life in Donora, in the whole Mon Valley, was harsh in the two decades between world wars. Lukasz and most men had trouble finding steady work, and what they did find was tough, dangerous, and dirty. Making matters worse, Lukasz developed a drinking problem. Mary managed the home, looking for bargains of any kind, buying in bulk when possible, and mending and re-mending clothes until they were outgrown or finally unwearable. At the same time, she was a loving, nurturing mother who made "baseballs" out of whatever she could wrap an old sock around and encouraged and played catch with little Stashu, who was showing athletic ability at an early age.

Going through the public schools in Donora, taking the nonacademic curriculum, and by his own admission not studying much, Stan (a bit shy and with a slight stutter) was only an average student, although his constant winning smile and easy disposition made him popular with everyone. He excelled in wood shop, but he just wasn't interested in schoolwork. His passion was sports, starting with the skill in gymnastics that he had acquired from the almost obligatory training he and many boys had received from the Polish Falcons Society. In high school he was beginning to make a name for himself in basketball and baseball, playing not only on school teams but also on local clubs. A frequently told story in the Musial legend has it that the University of Pittsburgh, coached by the legendary Dr. Henry C. "Doc" Carlson, offered Stan a basketball scholarship. The story goes on that Lukasz tried to force his son, who wanted to play baseball professionally, to accept the scholarship. Only after tears and lamentations on Stan's part and Mary's dramatic intercession ("Lukasz," she reportedly said, "this is America, and he has the right not to go to college.") in true Hollywood fashion, did the stern father relent and give his son his blessing to pursue his dream.[3] There was no immediate happy ending, however, as father and son barely spoke for several years.[4]

Stan Musial broke the all-time hits records in the National League on May 19, 1962, at Dodger Stadium. Honus Wagner previously held the mark. Greeting Musial is a smiling Ernie Broglio, with Larry Jackson and trainer Bob Bauman.

It's a fine story, but it's more likely that Lukasz wasn't pleased with his son's playing basketball, baseball, or any sport. From his point of view, he was making a tremendous concession in allowing the boy to finish high school (Stan was the only one of the six Musial children to graduate from high school) before getting a "real" job in the steel mill or zinc works. Moreover, as Giglio has shown, Stan was already a professional ballplayer even before high-school play, having "signed a contract with the St. Louis Cardinals' Monessen ball club of the Class-D Penn[sylvania] State League on September 29, 1937, several months before the start of the … high school basketball and baseball seasons and about two months before his seventeenth birthday."[5]

The signing wasn't made public until the following February. In addition, while he promised considerable potential, Stan hadn't really shown what he could do on the basketball floor, so a scholarship probably wasn't yet in the offing. In any case, his having signed the contract would have rendered him ineligible to play basketball at Pitt or any other college.

At the same time, Stan's having signed the contract by no means ended the maneuvering, much or most of it on his part. In the first place, he had some misgivings about the Cardinals organization after Commissioner Kenesaw Mountain Landis, having found St. Louis general manager Branch Rickey's machinations (among other byzantine activities, owning more than one ballclub in the same minor league) illegal, ordered the release and free agency of 74 players in St. Louis's farm system. Exacerbating the situation, Musial worked out with the Pirates and waited for what he thought would be a tryout with the Yankees. Then again, maybe he'd just stay home and pitch for the local zinc works team.[6]

The fiasco ended in the late spring of 1938 when Stan reported to the Williamson (West Virginia) Colts of the Class-D Mountain State League. He could have gone to the nearby Greensburg Green Sox of the Class-D Pennsylvania State Association but chose Williamson, for two likely reasons. First, Greensburg (the Monessen team ceased to exist after the 1937 season) was managed by Ollie Vanek, who had signed him and incurred the wrath of Mary Musial, who never failed to remind him that he hadn't given Stan enough money. Second, and perhaps even more important, Williamson was considerably farther from home in case he failed.

Musial's first season with Williamson didn't presage a brilliant career on the mound or at bat. As a pitcher he finished 6-6 with an ERA of 4.66 in 20 games. What stuck out, and not well, were 114 hits, 80 walks, and 66 strikeouts in 110 innings. Things weren't much better at the plate, 16 hits in 62 at-bats for a .258 average, with 3 doubles, a homer, 7 strikeouts, and only 3 walks.[7] At 17 years old and nowhere near his full height or weight, Stan's being overmatched comes as no surprise.

Even though he was playing minor-league ball, Stan was also playing for Donora High. Donora's coach was Michael "Ki" Duda, a man wise enough to know what he didn't know, and that was baseball. Duda brought in Charles "Chuck" Schmidt, himself just a few years out of high school but a fine shortstop in local leagues, to help coach the team. Musial and Schmidt remained friends until Schmidt's death.

Musial, said Schmidt, "was a born natural." "Even then," he told interviewer Gregory Ryhal, "you could tell he was going to be one of the greats." Asked what made Musial so good, he answered simply, "God."[8] Perhaps, but Musial deserves some of the credit, too. Curt Flood, a teammate late in Musial's career, describes a man who worked to develop and sharpen his inherent talents: "Musial also helped – mainly by working as hard as he did on his own perfect swing. If this immortal felt the need for frequent extra practice, how could I hope to prosper on less effort?"[9] The picture that emerges – one not often seen by the public – is of a Musial with raw, bleeding hands, the result of time spent in the batting cage honing his "natural" or "God-given" abilities.

Not all of Stan's time was taken up with sports. He was playing good basketball in the winter and pitching well in the spring and summer, helping to lead his teams to regional championships, not to mention dazzling everyone at the Ping-Pong table and on the dance floor. Not surprisingly, someone had caught his attention. In her last year at Donora High, only a few weeks older but a year ahead of Stan in school, was a petite brunette named Lillian Susan Labash. She was of Russian ancestry (with a touch of Czech), one of eight children, and called "Shrimp" by her family; her father, Sam, had a grocery store where Stan worked occasionally and could grab a quick bite. She was also stunningly beautiful.

Some things had changed when Stan returned to Williamson in 1939. No longer the Colts, the Williamson team was now the Red Birds and part of the Cardinals organization. Too, Stan was a year older, maturing nicely, and possessing more confidence. With a better team behind him, he improved to 9-2 in 13 games, 12 of them starts, but some signs again suggested he might not have a great future as a pitcher. The 4.30 ERA in 92 innings was tempered by his surrendering 71 hits; while his 86 strikeouts looked good, his 85 walks did not. He was now playing the outfield when he wasn't pitching, and his .352 batting average (25-for-71) was almost 100 points better than his 1938 performance. He showed some extra-base power with 3 doubles and 3 triples but again hit just one home run. Two red flags emerged from the numbers: 16 strikeouts and just one walk. The young man had a lot to learn.

Now 19, Musial was eager for the 1940 season to begin. Having graduated from high school, he'd be able to play a full season for the first time. It wouldn't be easy, as Giglio shows in his description of the circle of events that spring:

> The Albany ball club, which owned his contract and had optioned him to Williamson in 1939, now sold him to Asheville, North Carolina, of the Class B Piedmont League. Following spring training for Cardinal Class B and C clubs at Columbus, Georgia, Asheville optioned him to the Class D team in Daytona Beach, Florida.

His salary rose from seventy to one hundred dollars a month, but the demotion proved a disappointment to Musial, who, believing he could pitch at B level, felt that he was given no chance of making the Asheville club.[10]

Disappointment aside, 1940 was a pivotal year, and a blessing, for the young man came under the wing of one of the great benefactors of his life, Daytona Beach manager Dickey Kerr. As a rookie southpaw in 1919, Kerr had won two games for the White Sox in the World Series, no mean feat since three-quarters of his infield and two-thirds of his outfield had conspired to throw games as part of the infamous Black Sox scandal. Kerr, a small man, brought to managing the same backbone that had helped him in the Series, and combined it with insight, wisdom, patience, and compassion. He and Musial hit it off from the start.

Kerr and his wife, Cora, took such a shine to the young man that they stood up as witnesses when Stan and Lil were married in St. Paul's Roman Catholic Church in Daytona Beach on May 25, 1940. The young couple's son Richard (named after Kerr) was born within a year and was followed by sisters Geraldine (Gerry), Janet, and Jean.

Musial gave everything he had under the watchful eye of the fatherly Kerr and improved dramatically. He finished 18-5 with a 2.62 ERA in 223 innings with 19 complete games, but there were danger signs. Although he gave up only 179 hits while striking out 176, he also surrendered 145 walks and 43 unearned runs. Nevertheless, he was one of the top southpaws along with Frank Hudson (19-12, 2.91) of Sanford in the Florida State League. Because the team had only 14 men on the roster, Stan – and the other pitchers – would play in the field when he wasn't pitching. It was there that his talents really began to show. Hitting line drives all over the field, he batted .311 in 113 games, striking out just 28 times in 405 at-bats. Ten triples and 70 RBIs balanced out his meager 17 walks and single home run.

Everything came crashing down on August 11 in the second game of a doubleheader against Orlando. Playing center field, Musial went after a low, sinking line drive to left-center and attempted a somersault catch, something he'd been able to do from an early age due to his tumbling and gymnastics training. This time, though, his spikes caught, sending him shoulder-first to the ground. The pain and swelling in his shoulder were almost immediate, and it was soon determined that Musial was finished as a pitcher. Missing more than 20 games and trying to pitch only once, he played out the season as best he could, and finished what should have been a joyful year with a wife, impending fatherhood, and a dead arm.

Fortunately for all concerned, Kerr and Branch Rickey had seen the obvious: Stan Musial was not a pitcher, he was an outfielder. Because of the injury, his throwing arm would keep him from being a so-called "five-tool player" (he could certainly hit, hit for power, run, and field), but he compensated for the weakness by getting rid of the ball quickly and accurately.

Musial's stance was all his own, one he'd adopted because he believed it allowed him to cover the outside of the plate. Early in his career, teammate Harry Walker looked at him and said he'd never last in the majors with it. Hall of Fame pitcher Ted Lyons likened his plate appearance to a kid peeking around the corner to see if the cops were coming, a description that writers of the day took up with alacrity. Opposing pitchers thought he looked like a coiled rattlesnake. However Musial looked, he became a great hitter at age 21. Paul Warburton's description is spot-on:

> A lefty, he dug in with his left foot on the back line of the batter's box, and assumed a closed stance with his right foot about twelve inches in front of his left. He took three or four practice swings and followed up with a silly-looking hula wiggle to help him relax. He crouched, stirring his bat like a weapon in a low, slow-moving arc away from his body. As the pitcher let loose with his fling, "The Man" would quickly cock his bat in a steady position and twist his body away from the pitcher so that he was concentrating on his adversary's delivery out of the corner of his deadly keen eyes. He would then uncoil with an explosion of power. His line drives were bullets.[11]

The Musial the world came to know emerged in the 1941 season. His work under Kerr had won him a promotion to Springfield, Missouri, in the Class-C Western Association, where he was reunited with Ollie Vanek. Free from pitching and now a full-time outfielder, Musial proceeded to tear the Western Association apart with a league-leading .379 average, 27 doubles, 10 triples, a league-best 26 homers, 94 RBIs, and 100 runs scored in a mere 87 games. Promoted after a July 20 doubleheader to Rochester, New York, in the Double-A International League, he kept up the pace, hitting .326 with 3 homers and 21 RBIs in 54 games. Clearly ready for the big leagues, he made his debut with the Cardinals on September 17, getting his first hit, a double in the second game of a doubleheader sweep (6-1, 3-2) of the Boston Braves. In 12 games he hit .426, and nailed his first home run, a two-run shot off Pittsburgh's Rip Sewell at Forbes Field in the nightcap of a doubleheader on September 23. As a bonus he struck out just once in 47 at-bats. Despite Musial's contributions, the Cardinals came up 2½ games short of the pennant-winning Dodgers in a wild finish to a close race.

Given Musial's performance, it's difficult to understand why the Cardinals waited until mid-September to bring him up. Talking to Donald Honig for *Baseball When the Grass Was Real*, Johnny Mize provided a cynical explanation for the delay:

> In '41 [Enos] Slaughter collided with Terry Moore, and Slaughter broke his shoulder. Here we're fighting the Dodgers for a pennant. [Branch] Rickey said we didn't have anybody in the minor leagues to help us. Then in September he brings up Musial. Why didn't he bring Musial up earlier? That's what all the players wanted to know. We might have gone ahead and won the pennant.

I'll tell you what the talk used to be about Rickey: Stay in the pennant race until the last week of the season, and then get beat. I heard some talk to the effect that that was what he preferred. That way he drew the crowds all year, and then later on the players couldn't come in and ask for the big raise for winning the pennant and maybe the World Series. I don't know if it's true or not, but that was the talk.[12]

That Musial rose from Class C to the majors in one season is unusual. However, lending credence to Mize's reading of the situation is the fact that after the season Rickey traded him to the Giants, a move that some might see as an effort to weaken the Cardinals just enough to keep them out of the throne room in 1942.

Rickey's machinations backfired. Even without Mize, the 1942 Cardinals (with Johnny Hopp and Ray Sanders splitting first-base duties) were so good that they stormed the National League, winning 106 games to finish two games ahead of the Dodgers. They then polished off the Yankees, winners of 103 games themselves, in a five-game World Series that was considered an upset at the time. Musial made a solid impact with 10 homers, 72 RBIs (10th in the league), and a .315 average that was second to Slaughter's league-best .318.[13] He started the season in April batting second. By mid-May he was batting third. After shuffling around in the third through sixth spots in the lineup for about a month, Musial settled into the cleanup spot in late June, remaining there the rest of the season and through the World Series.

The Cardinals' confidence was well-placed. Stan's 32 doubles and 10 triples (third in the league) – the first of seven consecutive seasons he reached double figures in that department – showed that he got out of the box fast even with his unique peekaboo stance.

Musial didn't have a good Series against the Yankees, hitting just .222 with a double and a Series-best four walks. He was of no help in Game One, a 7-4 loss that the Cardinals almost pulled out with a furious rally in the bottom of the ninth, making the first and third outs of the inning. However, in the bottom of the eighth in Game Two, he drove in Enos Slaughter with the winning run after the Yankees had rallied from a 3-0 deficit to tie the game in the top of the inning.

With many stars gone to war in 1943, Musial established himself as the premier player in the National League if not the whole game. He led the league in hitting (.357), slugging (.562), on-base percentage (.425), doubles (48), triples (20), and various other categories in the first of a string of years amassing eye-popping statistics. Not surprisingly, Musial's performance on a pennant-winning team led to his first Most Valuable Player Award. Once again, though, he didn't fare well in the World Series, posting just a .278 average with no extra-base hits as the Yankees took the Cardinals in five games.

During the offseason, Musial took part in the war effort, working at the American Steel & Wire Co. back in Donora.

Stan Musial won seven batting titles and three MVP awards in his storied career with the St. Louis Cardinals.

In addition, he and several other players went on a goodwill trip to the Aleutians to visit the troops. (The War Department had canceled a scheduled trip to the Pacific in September of 1943.) No evidence suggests that Musial sought or received any special treatment concerning the draft. Being a father and coming from an area with many draft-age men probably kept him out of military service for most of the war.

For Musial and the Cardinals, the 1944 season was largely a repeat of the previous two. The Cardinals won 100 games for the third straight year, a feat previously achieved only by the 1929-1931 Athletics and duplicated by the 1969-1971 Orioles and 2002-2004 Yankees. Musial hit .347 and led the league in hits (197), doubles (51), on-base percentage (.440), and slugging (.549) while increasing his RBIs to 94 and walks to 90. Shortstop Marty Marion became the third consecutive Cardinal to be named Most Valuable Player, following Mort Cooper and Musial.

Meanwhile, the St. Louis Browns, perennial doormat of the American League and landlord of Sportsman's Park, which they shared with the Cardinals, sneaked past the many war-decimated teams to win their first (and last) pennant of the twentieth

This statue stands outside the Busch Stadium gift stop, along with statues of other Cardinal greats. Photograph by Glen Sparks.

century. Musial had his best Series as the Cardinals defeated the Browns in six games. He tied for the Series lead with seven hits that included two doubles and his only Series home run, while hitting .304. More important, he turned the Series around in Game Four after the Browns had surprisingly taken two of three games. His two-run homer over Sportsman's Park's right-field pavilion off Sig Jakucki in the first inning gave Harry Brecheen all the runs he needed in a complete-game 5-1 win.

Musial enlisted and entered the Navy on January 22, 1945, spending the next 13 or so months in the service. Luckily – a word he used frequently – he was able to spend most of his stint playing ball and never saw combat. Indeed, at Pearl Harbor he played in an eight-team league that was largely staffed with major leaguers. Accordingly, even though he missed the 1945 season, he didn't suffer the considerable loss of career numbers that older contemporaries – Hank Greenberg, Bob Feller, Johnny Mize, Joe DiMaggio, and Ted Williams, among others – experienced.

Assigned to Bainbridge, Maryland, for basic training, Musial got into a few games and played first base for the first time, not knowing it was to become his second position. Upon completion of basic training, he was sent to Shoemaker (California) Naval Base, a place he didn't like at all. Assigned to Special Services, he was shipped to Honolulu to serve with a ship repair unit in the 14th Naval District. As Thomas E. Allen explains, "His job was to run a liberty launch transporting men and officers from the dock out to the ships needing repair and back. He did this in the morning and played ball in the afternoons. He was named to the 14th Naval District's all-star team while playing for the ship repair unit team. Musial was still stationed in Hawaii when VJ Day occurred."[14] One aspect of Musial's wartime service had an impact on his later career: Because his fellow sailors wanted to see home runs, he made a slight adjustment to his stance that gave him more power. National League pitchers wished he had spent the war at home.

Later in the year Lukasz became gravely ill, and Musial's mother requested and received an emergency leave for Stan. Lukasz survived, but Musial remained in the States, having been transferred to the Philadelphia Navy Yard to work in another ship repair unit. He didn't repair any ships in Philadelphia, either, asking for and receiving a transfer when he was assigned to take apart a destroyer, a task for which he had no training or experience. Musial was honorably discharged on March 1, 1946, at Bainbridge, thus coming full circle.

Back from the service, his skills undiminished, Musial approached spring training in St. Petersburg in 1946 in his usual fine shape. Devoted to keeping in condition during the offseason, he had no trouble maintaining his weight, having started his career at 175 pounds and perhaps weighing in at 180 in his last seasons. Not everything was rosy, though. Slipping on some sandy soil that spring, he strained some ligaments in his left knee, causing a problem that would haunt him the rest of his career.

As the season progressed, it was becoming evident that rookie Dick Sisler wasn't developing as hoped at first base, prompting manager Eddie Dyer to ask Musial to move there temporarily from his left-field position. The move wasn't as temporary as originally thought, as Musial wound up playing more than a thousand games at first base, making him the first player to appear in at least a thousand games at two different positions. Warming to the position and being a first-rate athlete, he became a solid first baseman, almost as comfortable there as he was in the outfield.

Distractions abounded off the field, too. The reserve clause that eternally bound players to their team, combined with a lack of bargaining power and the absence of either a minimum wage or a retirement plan, led to discontent if not outright rage in the players, especially those who had sacrificed a large portion of their careers to the war effort. The prospects of change and unionization were in the air. So, too, was temptation from south of the border with the Mexican League, the brainchild of importer-exporter Jorge Pasquel and his five brothers. Musial took a cautious approach to the former and seriously considered the latter, which was sweetened by a $50,000 signing bonus. Fortunately, he stayed put, as the players who went south were punished to the tune of five-year suspensions.

Things went much better on the field. Showing National League pitchers that he'd lost nothing by being away, he led the league with a .365 average, a .587 slugging percentage, and 228 hits. Fifty doubles and 20 triples showed he was off and running from the batter's box and was still the Donora Greyhound. In addition, he topped the 100-RBIs plateau for the first of many times with 103. It all added up to his second Most Valuable Player Award and another pennant for the Cardinals, their fourth in the four full years he'd been with the club, a run equaled only by the Joe DiMaggio Yankees of 1936-1939. The Cardinals took the World Series from the Red Sox in a seven-game thriller, but the anticipated matchup between league MVPs Musial and Ted Williams didn't materialize as the two stars hit .222 and .200 respectively.

The legendary Red Barber described the 1947 season as the "year all hell broke loose in baseball." Barber, of course, was referring to the arrival of Jackie Robinson and the integration of the game. As hard as it is to understand the furor after many decades, the advent of Robinson was traumatic both in and out of baseball, certainly in St. Louis, as the Cardinals' enormous radio network that blanketed the whole South made them America's "Southern" team. St. Louis didn't have a monopoly on bigotry, but some players and fans were particularly virulent, and rumors have long since persisted of a possible player strike.

James Giglio notes that although Stan wasn't impressed with what he saw as Robinson's "short, choppy swing and his lack of grace in the field,"[15] he remained aloof from the ugliness and became supportive. He'd had Black teammates Buddy Griffey and Grant Gray back in Donora and had stood up for them in difficult times.[16] With two Most Valuable Player Awards under his belt, he was clearly the best player in the National League, making Robinson no threat to him. Indeed, Robinson himself mentioned Musial and Hank Greenberg as two of the players who had encouraged him during that terrible, courageous year.

For all kinds of reasons vitriol ran especially high between the Cardinals and Dodgers, with Robinson the catalyst or lightning rod. A potential flashpoint at which Musial and Robinson's careers intersected on a personal level came in the seventh inning of a game on August 20 in which Enos Slaughter (depending upon which of the myriad versions one believes) did or did not deliberately spike Robinson, who was playing first base that year.[17] Robinson was under orders from Branch Rickey not to retaliate or fight back, but he was seething when he got to first base later in the game. He growled to fellow first baseman Musial what he'd like to do to Slaughter, to which Musial quietly replied, "I don't blame you. You have every right to do so."[18] While Robinson was articulating but controlling his anger, Musial was saying that playing the game right trumped team loyalty. With nothing to show for it in the box score, the situation was a defining moment, showing two great players at their best.

All hell was breaking loose for Musial, too, so much so that he would refer to the season as "that lousy year." Starting slowly, he had a miserable April, hitting .146. Something was clearly wrong, the culprit turning out to be an inflamed appendix and tonsilitis diagnosed on May 9 by St. Louis physician and surgeon Robert F. Hyland, whom former Commissioner Landis had dubbed "the surgeon general of baseball." Hyland "froze"[19] Musial's appendix, a procedure that allowed him to finish out the year before having his appendix and tonsils removed during the offseason.

Stan took five days off before returning to the field, but his recovery was slow. He was down to .139 on May 19 after a streak of 24 hitless at-bats. He didn't reach .200 until mid-June and didn't get to .300 until he recorded five hits in an August 10 doubleheader. Finally starting to hit, Musial finished at .312 (his lowest average since his first full year) with 19 homers and 95 RBIs. His on-base percentage of .398 and slugging percentage of .504 were good but not up to the standard he had set. The tear that got Musial to .312 included a five-hit game in an 11-1 win over the Cubs on September 3. Given Musial's final numbers, it's hard to work up much sympathy for his "lousy" year.

At the same time, having won four pennants and three World Series in five years, the Cardinals were beginning a barely perceptible decline, finishing in second place five games behind the energized Dodgers and remaining in the bridesmaid's position through 1948 and 1949 before falling all the way to fifth in 1950 (albeit with a 78-75 mark). Few would have predicted it at the time, but the Cardinals neither rebounded nor returned to the World Series during Musial's career.

His appendix and tonsils removed, unquestionably stronger than he'd been in a long time, and apparently feeling that his subpar 1947 season was better than most players' good ones (Joe DiMaggio won the American League MVP Award with almost identical numbers: .315-20-97), Musial held out, finally signing on March 4 for $31,000. Teammate and fellow holdout Harry Brecheen and the Cardinals agreed to a $16,500 package the next day. As it turned out, Musial and Brecheen were bargains, Brecheen finishing 20-7 with a league-leading 2.24 ERA and Musial putting together not only his greatest season but one of the greatest seasons anyone has ever had.

For openers, he more than doubled his highest home-run output, belting 39, one behind Ralph Kiner and Johnny Mize, who tied for the league lead. At that, he lost one and possibly two homers, one to a rainout, another on a strange play that Peter Golenbock quotes from Musial: "In '48 I came within one home run of the Triple Crown. I had one rained out, actually, and Red Schoendienst reminded me that I hit another ball in Shibe Park in Philadelphia that hit the speakers of the PA system above the fence, and [umpire] Frank Dascoli called it a two-base hit. Red said it should have been a home run, or else I'd have led the league in everything."[20] Had Musial received credit for a homer in either case, he would have achieved the Triple Crown with his career-best .376 average and 131 RBIs. In addition, he led the league in hits (230), total bases (429), doubles (46), triples (18), runs (135), on-base percentage (.450), and slugging (.702) – every significant batting category except home runs.

Few hitters since have so thoroughly dominated a major league. His dominance included four games in which he picked up five hits (April 30, May 19, June 22, and September 22), tying Ty Cobb's twentieth-century record for five-hit games in one season. For the havoc he raised in Ebbets Field that year, Dodgers fans christened him "Stan the Man," the name by which he'll always be known.[21] All he did was hit .522 with on-base and slugging percentages of .560 and 1.022 in Brooklyn and improved (.523/.632/1.114) in 1949. To the surprise of no one, he picked up his third Most Valuable Player Award. But his magnificent season wasn't enough to boost the Cardinals over the hump, as they came in second once again, a decisive 6½ games behind the Boston Braves, who were led by former Cardinals manager Billy Southworth.

Not every moment of the season was wonderful for Musial, however. The September 7 game in Pittsburgh was one such exception. In the top of the first, with Fritz Ostermueller on the mound, Red Schoendienst and Marty Marion reached base for the Cardinals. With the runners moving, Musial lined a 3-and-2 pitch to Pirates shortstop Stan Rojek for the first out. Rojek stepped on second to double up Schoendienst, then threw to first baseman Johnny Hopp, who nabbed Marion to complete the triple play. It was St. Louis' first and last gasp, as the Pirates won, 6-2.

The year ended on a sad note for the Musials. A thermal inversion at the zinc mill in October unleashed a smog over Donora that left people dropping in the street. Among the many affected was Lukasz Musial, who at 58 years old had been retired for four years, suffering from black lung disease and the effects of several strokes. He and Mary moved in with Stan and Lil in St. Louis to escape the deadly air, but it didn't help. Lukasz suffered a stroke on December 17, lapsed into a coma, and died on December 19.

For the next 10 years, 1949 to 1958, Musial was eerily consistent, putting together seasons that were essentially interchangeable. His average season consisted of a .335 average, .426 on-base percentage, .582 slugging percentage, 189 hits, 38 doubles, 7 triples, 29 home runs, 104 runs, and 105 RBIs. Not surprisingly, he led the league in all these categories except homers at least once. As would be expected, he always placed high in voting for the Most Valuable Player Award. (Bill James has pointed out – before the emergence of Barry Bonds – that Musial garnered more shares than any other player in Most Valuable Player voting.)[22]

During these years there were many remarkable days and at least one rib-tickler. On September 28, 1952, Musial took the mound for the only time in his major-league career and faced off against Frank Baumholtz of the Cubs, who was comfortably second to Musial in the batting race. Baumholtz, a lefty hitter, switched to the right side and reached base on an error. A gracious Musial maintained that it was as clean a hit as he ever saw. Baumholtz was the only batter Musial faced that day, or any other day in the majors – but his one mound appearance is in the books.

Musial's greatest single day on the diamond came on May 2, 1954, in a doubleheader in St. Louis against the eventual pennant and World Series winners, the New York Giants. He went 4-for-4 in the first game with three homers, including the game-winner, a three-run shot off Jim Hearn, and 2-for-4 in the second game (a Cardinals loss) with two more homers. Coincidentally, witnessing the five homers was an eight-year-old named Nate Colbert, who as a San Diego Padre would match Stan's record of five home runs in a doubleheader, in Atlanta on August 1, 1972.

The All-Star Game was a showcase for The Man, who played in 24 of them. The 1955 game in Milwaukee's County Stadium was particularly sweet. The National League had fallen behind, 4-0, when he was inserted in the fourth inning. The deficit reached 5-0 before Musial's mates rallied to send the game into extra innings. Finally, in the 12th inning, Stan took the Red Sox' Frank Sullivan deep to win the game, 6-5. It was his fourth of a record six homers in All-Star Game play.

Not only was Musial stellar, but he was durable, playing in his 823rd consecutive game on June 12, 1957, breaking Gus Suhr's National League record. The streak ended at 895 on August 22, when he tore a muscle and chipped a bone swinging at a pitch in the fifth inning of a 6-5 win in Pittsburgh.

On May 13, 1958, he pinch-hit a double off Moe Drabowsky in Wrigley Field to become the eighth player (and the first since Paul Waner on June 19, 1942) to reach the 3,000-hit mark. The milestone hit helped the Cardinals to a 5-3 win. It seemed appropriate, too, that number 3,000 was a double, since in the eyes of more than a few fans the image of Musial is a line-drive double off the wall.

After 17 years terrorizing National League pitchers, the decline came quickly and suddenly for Musial. His batting average fell all the way to .255 in 1959, and he bettered it to .275 and .288 in 1960 and 1961. He had a brief resurgence in 1962 with marks of .330-19-82 but fell back to .255 as he finished his brilliant career in 1963.

Despite the low numbers, Musial had some good moments in 1963. On September 10, after waiting up all night with Lil for the birth of their first grandchild, he homered in his first at-bat to become the first grandfather to homer in the majors. On September 25, Cardinals owner August Busch Jr. named Musial a vice president of the team and announced that his number 6 would be retired. He bowed out on September 29 with two hits against Cincinnati, the first a single in the fourth inning past a rookie second baseman named Pete Rose and the second a ground-ball single off 23-game winner Jim Maloney to drive in his last run before leaving for a pinch-runner.

Musial's career numbers are stunning: .331 average, .417 on-base percentage, .559 slugging percentage, 3,630 hits, 725 doubles, 177 triples, 475 homers, 1,949 runs, and 1,951 RBIs. He's the only player to finish his career in the top 25 in all these categories and owns or did own a slew of records and achievements. Several stand out. For example, he had 1,815 hits at home and 1,815 on the road, a feat that must have required years of planning. He hit .336 at home, .326 on the road, a barely significant difference. Of his 475 home runs, 252 came at home, with 223 away, in a total of 12 ballparks. He hit 318 homers off right-handers, 157 off southpaws, a high number that dispels any notion that he may have had problems with lefties. Indeed, his favorite victim was Warren Spahn (whose career coincided almost exactly with Musial's), 17 of whose pitches he helped leave the ballpark. It all gives the impression that Musial didn't care who was pitching or where he was hitting: He just hit. Even though he never led the league in homers, his 12 game-ending home runs are equaled (through 2024) only by Babe Ruth, Jimmie Foxx, Mickey Mantle, Frank Robinson, and Albert Pujols – and topped only by Jim Thome's 13.

The triple – that rarest and most exciting of all hits – was something of a subspecialty for Musial. He holds several National League records for triples: most with the bases loaded (7, Shano Collins has the American League record with 8); most seasons leading his league in triples (5); and is tied with many other National League players for twice unloading 20 triples in a season (he's also the last, having done so in 1943 and 1946).

Musial received the ultimate reward for his magnificent career on January 21, 1969, with election to the Hall of Fame on the first ballot. Named on 93.2 percent of the ballots (317 of 340), he was the first player to receive 300 votes on a Hall of Fame ballot. One can only wonder what 23 presumably knowledgeable writers were thinking.

Musial held a position in the Cardinals' front office for a few years. He was named general manager on January 23, 1967, but resigned in less than a year, on December 5. He's the only general manager of a team that won the World Series in his sole year on the job. One gets the impression that he was never comfortable in management, his having more than once remarked, "I have a darn good job, but please don't ask me what I do."[23]

The Musial family visits the Polo Grounds in 1962. Left to right are Stan's daughters Gerry and Janet, his mother Mary, daughter Jean, and wife Lil.

It was said of Ty Cobb when he retired that he left the game with more money and fewer friends than anyone before him. The line on Musial was that he left with more money and more friends than anyone before him. His friends weren't just any friends, either. Having been somewhat active in Democratic politics at state and local levels through his friendship with activist and businessman Julius "Biggie" Garangani, he became acquainted with President John F. Kennedy, who presented Musial with a PT-109 pin, prompting The Man afterward to refer to the president as "my buddy." Although they didn't see each other often, the two men seem to have been genuinely friendly. Lyndon B. Johnson, having succeeded Kennedy, on February 26, 1964, named Musial his physical fitness adviser, an appropriate choice since Musial had always kept himself fit during and after his playing days.

Moreover, having been advised well and making many connections in the St. Louis area, Musial became active in business. His interests were diversified, but his primary focuses were on real estate and Stan and Biggie's, the steak and seafood restaurant he and Garangani owned. In essence, Garangani ran the business while Stan made himself available to the patrons. Longtime friends, the two were involved in several other restaurants and the Ivanhoe Hotel in Miami Beach. Among other ventures, Musial owned a bowling alley with Joe Garagiola, called the Redbird Lanes.

In addition, Musial stayed in the public eye, going to major sports events like the Kentucky Derby and the Indianapolis 500 while maintaining his connection with the game that made him famous. He went to spring training to work with Cardinals hitters and promote goodwill talking to fans and signing autographs. He even joined the Society for American Baseball Research (SABR), in which he must have been the only member to list his expertise as "Hitting a Baseball!" Anyone who's seen Stan's ever-present smile and laughing eyes knows it's his private little joke. Besides, it happens to be true.

As a general thing (to quote Missourian Huck Finn), the years treated the Musials well. As would anyone in his financial position, Stan was involved in numerous deals and investments, most of which worked out nicely. There were the inevitable health problems. Lil spent much of her time confined to a wheelchair, the result of heart trouble and arthritis. Stan suffered through a gastric ulcer (1983) and prostate cancer (1989) but recovered completely. He walked with a limp, though, owing to the removal of ligaments in his left knee. He made it to Cooperstown for most Hall of Fame inductions, serving for many years on the Veterans Committee, always smiling, and entertaining all with his harmonica.

Well into their 80s, Stan and Lil lived comfortably, reconnecting with Donora while enjoying their extended family in the city where he achieved fame and the adulation of baseball fans everywhere. The honors kept coming. In a correction of one of the great blunders in baseball history, he belatedly made the Mastercard All-Century Team in 1999.[24] More significantly, he received the Presidential Medal of Freedom from Barack Obama in 2011.

Lillian Musial died in St, Louis on May 3, 2012, survived by four children, 11 grandchildren, and 12 great-grandchildren. She and Stan had been married for almost 72 years. A funeral Mass celebrating her life was held in the Cathedral Basilica of St. Louis on May 7.

Ravaged by Alzheimer's and under hospice care, Stan Musial died in St. Louis on January 19, 2013, and lies with his beloved Lil in a private family crypt close to the Mausoleum at the Bellerive Heritage Gardens in Creve Coeur, part of Greater St. Louis.

The statue of Stan outside Busch Stadium reminds all who go to Cardinals games that he was "the perfect warrior ... the perfect knight."

ACKNOWLEDGMENTS

Special thanks to Mark Armour, who toiled as my first editor, and to Bill Nowlin, who steered me through this updated version. Glen Sparks provided a superb late edit. Carl Riechers did a spectacular job of fact-checking. Len Levin's final edit was, as usual, masterful. Their wisdom, kindness, and gentle prodding made this a better piece. It's been a joy having their company along the way.

Jonathan Finkel found Derrick Gould's article that explains the procedure of freezing Musial's appendix.

As always, Judy is my best reader, my best editor, my best friend.

Thank you, all.

SOURCES

In addition to the sources cited in the Notes, the author also consulted the Stan Musial files at the National Baseball Hall of Fame and Museum in Cooperstown, New York.

Bearce, Stephanie. *Stan Musial: From Donora, PA, to St. Louis, MO and the Big Leagues.* (St. Louis: Reedy Press, LLC, 2016).

Benson, John. "Stan Musial–1948," John Benson and Tony Blangino, eds., *Baseball's Top 100: The Best Individual Seasons of All Time* (Wilton, Connecticut: Diamond Library, 1995).

Broeg, Bob. "The Mystery of Stan Musial," *Saturday Evening Post*, August 28, 1954.

Bullock, Steve. "The Statistical Impact of World War II on Position Players," in *The National Pastime: A Review of Baseball History*, 23 (2003), 97-105.

Burns, Bob. "On the Field or Off, Stan Musial Is Everybody's Favorite," *Catholic Boy*, May 1963.

Burnes, Robert L. "Story Infuriates Musial," *St. Louis Globe-Democrat*, July 14, 1980.

Cobb, Ty, with Joe Reichler. "Here's Why Musial Tops 'Em All!," *Baseball Stars*, 1953.

Crichton, Kyle. "Ace in the Hole," *Collier's*, September 13, 1947.

Flood, Curt, with Richard Carter. *The Way It Is* (New York: Pocket Books, 1971).

Huard, Kevin. "Stan 'The Man' Musial," *Sports Collectors Digest*, March 15, 1991.

Johnson, Lloyd, and Miles Wolff, eds. *The Encyclopedia of Minor League Baseball.* 2nd ed. (Durham, North Carolina: Baseball America, Inc., 1997).

Kahn, Roger. "The Man: Stan Musial Is Baseball's No. 1 Citizen," *Sport*, February 1958.

Lansche, Jerry. *Stan the Man Musial: Born to Be a Ballplayer* (Dallas: Taylor Publishing Company, 1994).

Mead, William B. "The Surgeon General of Baseball," in *The National Pastime: A Review of Baseball History.* 22 (2002), 95-98.

Miles, Jack. "Milestones in Sports: Stan the Man," *Catholic Boy*, October 1967.

Musial, Lillian (Mrs. Stan). "My Life with Stan," *Parade*, July 13, 1958.

Musial, Stan, as told to Bob Broeg. "The Man behind the Man," *Look*, April 21, 1964.

Musial, Stan, as told to Bob Broeg. *The Man Stan Musial: ... Then and Now* (St. Louis: Bethany Press: 1977).

Musial, Stan. *Stan Musial: "The Man's" Own Story as told to Bob Broeg* (Garden City, New York: Doubleday & Company, Inc., 1964).

Musial, Stan, Jack Buck, and Bob Broeg, *We Saw Stars* (St. Louis: Bethany Press, 1976).

Newman, Mark, and John Rawlings. "Man to Man," *The Sporting News*, July 28, 1997. (Conversation on the art and craft of hitting with Musial and Tony Gwynn).

O'Neil, Paul. "Sportsman of the Year For 1957 the Editors of *Sports Illustrated* Choose Stan Musial," *Sports Illustrated*, December 23, 1957.

Peary, Danny, ed. *We Played the Game: 65 Players Remember Baseball's Greatest Era, 1947-1964* (New York: Hyperion, 1994).

Reichler, Joe. "Stan Musial's Ten Greatest Days," *Sport,* October 1954.

Robinson, Ray. *Stan Musial: Baseball's Durable "Man"* (New York: G.P. Putnam's Sons, 1963).

Ryhal, Gregory. Interview with Charles "Chuck" Schmidt at Beverly Healthcare of Bloomington, Indiana, October 6, 2003.

Selter, Ron. "Sportsman's Park's Right-Field Pavilion and Screen," *The Baseball Research Journal*. 32 (2004), 77-80.

Stanton, Joseph. *Stan Musial: A Biography* (Westport, Connecticut, and London: Greenwood Press, 2007).

Stewart, Wayne. *Stan the Man: The Life and Times of Stan Musial* (Chicago: Triumph Books, 2010).

Stockton, J. Roy. "Rookie of the Year," *Saturday Evening Post*, September 12, 1942.

"That Man," *Time*, September 5, 1949.

Treder, Steve. "War Begone," *The Hardball Times* (www.hardballtimes.com). March 8, 2005. (Web article projecting season statistics for Musial and other World War II veterans and Willie Mays).

Vaughn, Gerald F., "Jorge Pasquel and the Evolution of the Mexican League," *The National Pastime: A Review of Baseball History*. 12 (1992), 9-13.

Vecsey, George. *Stan Musial: An American Life* (New York: ESPN Books, 2011).

Vincent, David, Lyle Spatz, and David W. Smith, *The Midsummer Classic: The Complete History of Baseball's All-Star Game* (Lincoln and London: University of Nebraska Press, 2001).

Weintraub, Robert. *The Victory Season: The End of World War II and the Birth of Baseball's Golden Age* (New York, Boston, and London: Little, Brown and Company, 2013). E-book edition, 2013.

NOTES

1   Paul Dickson, ed., *Baseball's Greatest Quotations: An Illustrated Treasury of Baseball Quotations and Historical Lore,* Rev. Ed. (New York: HarperCollins e-books), 390. From Dodger telecast from summer of 1989.

2   James N. Giglio, *Musial: From Stash to Stan the Man* (Columbia and London: University of Missouri Press, 2001), 4.

3   Giglio, 26-27.

4   Giglio, 27.

5   Giglio, 24-25.

6   Giglio, 27-28.

7   All statistics are from Baseball-Reference.com. Play-by-play game reports are from Retrosheet.org.

8   Interview with Charles "Chuck" Schmidt at Beverly Healthcare of Bloomington, Indiana, October 6, 2003.

9   Curt Flood with Richard Carter, *The Way It Is* (New York: Trident Press, 1971), 47.

10 Giglio, 34-35.

11 Paul Warburton, "Stan Musial's Spectacular 1948 Season," *Baseball Research Journal*. 30 (2001), 99-104.

12 Donald Honig, *A Donald Honig Reader* (New York, London, Toronto, Sydney, Tokyo: Simon & Schuster, Inc., 1988), 85.

13 Some sources list Boston's Ernie Lombardi with a .330 average as league leader, but he had only 309 at-bats.

14 Thomas E. Allen, *If They Hadn't Gone: How World War II Affected Major League Baseball* (Springfield: Southwest Missouri State University, 2004), 63-64.

15 Giglio, 151.

16 Giglio, 155.

17 Peter Golenbock, *The Spirit of St. Louis: A History of the Cardinals and Browns* (New York: Avon Books, 2000), 383-386.

18 Giglio, 157.

19 Derrick Gould, "Checkup: Stan Musial's 'Frozen' appendix [*sic*]," *St. Louis Post-Dispatch*, April 8, 2011.

20 Golenbock, 392. Schoendienst or Musial's memory may have been a bit off because no such play can be found in *The Sporting News, New York Times,* or Retrosheet.org.

21 As often happens with things mythical and legendary, the origins are cloaked in mystery. This seems to be the prevailing view, but St. Louis sportswriter Bob Broeg remembered Brooklyn fans conferring the epithet on Musial in June 1946 after he had ravaged the Dodgers with an 8-for-12 performance in a three-game series. In a similar vein, Hall of Famer Joe Morgan told ESPN viewers that the name had come from Chicago fans after Musial had beaten up on the Cubs. Morgan's is a minority view in that all other accounts give Brooklynites the honor. What is clear is that in baseball – as in the worlds of Homer, Virgil, King Arthur, Charlemagne, James Fenimore Cooper, and so on – honors, titles, and epithets are earned.

22 James, *Historical Abstract*, 379-380.

23 "They Said It," *Sports Illustrated*, June 20, 1988, 16.

24 Mastercard sponsored the selection of the All-Century Team as a popular vote. Unfortunately, many voters lacked sufficient knowledge of baseball history and elected several outstanding but lesser players over Honus Wagner, Lefty Grove, Warren Spahn, Christy Mathewson, and Stan Musial. Mastercard appointed a panel of baseball historians to correct the oversights.

STAN MUSIAL, PITCHER

BY BILL PRUDEN

Notwithstanding his ultimate status as one of the greatest hitters in major-league history, Stan Musial's early visions of a big-league career rested on his strong left arm. As he tried to persuade his father to allow him to sign with the St. Louis Cardinals, the young southpaw dreamed of translating the success he had enjoyed on the Donora, Pennsylvania, diamonds into a spot in a big-league rotation.

Like so many boys of that era, Musial played a full array of sports. In addition to baseball, he was a star on the Donora High School basketball team that won the sectional championship for the first time in school history.[1] Meanwhile, as a result of his father's prodding he was an active member of the Donora branch of the Polish Falcons, a club that offered training and competition in gymnastics and track and field. Musial would later look back with appreciation on the impactful "three body-building years [he] spent with the Falcons."[2] But his undeniable passion was baseball.

His early days in baseball were like that of countless kids scattered across the country. First introduced to the game when he was around 7 years old, he played in pickup games on makeshift fields with neighbors who in the beginning were usually older. For young Stan it did not matter, young or old, he just wanted to play, and he would wander from field to field looking for a game. But games were easier to find than quality equipment, and legend has it that Musial's mother would make baseballs for him by binding up a bunch of rags that were wetted down and then covered with tape. Similarly, real balls were kept in service by applying electrical tape after the stitches and cover had begun to split. And for the most part they originally came into play when one of the fleet-footed neighborhood kids snagged one that was hit over the fence at the local ballpark.[3]

While pickup games were his start, Musial's first real experience with organized baseball came with the Donora Zincs, a semipro entry in the local industrial league. One of Musial's neighbors, Joe Barbao Sr., was a semipro player and coach and after Stan waited for him to come home from work the older Barbao would play catch with the young Musial, while also teaching him about the game, from the basics to the fine points.[4] Eventually Barbao, who coached and pitched for the Zincs, made Stan the team's batboy. And it was there, in the words of one author, that the "legend of Musial [began] on August 4, 1936, when Barbao asked the slender boy, in a scene that could have been lifted from a modern sports movie, if he wanted to work mop-up duty after his team was trailing badly."[5]

An episode intended to offer some fun to the dutiful batboy instead became a revelation as the "man among boys" left an indelible impression.[6] While there are conflicting reports of exactly how well he did – one says he went six innings and struck out 13, while another says he recorded 12 outs, five of which were strikeouts – there was no denying that he opened a lot of eyes.[7] Indeed, observers quickly realized that, although he weighed only 140 pounds, the 5-foot-4-inch Musial could "throw BBs through a brick wall."[8] Ironically, his Zincs debut cost Barbao his job as manager at least briefly, for as impressive as Musial had been, the use of a nondues-paying member of the Donora Zinc Works A.A. angered some team members.[9] Ultimately however, the team was won over by the youngster's performance and he would pitch again, before the season was over, losing his first outing 7-5 when the Zincs made four errors but defeating the league-leading Fairhope team 2-1 with 11 strikeouts in a game not long before he joined the Cardinals farm team.[10]

Musial had only a single year of high-school baseball, playing on a team that in 1938 brought the game back to Donora High School after a 15-year hiatus.[11] Though the team was essentially created around Musial and as a way to showcase his skill, his career was cut short when he headed off to the Cardinals' farm system, thus becoming ineligible to return and play as a senior. But the one year he had was memorable, offering a preview of what was to be. Musial pitched, played the outfield, and batted cleanup. While he later recalled, "I didn't like to pitch, because I could always hit, but in high school if you have the best arm, they always make you the pitcher," he was the undisputed ace for a strong arm he did have.[12] As his coach, likely with a bit of hyperbole, observed, "The trouble with [Musial] as a schoolboy pitcher was that we couldn't find anyone who could catch him. He might strike out 18 men, but half of them would get to first on dropped first [sic] strikes."[13] On a Donora squad that went 9-3, Musial finished 4-2 with both losses coming as a result of major defensive lapses. Indeed, in one loss he struck out 14 batters, but three defensive misplays cost the team the game.[14]

Musial kicked off the revival of the school's baseball program with an impressive performance, giving up just three hits while striking out 17 in seven innings in a 3-1 Opening Day victory.[15] Just days later he followed that up with another stellar effort, striking out 14 and giving up just two hits in a 22-3 victory.[16] Reflective of Musial's status was his performance in the team's first loss of the season, one in which Musial appeared in relief with no outs in the third inning after the opposing Charleroi Cougars had already scored three runs in the frame. While he gave up only a single hit the rest of the way, the Dragons could not get their offense on track, falling 5-1.[17] For all of his pitching prowess, his hitting did not go unnoticed. Indeed, a grand slam that salvaged a late April win as well as a 3-for-3 performance that saved a subpar pitching effort were no less a part of his highlight reel than the pitching efforts that were capped by his season-ending win over Monongahela in which he gave up only two hits while striking out 12. And he walked only two.[18]

At season's end, Musial was selected to the All-Star Section VI baseball team with the local paper reporting, "Stan Musial, all-around player and general utility man for a Dragon crew that amazed the valley with theoretical five game winning streak, won honors hands down as the league's outstanding player. His play in the pasture and on the mound were highlights of the season."[19] The article added that he was "easily the league's ace player, better termed a 'minor leaguer.'"[20] In the end, Musial's one season pitching for Donora High offered significant evidence of why professional organizations saw him as a pitching prospect.

Despite all this, years later, when he wrote his autobiography, Musial wrote that he did not recall "much of his one season high school career."[21] While he did remember the team's first game, and his school-record 17 strikeouts in the win over Monessen, his bigger memory involved a later game and a "tremendous home run [he] hit."[22] Playing against Monongahela City, coming to the plate with the bases loaded and Donora trailing in the late innings, Musial stroked a low ball that hit the fence 450 feet away on one bounce.[23] In a comment that said much about the circuitous route Musial took to big-league stardom, he later wrote, "In spite of that famous clout, I was signed to a professional contract not as a hitter, but as a pitcher."[24]

Given the nature of baseball at the time, it was the combination of his efforts with Donora High, the Zincs, and in American Legion ball that put him on the radar of the local scouts beginning in 1937. The early scouting reports touted his strong arm but noted that like many left-handers Musial had trouble harnessing that strength and struggled with his control. The earliest Cardinals scouting report, submitted in June 1937 by scout A.J. French, said he had a "good" arm, "good" fielding skills, and was "fast" with a "good curve ball." He was termed a "green kid," and a future prospect. It was a positive enough report that after a few visits and watching him play during the summer, the team offered him a contract.[25] For Musial it was a dream come true and while he was contacted by other teams, including the Indians and Yankees, the direct and early contact by the Cardinals won him over.[26]

The bigger challenge was persuading his father to allow the 17-year-old pitcher-outfielder to sign. Ultimately, after an internal family battle in which his mother's advocacy won out over his father's hope that he would go to college or get a "real job," permission was granted for the 17-year-old Musial to sign with the Cardinals which, as was the practice of the time, did not file the contract with the commissioner's office until the following spring, allowing Musial to play a season for the revived Donora High program.[27] Ironically, it was an approach that almost backfired, for when the local high-school athletic association learned of the contract there was debate over whether Musial could still play, the June effective date notwithstanding. Musial's absence from the early days of practice while the matter was being settled led to some resentment among some of his teammates who felt he was "letting the school down."[28] However, his performance on the diamond, as well as his popularity among his peers, quickly rendered the issue moot.

Despite having a professional contract in hand, Musial spent a very active spring appearing in Zinc games in between the contests that comprised his only season of high-school baseball. But regardless of the venue, the young southpaw cemented his reputation as one of the area's star players, both on the mound and at the plate, and once school was done, the Cardinals sent Musial to one of their Class-D minor-league teams for the 1938 summer season.[29]

With his contract going into effect in time for the 1938 season, the organization initially wanted to send Musial to their farm club in Greensburg, Pennsylvania, only about an hour from Donora. But for reasons that are not clear – there is speculation that he did not want to be so close to home – the young pitcher successfully lobbied for a different assignment and was instead sent to the Cardinals' Williamson (West Virginia) team in the Class-D Mountain State League.[30] He did not wow anyone, finishing with a 6-6 record and an earned-run average of 4.66 in 110 innings, but it was a start. The wild left-hander walked 80 while striking out 66.[31] He did better with his bat, and looking back, he recalled not having any confidence in his pitching, but that his hitting was another story.[32]

Musial was again assigned to Williamson in 1939 but the familiarity of the venue did not result in any significantly greater success. Indeed, not only did he miss his high-school graduation (his longtime girlfriend and soon to be wife, Lil Labash, stood in for him and collected his diploma) but despite compiling a record of 9-2 while striking out 86, he also walked 85 in 92 innings, with an ERA of 4.30.[33] At the end of the season, the team's manager, Harrison Wickel, recommended that the Cardinals release him, noting "almost as an afterthought … that he was a nice young man who could hit – .352 with a home run."[34]

As the 1939 season came to a close, Lil, knowing that her boyfriend was not only struggling at his craft, but was far from home and making little money, wanted him to quit and get a full-time job.[35] Fortunately for Musial, Lil's father, Sam Labash, was in his future son-in-law's corner and with war on the horizon, urged Musial to give it one more shot and so, in the spring of 1940, Musial headed to Daytona Beach, Florida, a slight upgrade from his forays to Williamson.[36] There, accompanied by a noticeably pregnant Lil – the couple had secretly married on Musial's birthday, November 21, 1939 – he came under the tutelage of manager and former major-league pitcher Richard "Dickey" Kerr.[37] Kerr was something of a baseball legend for his role on the 1919 Chicago White Sox. A rookie and the number-three starter on the infamous Black Sox, Kerr won both the third and the sixth games while the core of the team was throwing the World Series.[38]

For Musial and his young pregnant wife, Dickie Kerr was a lifesaver. Not only did the manager offer the kind of support that the young player needed but Kerr and his wife took the young couple into their home, a kindness that was rewarded in August when the young couple named their first child Richard Stanley Musial in honor of their benefactor.[39] Kerr was no less a factor on the field.

Indeed, under Kerr's watchful and practiced eye, Musial made some major gains and finished the season with an 18-5 record and a sterling ERA of 2.62, although his control was little better as he walked 145 batters in 223 innings.[40]

Indeed, a close inspection made clear that it was a season of ups and downs, one that offered reasons for hope while also raising doubts about his long-term future on the mound. Perhaps no game better illustrated the roller coaster that was Musial's season than the team's 7-5 win over Orlando on June 3. Musial carried a no-hitter into the seventh when suddenly the team's defense, as well as his command, disappeared and while the team still secured the win, Musial's effort showed him at his best and worst.[41] Similarly, two weeks later he gave up eight walks, highlighted by a fifth-inning stretch in which he walked the bases loaded before giving up a two-run single, cementing a loss to the St. Augustine Saints.[42] And yet, at the end of July he boasted a 12-4 record that had propelled the team to the top of the standings.[43] And by the end of August, a preview of the league's all-star game tabbed him as the expected starter.[44]

At the same time that Musial was seeking to make his mark as a pitcher, the team's limited roster left manager Kerr little choice but to also use him in the outfield.[45] The split duty worked well for the young ballplayer until August 11, when in a game against Orlando, Musial, playing center field, "went after a low, sinking line drive to left center, and attempted a somersault catch, something he'd been able to do from an early age."[46] But unlike countless previous times, "his spikes caught, sending him shoulder-first to the ground."[47] The pain and swelling in his shoulder were almost immediate, and it was soon determined that Musial was finished as a pitcher. While he pitched through the pain, finishing what was, on paper, his best year ever, he had serious doubts about his baseball future.

As the season came to an end and he pondered his future after three seasons of minor-league ball, Musial saw a three-season record of 33-13 with an ERA of 3.52 in D-level ball. He had pitched 425 innings and had walked 310 batters.[48] Meanwhile, as just another body in the major leagues' largest minor-league system, he was unable to get any of the medical care that his shoulder needed or which might have helped. With Lil and the baby having headed back to Donora ahead of him, Musial began to talk of returning home to work in the mills.[49] But at the same time, Lil's father was telling him to stay with it, that he would take care of Lil and young Richard.[50] And Dickie Kerr was no less supportive or emphatic in his belief in Musial, telling the young ballplayer, "You won't make it to the top as a pitcher, but you'll get there some way because you are a damn fine ballplayer and a big-league hitter."[51] Little could Kerr, or anyone, have envisioned just how right he would be.

While Musial arrived at spring training in 1941, still listed as a pitcher, the effects of the previous season's injury remained along with the almost casual previous reports of his hitting prowess. When those reports were confirmed in the early going of spring training, the transition from Stan Musial the pitcher to Stan Musial the hitter was quickly completed. When camp broke, and after much discussion, Musial was sent to the Cardinals' Class-C club in Springfield, Missouri, to start what proved to be his final year in the minors. So well did the hitting "experiment" go – in 87 games he hit .379 – that in late July he was promoted to the Rochester Red Wings of the Double-A International League.[52] There he hit .326 in 54 games, leading the team into the playoffs.[53] Then, to his utter amazement, Musial was called up to the majors in September, walking into Sportsman's Park for the first time on September 17, 1941.[54] With his minor-league and pitching days behind him, his 12-game audition with the big-league St. Louis Cardinals, during which he hit .426, represented the start of a 22-season career that would ultimately see him recognized as one of the greatest hitters the game has ever known, while rendering his minor-league pitching exploits little more than soon-to-be-forgotten memories.[55]

But in fact, they were not forgotten by everybody, and no discussion of Musial's pitching career would be complete without at least a mention of the only time he took the mound in a major-league game. The historic moment took place on September 28, 1952, the last day of the season. While Musial was in hot pursuit of a sixth batting title, the Cardinals were stuck in third place, playing out the string of a disappointing season. In an effort to drum up a crowd for the finale of a disappointing season, the team decided to have Musial relive the early days of his professional career, turning the clock back to a time when it was thought that his left arm was the key to his making the big leagues.[56]

Hoping to further enhance the entertainment value of the event, the front office decided that Musial would pitch to the Cubs' Frank Baumholtz, who, when the plan was announced, was trailing Musial by only a point in the race for the batting crown. By the time game day arrived, Musial had widened the gap to 11 points. The lack of drama notwithstanding, the show went on.[57]

After the Cardinals starter, rookie left-hander Harvey Haddix, walked the Cubs' leadoff batter, shortstop Tommy Brown, Cardinals manager Eddie Stanky emerged from the dugout, walked toward Haddix, and called for Musial to take his place on the mound. Haddix took over in right, while right fielder Hal Rice shifted to center. As Musial took his warm-up pitches, an irritated Cubs manager Phil Cavarretta told Baumholtz that the Cardinals were trying to make a fool of him, but an unruffled Baumholtz told his manager, "I don't think so. I think it's just a gimmick to get a lot of people in the stands to watch two also-rans on the last day of the season."[58]

Meanwhile, on the mound, the 31-year old Musial, clearly anxious to complete the distasteful task, took fewer warm-up pitches than he was allowed as he prepared to face Baumholtz.

Indeed, years later he made clear that he had not been happy about the plan, thinking not only that it was nothing more than "contrived show," but no less importantly the ever-professional Musial did not want to be seen as showing up Baumholtz.[59] Much to his chagrin, those concerns had fallen on deaf ears.

But as he looked toward home plate, Musial found that the tables had been turned when the left-handed-hitting Baumholtz stepped into the right-handed batter's box to face his Cardinals nemesis. Later reports said that Baumholtz had decided to bat right-handed as a gesture of sportsmanship. He did not want "to try for a cheap hit" against the pseudo-pitcher; nor did he want "to get something for nothing."[60] Regardless of how either player felt, the whole spectacle was over in no time.

On the mound for the first time in over a decade, Musial threw a single pitch. He later said he "flipped the ball," while the *St. Louis Post Dispatch* called it a "fast ball."[61] Either way, Baumholtz hit "the ball squarely," but the potential double-play ball "bounced on a big hop" to third baseman Solly Hemus, who was unable to handle it and was charged with an error.[62]

And with that, Musial returned to center field, Rice to right, and Haddix to the mound, and the game continued. The Cubs ultimately won 3-0 while Musial won his sixth batting title.

The whole episode was an incongruous reminder that one of the greatest hitters of all time began his professional journey as a pitcher before he suffered one of the most fortuitous injuries in baseball history.

NOTES

1. Wayne Stewart, *Stan the Man: The Life and Times of Stan Musial* (Chicago: Triumph Books, 2010), 26.
2. Stan Musial and Bob Broeg, *Stan Musial: "The Man's" Own Story as Told to Bob Broeg* (Garden City, New York: Doubleday & Company, 1964), 11.
3. Stewart, 13-14.
4. Stewart, 27.
5. Stewart, 27.
6. Stewart, 27.
7. Musial and Broeg, 3; Stewart, 27; In his own autobiography Musial recalls his performance as six innings and 13 strikeouts.
8. Stewart, 28.
9. Musial and Broeg, 13.
10. Musial and Broeg 13; "Zincs Tumble Fairhope, 2-1," *Monongahela (Pennsylvania) Daily Republican*, May 26, 1938.
11. Stewart, 30.
12. Stewart, 32.
13. Stewart, 30.
14. Stewart, 32.
15. "Donora Tops Monessen in Loop Opener," *Monongahela Daily Republican*, April 14, 1938.
16. "Donora Routs Rostraver by 22-3 Decision," *Monongahela Daily Republican*, April 20, 1938.
17. "Cougars Hand Donora First Loop Loss, 5-1," *Monongahela Daily Republican*, April 23, 1938.
18. "Musial Halts Wildcats, 4-1 to Close Schoolboy Season," *Monongahela Daily Republican*, May 14, 1938.
19. "McGinty, Paver Are Named to All-Star Section VI Squad," *Monongahela Daily Republican*, May 16, 1938.
20. "McGinty, Paver Are Named to All-Star Section VI Squad."
21. Musial and Broeg, 14.
22. Musial and Broeg, 14-15.
23. Musial and Broeg, 14-15.
24. Musial and Broeg, 15.
25. Musial and Broeg, 15-16.
26. Musial and Broeg, 15-16.
27. Musial and Broeg, 20.
28. Phil Fair, "Speaking of Sports," *Monongahela Daily Republican*, March 24, 1938.
29. Musial and Broeg, 18; Stewart 29-30.
30. George Vecsey, *Stan Musial: An American Life* (New York: Ballantine Books, 2011), 70.
31. Vecsey, 71.
32. Vecsey, 71.
33. Vecsey, 71, says that Musial's record was 9-1, but Baseball-Reference reports it as 9-2. https://www.baseball-reference.com/register/player.fcgi?id=musial001sta.
34. Vecsey, 71.
35. Vecsey, 71.
36. Vecsey, 71.
37. Vecsey, 72.
38. Adrian Marcewicz, "Dickey Kerr," SABR BioProject; https://sabr.org/bioproj/person/dickey-kerr/.
39. Vecsey, 73.
40. "Stan Musial," Baseball Reference; https://www.baseball-reference.com/register/player.fcgi?id=musial001sta.
41. "Daytona Whips Orlando, 7-5, Nationals Getting But 3 Hits," *Orlando Sentinel*, June 4, 1940.
42. "Saints Drop Islands," *Orlando Evening Star*, June 16, 1940.
43. "Toenes to See Duty on Mound Part of Game," *Tampa Times*, August 30, 1940.
44. Danny Bickford, "Speaking of Sports," *Monongahela Daily Republican*, July 24, 1940.
45. Vecsey, 73.
46. Jan Finkel, "Stan Musial," SABR BioProject; https://sabr.org/bioproj/person/stan-musial/.
47. Finkel.
48. Stan Musial, Baseball Reference; https://www.baseball-reference.com/register/player.fcgi?id=musial001sta.
49. Vecsey, 73.
50. Vecsey, 73.
51. Vecsey, 73.
52. Vecsey, 81.
53. Vecsey, 82.
54. Musial and Broeg, 47.

55 Stan Musial, Baseball Reference; https://www.baseball-reference.com/register/player.fcgi?id=musial001sta.

56 Musial and Broeg, 153.

57 Tom Larwin, "September 20, 1952: Musial, Baumholtz Compete for National League Batting Title." Society for American Baseball Research Games Project. https://sabr.org/gamesproj/game/september-20-1952-musial-baumholtz-compete-for-national-league-batting-title/; "Attention, Now Pitching for the Cardinals – Stan Musial"; RetroSimba: Cardinals History Beyond the Box Score, September 20, 2022; https://retrosimba.com/2022/09/20/attention-now-pitching-for-the-cardinals-_-stan-musial/.

58 "Attention Now Pitching…"

59 "Attention Now Pitching…"; Musial and Broeg, 153.

60 "Attention Now Pitching…"

61 "Attention Now Pitching…"

62 "Attention Now Pitching…"

MUSIAL PICKS UP THE NICKNAME "STAN THE MAN"
SEPTEMBER 1946

BY RICK ZUCKER

Almost exactly five years after Stan Musial made his major-league debut, *St. Louis Post-Dispatch* sportswriter Bob Broeg wrote an article that forever transformed Musial into Stan the Man. Published on September 20, 1946, the article referred to comments made by Brooklyn Dodgers fans and heard by Broeg and St. Louis Cardinals traveling secretary Leo Ward during a series in Brooklyn the week before.[1] Brooklyn fans named Musial "The Man" in 1946, even before he reached his peak at Ebbets Field in 1948-49, when he creamed Dodgers pitching to the tune of an incredible .522 batting average and 1.067 slugging average.[2]

The Cardinals and Dodgers waged a battle for supremacy in the National League in the 1940s. The Dodgers nosed out the Cardinals in 1941, and the Cardinals returned the favor in 1942. After an interruption caused by World War II, the teams resumed their battle in 1946. Musial, who had spent the 1945 season in the US Navy, returned in 1946 and quickly asserted himself as the best player in the NL and a thorn in Brooklyn's side.

In eight games at Ebbets Field in 1946 prior to September, Musial hit .419 and slugged .548 to help the Cardinals win five of the games. As St. Louis headed into Brooklyn for the final scheduled series of the season, on September 12-14, the Cardinals held a slim 1½-game lead over the second-place Dodgers.

On Thursday, September 12, a crowd of 32,643 showed up at Ebbets Field to see the Dodgers' Kirby Higbe oppose Cardinals hurler Howard Pollet.[3] Higbe got two quick outs in the top of the first, but Musial, batting third, doubled off the right-field wall. This was followed by a walk to Enos Slaughter, Whitey Kurowski's infield hit, Dick Sisler's line single to right that drove in two runs, and a three-run homer by rookie Joe Garagiola, staking the Cardinals to a 5-0 lead.

The Dodgers got two runs back in the second, but after Musial led off the third with an unsuccessful attempt to bunt for a hit, the Cardinals scored a run and knocked Higbe out of the game. Musial popped out to shortstop in the fourth and walloped a second double to right field in the seventh. The score remained 6-2 into the eighth, when the Cardinals put the game away with four more runs. Musial drove in one of them with a single to right for his third hit of the game, and scored another on a hit by Kurowski. The Cardinals won 10-2. Musial was 3-for-5 with two doubles, two runs scored, and an RBI.

With the Dodgers falling to 2½ back, only 22,549 (21,935 paid) came to see game two of the series on Friday the 13th. Brooklyn sent southpaw Joe Hatten to the mound to oppose the Cardinals' Red Munger. The crowd saw the Dodgers turn the tables on the Cardinals. After St. Louis went down in order in the top of the first, the Dodgers scored four times, knocking out Munger after two-thirds of an inning. With the Dodgers ahead 4-0, Cardinals relievers Alpha Brazle, Ted Wilks, and Ken Burkhart held Brooklyn scoreless for the next 7⅓ innings as the Dodgers clung desperately to their lead. The Cardinals scored a run in the fourth but should have scored more. Musial tripled off the right-field scoreboard to lead off the inning. He was thrown out at the plate on Slaughter's short fly ball to center field when he mistakenly thought third-base coach Mike Gonzales was saying, "Go, go, go!" instead of "No, no, no!"

Terry Moore doubled with one out in the fifth. The nervous Brooklyn fans swallowed hard as they saw Musial advancing to the plate. He already had four hits in the first 13 innings of the series, including two doubles and a triple. Musial drove Moore home with yet another double to right field to make the score 4-2. It was still 4-2 as the Cardinals came to bat in the seventh. Musial led off the inning by belting a long drive to left field that was caught by Dick Whitman. By the ninth inning the Dodgers' lead was down to one run at 4-3. With one out, Moore drew a walk to put the tying run on base. Who was coming to the plate, batting .369 and holding a lock on the NL MVP? It was Musial again. The fans held their collective breath as Musial launched one to deep right-center. They breathed a sigh of relief as Dixie Walker hauled it in. Higbe, a goat the day before, came on in relief in the seventh inning and finished the game. On Saturday, September 14, Musial turned in an ordinary 1-for-4 as the Dodgers shut out the Cardinals, 5-0, to pull within one-half game of St. Louis.

After the Cardinals-Dodgers series, Broeg asked Leo Ward what the Dodgers fans were saying when Musial came to the plate. Broeg thought he heard, "Here comes that man." But Ward corrected him, indicating that the fans were uttering with trepidation, "Here comes the man."[4] On September 20, 1946, precisely five years and three days after Musial's debut, Broeg wrote an article in the *Post-Dispatch* lauding Musial for leading the Cardinals to a 5-4 win over the Braves one day earlier. Musial had contributed five hits to the cause, including two doubles. Broeg started the article by crediting Dodgers fans with bestowing a new nickname on Musial:

"It took the baseball-batty borough of Brooklyn … to supply with begrudging respect the best nickname yet bestowed upon

Stanley Frank Musial. To Brooklyn's fanatical baseball followers, Musial is simply 'The Man.'

In the recent series at Flatbush ... the appearance at the plate of the Cardinals' apple-cheeked first baseman frequently brought from several sections of the Ebbets Field stands a distinct: 'O-O-h, here comes The Man, again.'

Not that man, but THE man. And the nickname so aptly applied to a self-effacing player ... summarized the around-the-league regard for Musial, unquestionably THE man in the Redbirds' race to the wire against the Dodgers."[5]

And there it was. But would it catch on? The *Brooklyn Daily Eagle* ran Broeg's article in its sports section the same day. But in the battle for newspaper supremacy in St. Louis among the *Post-Dispatch*, its archrival the *Globe-Democrat,* and the *Star-Times*, would the other papers adopt the nickname that Broeg proposed? On September 21, the *Post-Dispatch* repeated Broeg's nickname, stating, "When it comes to naming the Cards' most valuable player, it should not be hard to name 'The Man.'"[6]

At the same time, Joe Trimble of the *New York Daily News* was trying to hang a different moniker on Musial. Three times between September 16 and 21, Trimble referred to him as "Musial the Menace."[7] It didn't catch on.

Back in St. Louis, on September 27, Sid Keener of the *St. Louis Star-Times* wrote a column with a section heading that read "Musial's The Man." However, rather than refer to Musial as "The Man" in the article, Keener twice referred to him as "Mr. Base-Hit," another moniker that didn't stick.[8] On September 29 Broeg wrote a feature article on Musial that included the following: "Now, however, The Man, as Brooklyn's rabid followers respectfully nicknamed Musial, expects to be with the Cardinals for years."[9] On September 30 the *Star-Times,* referring to Musial as 'Stanley Frank Musial, The Man among men," began to bow to the inevitable.[10]

But how did the nickname go from "The Man" to "Stan the Man?" Broeg had a simple explanation. Noting that admiring Brooklyn fans had dubbed Musial "The Man," Broeg stated "You didn't have to be a brain scientist to make it "Stan the Man.""[11]

In October *The Sporting News* reported, "They're now calling Stan Musial, 1946 National League batting champion, The Man."[12] After the Cardinals were crowned World Series champions, the nickname followed Musial into the barnstorming season. In late October the Kansas City Royals, an African American team featuring Satchel Paige, faced off against the Bobby Feller All-Stars, a team promoted as including "Stan (The Man) Musial."[13] On November 22 Musial was named the NL's Most Valuable Player. The *Post-Dispatch* announcement included a drawing of Musial by *Post-Dispatch* artist Amadee Wohlschlaeger, captioned "Stan The Man Musial."[14] The *Star-Times* also appeared to be on board, referring to the new MVP as "Stanley Frank Musial, The Man."[15]

By December it was official. Referring to contract talks between Musial and Cardinals President Sam Breadon, the

Stan the Man remains a legend in St. Louis and throughout Cardinal nation. Photograph by Glen Sparks.

Star-Times referred to the player as "Stan (The Man) Musial.'"[16] However, the *Globe-Democrat* and its main baseball writer, Robert L. Burnes, declined to give its rival the satisfaction of using the new nickname. The *Star-Times* was willing to adopt "The Man" because it denied that Broeg had popularized the moniker. Instead, Keener offered general attribution for the nickname. He asserted that "Press Box wise-crackers around the National League circuit tabbed our Stanley Musial 'The Man' after watching the Cardinals' all-star performer in action last season."[17]

Despite Burnes's denial and Keener's guile, the record should show that "Stan the Man" was originated by Dodgers fans and popularized by Bob Broeg.

SOURCES

Thanks to Bob Tiemann for his helpful insight.

In addition to the sources cited in the Notes, the author also consulted Baseball-reference.com.

NOTES

1. Bob Broeg, "Musial (The Man) Gives Boston Fans an Eyeful; Birds Play Cubs Next," *St. Louis Post-Dispatch,* September 20, 1946: 2E.

2. Bob Broeg and Jerry Vickery, *St. Louis Cardinals Encyclopedia* (Lincolnwood, Illinois: Contemporary Books, 1998), 260; Robert L. Tiemann, "At the Top of His Game – Stan Musial at Ebbets Field – 1948 & 1949," presented at a Bob Broeg St. Louis SABR Chapter Meeting, May 16, 2022.

3. The paid attendance was 31,303.

4. James N. Giglio, *Musial – From Stash to Stan the Man* (Columbia: University of Missouri Press, 2001), 136-37.

5. Bob Broeg, "Musial (The Man) Gives Boston Fans an Eyeful; Birds Play Cubs Next."

6. "Wray's Column – 'From Greenland's Icy Mountains,' Etc.," *St. Louis Post-Dispatch,*" September 21, 1946: 6.

7. Joe Trimble, "Cardinals Sweep Giants, 3-0, 7-4; Increase Lead," *New York Daily News,* September 16, 1946: C17; Joe Trimble, "Cards Win in Ninth, 5-4, on Musial's 5th Hit," *New York Daily News,* September 20, 1946: 71, 74; Joe Trimble, "Slats OK for Cub Series; Card Flag Hopes Buoyed," *New York Daily News,* September 21, 1946: C17.

8. Sid Keener, untitled column, *St. Louis Star-Times,* September 27, 1946: 24.

9. Bob Broeg, "Musial No Big Silent Hero," *St. Louis Post-Dispatch,* September 29, 1946: 1H.

10. W. Vernon Tietjen, "Pollet or Dickson to Open Here Tomorrow; Year's Top Crowd Sees Cubs Tame Birds," *St. Louis Star-Times,* September 30, 1946: 20.

11. Bob Broeg and Jerry Vickery, *St. Louis Cardinals Encyclopedia,* 260.

12. Fred Lieb, "Stan Musial, National League batting Champion," *The Sporting News,* October 9, 1946: 25.

13. "Feller All-Stars to Play Kansas City Nine Tonight," *Bakersfield Californian,* October 23, 1946: 15. Paige's team was sometimes dubbed the Monarchs, but in California newspaper advertisements was listed as the Royals.

14. "Our Man Stan," *St. Louis Post-Dispatch,* November 22, 1946: 2E.

15. W. Vernon Tietjen, "Cards' First Basemen Polls 319 Votes in Winning Award for Second Time in 4 Years," *St. Louis Star-Times,* November 22, 1946: 24.

16. Franz Wippold, "Musial and Breadon Confer, Reach No Agreement for 1947," *St. Louis Star-Times,* December 19, 1946: 28.

17. Sid Keener, untitled column, *St. Louis Star-Times,* December 20, 1946: 24.

STAN MUSIAL MVP YEARS (1943, 1946, 1948)

BY JEREMY GIBBS

Year	G	PA	AB	H	HR	RBI	SB	BB	BA	OBP	SLG	OPS	OPS+
1943	157	701	617	220	13	81	9	72	.357	.425	.562	.988	177
1946	156	702	624	228	16	103	7	73	.365	.434	.587	1.021	183
1948	155	698	611	230	39	131	7	79	.376	.450	.702	1.152	200

Vote Points	1st Place	Share%	WAR
267	13	79%	9.5
319	22	95%	9.3
303	18	90%	11.3

St. Louis Cardinals vs. Brooklyn Dodgers (1940 - 1949)

Year	Cards Wins	Cards Losses	Ties	Winning Percentage
1940	13	9	1	.591
1941	11	11	1	.500
1942	13	9		.591
1943	15	7		.682
1944	18	4		.818
1945	13	9		.591
1946	16	8		.667
1947	11	11	1	.500
1948	10	12		.455
1949	12	10	2	.545
Total	132	90	5	.595

INTRODUCTION

Stan Musial is undeniably one of the greatest baseball players of all time. With 24 All-Star appearances, just one behind Hank Aaron for the most ever, and three MVP awards – while finishing in the top 10 a record 14 times – Musial's legacy is noteworthy.

In his great book *The Baseball 100*, Joe Posnanski ranked Musial ninth. His accomplishments speak for themselves. Yet, for many he has gone unnoticed.

> "Stan Musial didn't hit in 56 straight games," says Musial's friend Bob Costas, who began his broadcasting career with KMOX in St. Louis. "He didn't hit .400 for a season. He didn't get 4,000 hits. He didn't hit 500 home runs. He didn't hit a home run in his last at-bat, just a single. He didn't marry Marilyn Monroe; he married his high school sweetheart. His excellence was a quiet excellence."[1]

This article will examine the three seasons in which Musial won the MVP (1943, 1946, 1948), putting his accomplishments in historical perspective.

–1943–

During his rookie season (1942), Stan Musial made just $4,500. Knowing that center fielder Terry Moore and right fielder Enos Slaughter would be serving in the armed forces during the war, Stan Musial asked team owner Sam Breadon for a raise. He hoped

Musial batted .365 in 1946 and won his second NL MVP award.

to make $10,000, but was disappointed when Breadon offered only $5,500. Breadon voiced his disapproval this way: "You will have no more to do this year than you had last year. I thought you were the kind of ballplayer that gave all you had in every ball game. Of course, we expect the same in 1943, if you sign a contract with us."[2]

Musial signed a contract to stay with the Cardinals in 1943. And although he did not make $10,000, he gave Breadon no reason to deny this same request in 1944.

Musial's 1943 season did not start as well as he would have liked. In his first 10 games, he had just 11 hits in 40 at-bats (.275) with no home runs and just 2 RBIs. This was likely due to the new baseballs that were being used at the start of this season. Because of the war, rubber was scarce. As a result, A.G. Spalding & Brothers used reprocessed rubber for its baseballs – the infamous balata ball.[3] With the perceived decrease in runs scored per game, National League President Ford Frick allowed teams to start using the 1942 baseballs again or order some if they did not have any on hand, while American League President Will Harrage chose to keep the balata ball throughout the season.[4]

The result of these decisions is that the American League scored 400 fewer runs than in 1942 (5,211 vs. 4,795), seeing a decrease in runs per game by over one-third of a run per game (4.26 – 3.89 = 0.37 runs/game), while the National League saw its total runs scored increase from 4,784 to 4,892, an average of 0.04 runs per game. Musial's hitting improved after the ball was changed.

From May 10 until the end of the season, Musial hit .362/.427/.570. He finished the season with a 177 OPS+, which ranks 11th among all major-league players in the 1940s.

During the 1940s, the Cardinals and Dodgers built an intense rivalry. Each team fought for the pennant, with the Cardinals finishing atop the standings four times and the Dodgers taking the top spot three times. This competition set the stage for some of the most exciting and memorable moments in baseball history.

In August 1942 Dodgers President Larry MacPhail visited the clubhouse after a Dodgers 1-0 win over the Phillies and said, "I'm telling you boys, the Cardinals are going to beat you if you're not careful. You guys are getting lackadaisical, you think you have it clinched, and before you know it, they are going to beat you out."[5]

The Cardinals did just that, clinching the pennant on the final day of the season en route to their World Series championship over the Yankees. That set the stage for the 1943 pennant race.

At the end of May, the Cardinals were 22-13 (.629) – 1½ games behind the Dodgers.

In June the Cardinals had a decent record of 15-11, but it didn't translate into progress in the standings – they stayed 1½ games behind the Dodgers. Musial's performance was also lackluster during this period; he batted .278 with a .333 OBP, which was relatively pedestrian by his standards. Despite the team's solid play, the Cardinals couldn't close the gap on the Dodgers.

Reminiscent of 1942, when they finished 68-21 in the final three months, the Cardinals really started rolling in July. They were an impressive 24-7 (.774) pushing them a full 10½ games ahead of the Dodgers, who were a miserable 10-19 (.345), virtually ending the pennant race. It is no surprise that Musial excelled during this month. He slashed an impressive .374/.423/.557, racking up 49 hits in a single month.

One of the best games of his 1943 season took place on July 21. After going 0-for-4 in the first game of a doubleheader, Musial came alive in the second game. Going 5-for-6 with two singles, two doubles, and a triple, knocking in 4 runs, and even picking up a stolen base. The Giants used five pitchers in the game and Musial got a hit off four of them, not getting a chance to face Harry Feldman. who faced only three batters.

On July 13 Musial made his first All-Star Game appearance, batting third and starting in left field. He finished the game 1-for-4 with one RBI.

For the season, Musial played 157 games, leading all of major-league baseball with 701 plate appearances (four more than Tommy Holmes and Dick Wakefield), 220 hits (20 more than Dick Wakefield), 48 doubles (7 more than Billy Herman and Vince DiMaggio), 20 triples (6 more than Lou Klein, and 128 RBIs (10 more than Rudy York), while leading the National

League in batting average, batting .357 (27 points better than Herman), OBP (.425), and slugging (.562).

The only two categories of note in which Musial did not lead the league were home runs (13 vs. 29 for Bill Nicholson) and stolen bases (9 vs. 20 for Arky Vaughn). In every sense of the word, Musial was the most valuable player, carrying the Cardinals to their second consecutive pennant. Yet he was also a relatively fresh face, having come from Class D to make the majors just three years earlier. Thus, he received only 13 of the 24 first-place votes while his teammate Walker Cooper finished second with 5 first-place votes. (Walker's brother, Cardinals pitcher Mort Cooper, won the NL MVP Award in 1942.)

GAMES VS. DODGERS

Playing against his biggest rival seemed to bring out the best in Musial. In 22 games, Musial hit an impressive .373 (31-for-83) with a .480 on-base percentage. He scored 17 times while knocking in 13 runs. His numbers against the Dodgers were better than his overall season stats (.357/.425/.562).

The Cardinals finished 15-7 against the Dodgers.

Best Game

Musial's best game of the season took place on August 15, the first game of a doubleheader. Conveniently, this was against the Dodgers. Musial hit two home runs, producing five RBIs. He finished with three hits for the day with three runs.

–1946–

After spending 1945 in the Navy – where he often played baseball to the delight of his fellow servicemen – Musial returned to action for the 1946 season. He quickly found his groove again. In the 13 April games, he went hitless only twice, notching 20 hits with a slash line of .370/.404/.574, along with one home run and 11 RBIs.

Musial's performance improved even more in May, when he slashed .323/.411/.473, hitting one home run and driving in 15 runs. By June he was on fire, posting a slash line of .388/.437/.629, hitting 4 home runs and racking up 24 RBIs.

In July, Musial maintained his stellar form with a .359/.432/.556 slash line, hitting 3 home runs and adding 19 RBIs in 30 games. August was even more remarkable: He slashed .403/.493/.656 with 3 home runs and 15 RBIs. By September, Musial continued to shine, hitting .344/.400/.600, adding 4 home runs and 19 RBIs.

It was during this impressive stretch that Musial earned the nickname The Man. This came about after Dodgers fans, tired of watching Musial tear up their pitching, started saying, "Here comes the man again" each time he came to bat. *St. Louis Post-Dispatch* columnist Bob Broeg later included this nickname parenthetically in his September 20, 1946, column. Musial's performance was so outstanding that when he knocked out five hits in five at-bats at Ebbets Field, even the opposing fans had to acknowledge his greatness.

Musial led the league in games played (156), plate appearances (702), at-bats (624), runs (124), hits (228), doubles (50), triples (20), batting average (.365), slugging percentage (.587), and OPS (1.152).

He received 22 out of 24 first-place votes and 319 of the 336 (95 percent) maximum points he could have received. The two votes he did not receive were given to Musial's teammate, Enos Slaughter, likely because he led the league with 130 RBIs.

GAMES VS. DODGERS

The Cardinals played the Dodgers 24 games in 1946. (They finished the season tied and swept Brooklyn in a best-of-three playoff.) Musial played in all 24 of those games and produced unfathomable results. He hit .418, racking up 41 hits in 98 at-bats, which included 17 extra-base hits and a .714 slugging percentage. He also had 13 walks in those games, resulting in an unbelievable .491 OBP. All these numbers are better than his league totals (.365/.434/.587). He produced these numbers against a team that finished just two games behind the Cardinals in the standings.

BEST GAME

Musial's best game of the season took place on July 15 against the Dodgers. He went 4-for-5 with a triple and a home run and knocked in two runs while scoring once.

–1948–

Only eight games were played in April 1948. Even though Musial did not get a hit in two of them and was batting only .250 after six games, he still managed to end the month with a slash line of .400/.447/.800 with 2 home runs and 12 RBIs. When you collect eight hits with eight RBIs in the final two games of the month, that's a quick way to fix what was broken.

Nothing was broken for Musial in May. He was seemingly unstoppable, failing to get a hit in only four games while racking up at least one hit in the other 24 games. His slash line was a stunning .391/.481/.746, with 8 home runs and 22 RBIs. This power surge was relatively new for him – before August 1947, he had never hit more than four home runs in a month.

In 1948 Musial's consistency with the long ball improved. In June he hit .412/.508/.726 with 7 home runs and 17 RBIs. In July he posted a slash line of .367/.411/.650 with 7 home runs and 28 RBIs. Musial's hot streak continued in August, arguably his most productive month ever. In 33 games, he scored 31 runs, hitting .348/.427/.725 with 10 home runs and 30 RBIs. September kept the momentum going, with a .368/.451/.632 slash line, 5 home runs, and 22 RBIs. Month after month, Musial displayed remarkable consistency, proving he was one of the most reliable hitters in the game. He delivered standout performances with unwavering regularity, establishing himself as a player who could be counted on for consistent production throughout the season.

Musial concluded the greatest season of his career by leading the league in an impressive array of statistical categories: hits (230), doubles (46), triples (18), runs (135), RBIs (131), batting average (.376), on-base percentage (.450), and slugging percentage (.702). All those, with the exception of doubles and triples, would be career highs. His outstanding performance across the board showcased his dominance on the field. Musial narrowly missed winning the Triple Crown, hitting 39 home runs, while Johnny Mize and Ralph Kiner each hit 40. Despite this, Musial's remarkable season solidified his status as one of the premier players in baseball history.

The new power numbers were a surprise to Musial as much as it was to his fans. "After the 1948 season, I got to thinking about the 39 home runs and asked myself, if I hit 39 without trying, how many could I hit with an earnest effort?"[6]

Musial's OPS+ was an astonishing 200, indicating he was twice as effective as the average major-league hitter. According to this metric, his 200 OPS+ ranks as the 48th best individual season in baseball history. This level of performance underscores Musial's extraordinary talent and impact on the game.

His 11.3 WAR ranks 16th in baseball history, behind such greats as Ruth, Gehrig, and Bonds, among others.

Even though Musial produced one of the best seasons in baseball history, he received only 18 of the 24 first-place votes and 303 of the 336 (90 percent) possible points. Boston Braves ace Johnny Sain received five first-place votes, while his rookie teammate, Al Dark, received two. Sain led the league in wins (24) and complete games (28), which helped the Braves win the pennant under the direction of former Cardinals manager, Billy Southworth.

BEST GAME

Musial played his best game of the season on April 30. Next to when he hit for the cycle on July 24, 1949, this was probably his best game of the decade and one of the best in his career. He tallied five hits in six at-bats, knocking in four runs while scoring three times. Musial ended the day with 10 total bases (two singles, two doubles, one home run), which tied with two other games for his most in the decade.[7]

GAMES VS. DODGERS

For the first and only time that decade, the Cardinals finished with a losing record against the Dodgers, winning 10 of 22 games (.455). However, this outcome was not because of Musial's performance; he delivered one of his best offensive showings against the Dodgers, displaying notable power. In 22 games he collected 34 hits in 87 at-bats, with 22 of those for extra bases, leading to an impressive .391 batting average and an astonishing .851 slugging percentage. His 11 walks contributed to a .465 on-base percentage.

Musial's production against the Cardinals' primary rival far exceeded his season stats, demonstrating an ability to elevate his game in high-stakes matchups. Despite the team's overall record, Musial's performance against the Dodgers solidified his status as a consistently dominant player, capable of stepping up against the toughest competition.

SOURCES

In addition to the sources cited in the Notes, the author consulted a number of publications, including

Broeg, Bob. "Musial (The Man) Gives Boston Fans an Eyeful." *St. Louis Post-Dispatch*, September 20, 1946. https://www.newspapers.com/article/st-louis-post-dispatch-stan-becomes-the/34876198/. Accessed April 28, 2024.

James, Bill, and Jim Henzler. *Win Shares*. (N.p.: STATS Pub., 2002).

Jasper, Kyle. "St. Louis Cardinals: Stan Musial's Time in the Navy," *Redbird Rants,* November 11, 2022. https://redbirdrants.com/2022/11/11/st-louis-cardinals-stan-musials-navy/.

Livacari, Gary. "Stan Musial Named 1948 MVP! | Baseball History Comes Alive." *Baseball History Comes Alive!* 2023. https://www.baseball-historycomesalive.com/stan-musial-named-1948-mvp-2/.

Mileur, Jerome M. *High-Flying Birds: The 1942 St. Louis Cardinals* (Columbia: University of Missouri Press, 2009).

Muder, Craig. "Musial's Historic 1948 Season Nets Him Third NL MVP," Baseball Hall of Fame. https://baseballhall.org/discover/inside-pitch/stan-musials-historic-1948-season-nets-him-third-nl-mvp. Accessed April 28, 2024.

"1948 – Stan Musial of the St. Louis Cardinals is named National League Most Valuable Player. In one of the best seasons ever, Musial led the NL in batting average (.365), runs (135), RBI (131), hits (230), doubles (46), triples (18) and slugging (.702). Hi." This Day in Baseball, 2023. https://thisdayinbaseball.com/stan-musial-of-the-st-louis-cardinals-is-named-1948-n-l-most-valuable-player/.

Posnanski, Joe. "Where Are They Now: Stan Musial," *Sports Illustrated*, August 2, 2010. https://vault.si.com/vault/2010/08/02/where-are-they-now.

Posnanski, Joe. *Why We Love Baseball: A History in 50 Moments* (New York: Dutton, 2023).

Reidenbaugh, Lowell. *Cooperstown: Baseball Hall of Fame: Editions of Sporting News* (New York: Random House Value Publishing, 2001).

Rogers, Anne. "How Cards' Legend Musial Became 'The Man.'" mlb.com, November 19, 2020. Accessed April 28, 2024. https://www.mlb.com/news/stan-musial-the-man-nickname-origin?partnerID=web_article-share.

"Sam Breadon." n.d. Cooperstown Expert. Accessed April 28, 2024. https://www.cooperstownexpert.com/player/sam-breadon/.

Vecsey, George. *Stan Musial: An American Life* (New York: Ballantine Books. 2011).

NOTES

1 Joe Posnanski, "Musial," November 21, 2012. https://medium.com/joeblogs/musial-637c8d9fee2f

2 Frank Cusumano, "Cardinals, Stan Musial Disagreed on Pay Early in His MLB Career," KSDK.com, May 24, 2023. https://www.ksdk.

com/article/sports/local-sports/sports-plus/cardinals-stan-musial-disagreed-on-pay-1943/63-ec4968c2-0e12-4e4c-bbf6-7a58acfa772a.

3   Jerry Lansche, *Stan "The Man" Musial: Born to be a Ballplayer* (Dallas, Texas: Taylor Publishing Company, 1994), 47.

4   Steven P. Gietscher, *Baseball: The Turbulent Midcentury Years* (Lincoln: University of Nebraska Press, 2023), 247.

5   Lansche, 33.

6   John Benson and Tony Blengino, *Baseball's Top 100: The Best Individual Seasons of All Time.* (Diamond Library, 1995), 131.

7   The other two games were on May 1, 1942, and April 30, 1948.

MUSIAL AND THE WORLD SERIES

BY PAUL HOFMANN

Stan Musial was involved in 13 World Series with the St. Louis Cardinals as a player, member of the front office, and later as the team's senior ambassador – Mr. Cardinal. The 13 World Series, of which the Cardinals won eight, were spread out over eight different decades, making his affiliation with the Cardinals one of the longest with a single team in baseball history.

Musial played in four World Series before the age of 26. Given that he had already won two National League batting titles and cemented his position as one of the National League's best players, it seemed certain that he and the Cardinals would continue to make frequent appearances in the World Series. Testament to how difficult it is to win a pennant and how nothing should be taken for granted, the 1946 fall classic was Musial's last as a player in his 22-year Hall of Fame career in which he batted .331, hit 475 home runs, and drove in 1,951 runs.

In his first full season, 1942, Musial hit .315 with 32 doubles, 10 triples, 10 home runs, and 72 RBIs to help the Cardinals capture their first National League pennant and advance to the World Series for the first time since the Gas House Gang defeated the Detroit Tigers in the 1934 World Series.

1942 WORLD SERIES

The World Series was a matchup between two teams that won more than 100 games. The Cardinals, who trailed the National League-leading Brooklyn Dodgers by 10 games on August 5, rallied down the stretch - winning 43 of their last 51 games - to finish with a record of 106-48 (with two ties), two games ahead of the Dodgers.[1] The Cardinals' 106 victories remain the franchise record.

In Game One at Sportsman's Park III, the Yankees' Red Ruffing, threw 7⅔ innings of no-hit ball before giving up a single to center fielder Terry Moore. Entering the bottom of the ninth, the Yankees led 7-0. Musial fouled out to lead off the bottom of the ninth before the Cardinals mounted an improbable comeback that fell just short. They scored four runs and had the bases loaded when he came to bat once more, representing the winning run. He hit a grounder to first baseman Buddy Hassett, who tossed the ball to reliever Spud Chandler for the game's final out. Despite being angered at his own performance, going 0-for-4 and making two outs in the bottom of the ninth, "Musial took heart at the late-inning rally, believing more than ever that the Yankees were beatable."[2] In fact, the Cardinals' ninth-inning near comeback "showed the Yankees that they were indeed, a worthy contender."[3]

In Game Two, the Cardinals led 3-0 into the eighth inning only to see it evaporate on a run-scoring single by Joe DiMaggio and a two-run homer to deep right field by Charlie Keller.

In the bottom of the eighth, Enos Slaughter hit a two-out double and Musial followed with an RBI single to center. Musial's first hit of the Series gave the Cardinals a 4-3 lead, which held up and evened the Series at a game each. Musial finished the day 1-for-4.

October 2 was a travel day for the two teams as the Series shifted to Yankee Stadium. The next day, a World Series-record crowd of 69,123 filled the ballpark for the pivotal Game Three.

According to Musial biographer James Giglio, Musial admitted to feeling numb on the occasion of his first visit to Yankee Stadium, "not only because he was a twenty-one-year-old only one season removed from Class C ball. The three-tiered stadium created an enormous obstacle for left fielders because of the haze of cigarette smoke and the shadows created by the October sun, which blanketed left field, making it difficult to see batted balls."[4]

Game Three was a matchup between injury-plagued left-hander Ernie White, who was 7-5 with a 2.52 ERA in 1942 following a 17-win season in 1941. The Yankees countered with the right-handed Chandler, who went 16-5 with a 2.38 ERA during the regular season, and earned the save in Game One.

Ernie White scattered six hits and struck out six, tossing a shutout to outduel Chandler, who gave up only three hits and one run over eight innings. The Cardinals manufactured a run in the third on a walk, a bunt single, a sacrifice, and a groundout, and added an unearned run in the ninth to win 2-0. Musial finished the day 1-for-3, with a fourth-inning single to center. He was also intentionally walked in the top of the ninth with runners on second and third with nobody out.

Another World Series attendance record was established when 69,902 fans packed Yankee Stadium for Game Four, a matchup between Mort Cooper, who was making his second start of the Series, and right-handed rookie Hank Borowy, who was 15-4 with a 2.52 ERA during the regular season for the Yankees.

The Yankees took a first-inning lead and held it until the fourth inning when the Cardinals exploded for six runs.

Musial led off with a bunt single to the left side of the infield. A single and a walk followed, with Whitey Kurowski singling to give the Cardinals a 2-1 lead. Marty Marion walked to reload the bases before Mort Cooper hit a two-run bloop single to right field that ended the day for starter Borowy. Atley Donald came on in relief.

Whitey Kurowski, Marty Marion, Stan Musial, and Ray Sanders get together during the 1944 World Series against the St. Louis Browns.

Terry Moore's single to left field increased the Cardinals' lead to 5-1. After Slaughter grounded into a force for the second out, Musial doubled to right to drive in Cooper with the Cardinals' sixth run of the inning, tying the Word Series record for the most hits in an inning.[5]

In the sixth, the Yankees scored five runs and tied it, 6-6,. the big blow Keller's three-run homer.

The Cardinals scored two runs in the top of the seventh to regain the lead. Musial, who drew a walk, scored the second run of the inning on a fly out to center by Marion. The Cardinals added an insurance run in the ninth and won 9-6, taking a three-games-to-one lead. Musial finished the day 2-for-3 with one RBI and two walks, including an intentional pass in the top of the eighth.

Game Five was a low-scoring back-and-forth affair that stood 2-2 until the top of the ninth, when Whitey Kurowski hit a two-run homer to put the Cardinals ahead 4-2, and ultimately secured the World Series title. Musial was 0-for-4 in the series-clinching game.

As a batter, Musial didn't have a great Series. He was 4-for-18 (.222), with a double, a Series-leading four walks that gave him an OPS of .364, and two runs batted in. The Cardinals players' share for winning the World Series was $6,192.50, which easily surpassed the $4,250 salary Musial received during his rookie year.[6]

Musial ranked the Cardinals' victory among his greatest sports moments. In an interview later in life he pointed to the five-game triumph as one of his biggest thrills. "Well, I guess winning the World Series as a rookie (1942). Beating the Yankees."[7] He also included his induction into the Hall of Fame and the first time he put on a Cardinals uniform.

After the Series, Musial, accompanied by his parents, returned to his home in Donora, Pennsylvania, where he worked part-time as a clerk in his father-in-law's grocery store.[8] Giglio recounted Musial's farewell to his teammates at New York's Pennsylvania Station: "Musial said his final good-byes to teammates who were heading back to St. Louis. (Marty) Marion remembered him 'crying like a baby, shaking hands with everyone.'"[9] This may have been in part due to the escalation of World War II and the uncertainty surrounding which players would be in the armed forces or would return to the Cardinals for the 1943 season.

1943 WORLD SERIES

In 1943, with many stars off serving in World War II, "Musial established himself as the premier player in the National League if not the whole game."[10] He led the league in games played (157), plate appearances (701), batting (.357), slugging (.562), on-base percentage (.425), on-base plus slugging percentage, or OPS (.988), hits (220), doubles (48), triples (20), total bases (347), and WAR (9.5).[11] Not surprisingly, Musial won the first of his three Most Valuable Player awards and a second consecutive trip to the fall classic.

The Series was a rematch between the Cardinals and Yankees. The Cardinals were runaway winners in the National League, finishing with a record of 105-49, 18 games ahead of the second-place Cincinnati Reds. The Yankees won the pennant with a record of 98-56 and finished 13½ games ahead of the Washington Senators. Both teams were missing key players in their lineups who were away on military service. Given the results of the 1942 Series and the fact that the Cardinals had the finest pitching in the National League – Howie Pollet, Max Lanier, and Mort Cooper ranked one-two-three in the league in ERA at 1.75, 1.90 and 2.30 respectively[12] – the Cardinals were favored to repeat as World Series champions.

The Yankees took Game One, 4-2, behind the pitching of 1943 American League MVP Spud Chandler (20-4, 1.64 ERA, 20 complete games). Joe Gordon homered for the Yankees, who scored the winning run on a wild pitch in the bottom of the sixth. Musial went 1-for-4, hitting a single to right in the eighth inning.

The next day the Cardinals evened the Series with a 4-3 victory. Mort Cooper pitched a complete game, backed by Marion's third-inning solo home run and a two-run homer by Sanders. Musial was again 1-for-4; he led off the fourth with a single to center and scored on Kurowski's single to center.

Because of wartime travel restrictions, Game Three was also played in New York. The Cardinals took a 2-0 lead in the top of the fourth. Musial led off with a single to left and went to third on a one-out double by Kurowski. After an intentional walk to Sanders, Danny Litwhiler singled to left, scoring Musial and Kurowski.

The Cardinals managed only one hit the rest of the way and made four errors as the Yankees scored three unearned runs. Musial finished 1-for-3 with a walk.

After a two-day break the Series resumed on October 10 at Sportsman's Park. The Yankees took a commanding three-games-to-one lead with a 2-1 victory. Musial collected two hits without hitting the ball out of the infield. He lined out to second in the first inning, had a one-out bunt single in the fourth inning, grounded out to second in the sixth inning, and had a one-out infield single to third in the eighth.

The Series ended the next day when Chandler pitched his second complete game in a week, a 2-0 shutout. Dickey was the hitting hero with a sixth-inning two-run homer. Musial went 0-for-3 with a walk.

Musial finished the Series with a .278 batting average (5-for-18). He had no extra-base hits or RBIs and drew two walks. His performance was not what Cardinal fans had come to expect during the 1943 season. After the Series Musial often said that the Yankees "deserved to win" because they "played better ball" and "had the better pitching."[13] The reality that every game was close and could have gone either way was testament to Musial's graciousness.

1944 WORLD SERIES

Musial helped the Cardinals win a third consecutive pennant with a season that was very similar to his MVP year of 1943. He hit .347 and led the National League in hits (197), doubles (51), on-base percentage (.440), slugging percentage (.549), OPS (.990), and WAR (8.9).[14]

The Series was an all-St. Louis affair as the city's second-class citizens, the Browns, won their first and only American League pennant.[15]

Both teams played at Sportsman's Park. The Browns owned the ballpark until they moved to Baltimore in 1953; the Cardinals were a tenant. In the opener, on Wednesday, October 4, a crowd of 33,242 watched right-handed "Sunday pitcher" Denny Galehouse, who was just 9-10 with a 3.12 ERA during the regular season, outduel Mort Cooper.[16]

Galehouse scattered seven hits on his way to a 2-1 complete-game victory. He lost his bid for a shutout in the ninth inning when the Cardinals scored their only run on a fly ball by Ken O'Dea, pinch-hitting for relief pitcher Blix Donnelly. The difference in the game was a fourth-inning, two-run homer by first baseman George McQuinn. Musial went 1-for-3. He singled to center in the first inning and laid down a sacrifice bunt in the third that advanced baserunners to second and third, only to be stranded.

The Cardinals evened the series with a 3-2, 11-inning Game Two victory that saw one of the greatest defensive plays in World Series history.[17]

Sanders led off the bottom of the 11th with a with a single to center and was sacrificed to second by Kurowski. O'Dea, pinch-hitting for the second consecutive game, singled to center to drive in the winning run. Musial was 1-for-5. His only hit was an eighth-inning leadoff single to center.

The two teams switched dugouts for Game Three, with the Browns assuming the role of the home team. The game was a matchup between a pair of 17-game winners. The Browns chased rookie Ted Wilks when they scored four in the fourth and added two insurance runs in the seventh to beat the Cardinals 6-2.

Musial was held to one hit, a single to right field in the top of the third, in four trips to the plate. The Browns' Jack Kramer threw a complete game, scattering seven hits and striking out 10.

The Cardinals tied the Series again with a 5-1 Game Four victory. Musial was their hitting star, going 3-for-4 with two runs scored and two RBIs on his only World Series home run, to right field in the first inning off Sig Jakucki.

The pivotal fifth game was a rematch between Game One starters Mort Cooper and Galehouse. Both starters went the distance, with Cooper tossing a 2-0 shutout to give the Cardinals a three-games-to-two lead, on solo home runs by Sanders and Danny Litwhiler. Although he didn't factor into the scoring, Musial was 1-for-3 with a first-inning walk and a two-out double in the third.

The Series ended on October 9 when Max Lanier limited the Browns to one run in 5⅓ innings and Wilks atoned for his Game Three struggles with 3⅔ no-hit innings. Musial went 0-for-4 in the Cardinals' 3-1 victory.

While still below the performance Cardinal fans had come to expect from him, the 1944 World Series was Musial's best from a statistical perspective. He hit .304 (7-for-23) with two doubles, a home run, two RBIs, and a .552 slugging percentage.

The Cardinals' and Musial's run of three consecutive trips to the World Series came to an end in 1945. Probably not coincidentally, Musial was inducted into the Navy in January of that year.[18]

With Musial out of the lineup, the Cardinals fell to second place in the National League. The team still finished with an admirable record of 95-59, three games behind the pennant-winning Chicago Cubs. Given Musial's combined WAR of 44.1 in five full seasons between 1943 and 1948 (an average WAR of 8.8) his presence might have pushed the Cardinals to a fourth consecutive pennant in 1945.

1946 WORLD SERIES

Musial was discharged from the Navy in March 1946 and immediately rejoined the Cardinals. Enjoying one of the best years of his career, he led the National League in games played (156), plate appearances (702), at-bats (624), runs scored (124), hits (228), doubles (50), triples (20), batting average (.365), slugging percentage (.587), OPS (1.021), total bases (366), WAR (9.3), and oWAR (9.6).[19] He drove in 103 runs in the first of 10 seasons in which he had 100 or more RBIs. For his efforts he earned his second NL MVP award.

With Musial and many of his Cardinals teammates back in the lineup, the Cardinals returned to the top of the National League standings with a record of 98-58, narrowly edging the Brooklyn Dodgers by two games and earning their fourth trip to the World Series in five years.[20]

In the American League, the Boston Red Sox finally got over the hump and won the pennant going away, 104-50, 12 games ahead of the Detroit Tigers.

The much-anticipated Series offered a matchup between two of the game's biggest stars at the prime of their careers. Ted Williams, the Red Sox left fielder, who had missed the 1943, '44, and '45 seasons while serving in the US Navy and Marine Corps, made a triumphant return with an MVP season of his own.[21]

Before the Series there was a great deal of discussion as to who was the better hitter. Dodgers manager Leo Durocher said, "Musial is two to one a better hitter. You can pitch to Williams, crowd him and keep the ball on the handle. Williams can hit to only one field. Musial can hit to all fields and you can't fool him. Williams has only one advantage. He has more power and power worries you. You are afraid to make one mistake. But I'll take Musial any day – and what is more, I'm not comparing dispositions."[22]

Game One featured a pair of 20-game winners as starting pitchers, Howie Pollet (21-10, 2.10 ERA) against Boston's Tex Hughson (20-11 2.75).

The Red Sox held a 1-0 lead until the bottom of the sixth, when Red Schoendienst, Musial's roommate, reached on a one-out weak roller to shortstop. He advanced to second when Moore grounded out to second. Musial tied the game with a double to right.

Tied 2-2 after nine innings, the game was decided in the 10th when Rudy York hit a two-out home run to left. 3-2, Red Sox. Musial came to the plate with a man on second and one out in the bottom of the inning and grounded out, finishing the game 1-for-5.

Game Two saw Harry Brecheen outpitch Mickey Harris, with a four-hit shutout. He helped his own cause at the plate. After Del Rice led off the bottom of the third with a double to left field, Brecheen singled to right to give the Cardinals a 1-0 lead. In the bottom of the fifth, with Rice again on base, Brecheen bunted and reached second on a bad throw on a force play. Moore's single brought Rice home with the game's second run, and Musial's force-play grounder scored Brecheen, making it 3-0, the game's final score. Musial finished 0-for-4 with an RBI.

At Fenway Park, Dave Ferriss (25-6, 3.25 ERA) tossed a 4-0 shutout, beating Murry Dickson. York, the hitting hero in Game One, hit a three-run home run to left field in the bottom of the first to give the Red Sox all the runs they needed.

Musial was 1-for-3 with a first-inning walk. He then stole second before being picked off by Ferriss as he tried to steal third.[23] Musial's hit was a two-out triple in the ninth. Slaughter struck out to end the game, stranding Musial at third.

The Cardinals scored 12 runs on a World Series record-tying 20 hits in Game Four. The final score was 12-3. Cardinals righthander Red Munger surrendered nine hits but yielded only one earned run. Musial was 1-for-5 with a walk, one run scored, and a two-run third-inning double that scored Schoendienst and Moore.

Pollet failed to get out of the first inning in Game Five. Down 1-0 and with just one out and two runners on base, Al Brazle came on in relief. Joe Dobson started for Boston. The Cardinals tied the score in the second when Harry Walker doubled to left field, driving in Joe Garagiola. In the bottom of the second, the Red Sox' Don Gutteridge drove in Roy Partee to give the Red Sox a 2-1 lead. Boston added one more run in the sixth and three in the seventh.

Down 6-1, the Cardinals made one last effort to get back into the game in the ninth. Musial led off with a walk and later scored on Walker's two-run single, but the scoring ended. 6-3 victors, the Red Sox led three games to two.

Musial was 1-for-3 with a walk. His lone hit was a two-out double to center in the sixth inning.

The series resumed in St. Louis with a Game Six rematch of Game Two starters Harris and Brecheen. The Cardinals scored three runs in the bottom of the third inning. After they scored their first run, Musial kept the inning going with an infield single that moved Schoendienst to third. RBI singles by Kurowski and Slaughter followed. The Cardinals held a 3-0 lead. The game ended with a 4-1 Cardinals victory. Musial was 1-for-4 with one run scored.

One thing about Game Seven of the World Series is that it is often close. Of the 40 winner-take-all World Series contests, 15 have been decided by a single run.[24] Game Seven of the 1946 World Series was one of those 15 instances.

The Red Sox scored once in the top of the first, and the Cardinals tied the score in the second. They took a 3-1 lead in the bottom of the fifth when pitcher Dickson hit an RBI double and Schoendienst followed with an RBI single.

In the Red Sox eighth, Dom DiMaggio hit a two-run double to right to tie the game at 3-3. In the process of legging out the double, DiMaggio pulled a hamstring. With Williams due to hit, the Red Sox' Leon Culberson ran for DiMaggio – a move that would play a huge role in what transpired in the bottom of the inning. Williams, who was playing hurt, ended the inning with a pop fly to second base.[25]

The events in the bottom of the eighth included one of the most analyzed plays in baseball history – the "mad dash" by Enos Slaughter, who singled and then scored the go-ahead run from first base on a two-out base hit to center by Harry Walker. Did Johnny Pesky "hold the ball" and fail to throw home in time to get Slaughter? Should Walker's hit have been scored a double (as it was) or a single? The indisputable fact was that the Cardinals took a 4-3 lead and, though Boston batters led off the ninth with back-to-back singles, they could not get the tying run home.[26]

Musial finished the Series 6-for-27 with four walks, and four RBIs. His MVP counterpart, Williams, finished 5-for-25 with five walks and one RBI.

The 1946 World Series turned out to Musial's last appearance in the postseason as a player. Who would have thought that possible at the time, considering that the 26-year-old had already played in four World Series?

Reflecting back on the 1946 season and World Series, Musial considered it one of "the best years of our lives."[27] Shortly after the Series, Musial decided to move to St. Louis from his hometown of Donora. He said, "I think it's wise for a baseball player to make his home where he's made his reputation. I always worried about my baseball career, about getting hurt, and I wanted a business to fall back on."

Summary of Musial's World Series Playing Career

Despite winning three of the four World Series he appeared in, Musial's Series statistics were far off his career performance. In his 23 World Series games, he hit just .256 (22-for-86) with 7 doubles, a triple, one home run, and 8 RBIs. His .742 OPS in 99 plate appearances was more than 200 points lower than his career OPS of .976.

Joseph Stanton, a Musial biographer, addressed the discrepancy between Musial's regular-season statistics and his World Series performances. "He always found it difficult to hit in championship games when white-shirted spectators crowed into the center field seats. … Musial's knack for seeing and interpreting the emergence of the ball out of the pitcher's hand was one of the keys to his greatness as a hitter. With that edge compromised he tended to underperform in World Series contests."[28] This, coupled with the fact that he was facing superior pitchers, may explain the difference.

Musial's home and away splits in World Series competition support Stanton's claim. In 14 World Series games at Sportsman's Park, Musial hit .241 (13-for-54) with 4 doubles, 1 home run, 5 RBIs, 5 bases on balls, and 4 strikeouts. In nine World Series games contested on the road, Musial hit .281 (9-for-32) with 3 doubles, 1 triple, 7 bases on balls, and no strikeouts.

Defensively, Musial was a solid World Series performer. In 96 total chances at three different positions (left field, right field, and first base) he made only one error, a miscue in right field in Game Five of the 1944 World Series that did not factor into the scoring. He finished his World Series career with a .990 fielding percentage.

For the remainder of Musial's career, the Cardinals finished no higher than second place (five times) in the National League.

When he announced his retirement in August of 1963, Musial declared that he would "like to go out on a winner," noting, "Our 1942 club was farther behind and won. … I've dreamed for a long time of playing in one more World Series. I think we still have a chance to do it."[29] Despite winning 19 of 20 from August 30 to September 15 to pull within one game of the Los Angeles Dodgers, the Cardinals were 2-8 over their final 10 games and finished six games behind, ending Musial's hope of returning to the fall classic.

The final Cardinals game of the season, which took place in St. Louis, was a grand farewell party for Musial. The pregame festivities included numerous speakers, including Commissioner Ford Frick, who bestowed tributes on Musial. Teammate Ken Boyer presented Musial with a ring from the players with the number 6, Musial's jersey number, set in diamonds, "a gift Stan especially appreciated because his World Series rings from the 1940s had been stolen from his home several years before."[30]

1964 WORLD SERIES

After retiring, Musial moved into the Cardinals front office as a team vice president, but primarily in a public-relations role. The

Cardinals won the pennant in 1964 with a record of 93-69, one game ahead of the Cincinnati Reds and Philadelphia Phillies.

The Cardinals faced a familiar World Series foe, the Yankees, pennant winners by one game over the Chicago White Sox. Led by Boyer, the Cardinals defeated the Yankees in seven games to capture their first World Series title in 18 years.

After the Cardinals' victory, Musial was often asked if he regretted retiring after the 1963 season. With typical modesty, he noted that had he not retired, the Cardinals would not have acquired Lou Brock, and claimed that a 1964 Cardinals team with a Musial instead of a Brock would not have won the World Series.[31] While the answer was effective at fending off the frequently asked question, "there must have been some moments in which he thought about how satisfying it would have been to have been on the field for one more championship season."[32]

On January 23, 1967, Musial was named the Cardinals' general manager. Once he remarked, "I have a darn good job, but please don't ask me what I do."[33] This gave some the impression that he may not have been comfortable in his new role.

The Cardinals won the 1967 pennant with a 101-60 record, an 18½-game improvement over 1966, and advanced to World Series against the Boston Red Sox – a rematch of the 1946 Series, Musial's last as a player.

1967 WORLD SERIES

Just as in 1946, the Cardinals defeated the Red Sox four games to three, the Cardinals' fifth World Series title during Musial's tenure with the team. Despite the team's success, Musial resigned as general manager on December 5, less than a year after accepting the job. He remains the only general manager of a team that won the World Series in his only year on the job.

When asked what the difference in the Series was after the Cardinals' Game Seven victory, Musial praised the manager, his former teammate and longtime roommate Red Schoendienst. "If there was a turning point in the Series," Musial said, "it was in Red pitching Gibson on Sunday so he would be ready if there was a seventh game."[34] Right-hander Bob Gibson won three games to capture his second World Series MVP Award.

Musial's departure from the general manager position came as a surprise to fans and the press. He later provided plausible reasons for his "retirement," including the sudden death of his business partner Biggie Garagnani, which Stan said required him to devote more of hist time to their restaurant.[35]

The media did not completely buy Musial's explanation and there were rumors of a rift in the front office. *The Sporting News* reported that "emerging differences came to a head involving Musial over the distribution of World Series tickets." Those close to Musial seemed to agree that the supposed conflict over the releasing of too many World Series tickets was not the actual reason for his departure. More likely, Augie Busch, the team owner, probably told Musial, who enjoyed the public-relations part of the job, that he needed to master the paperwork, baseball law, and other intricacies of the position.[36] No longer the team's general manager, Musial remained Mr. Cardinal, the team's senior ambassador for the remainder of his life.

MR. CARDINAL AND THE WORLD SERIES

The Cardinals played in seven more World Series during the remainder of Musial's lifelong tenure as Mr. Cardinal, winning three and losing four.

On August 4, 1968, a statue of Musial was erected outside Busch Memorial Stadium. That year the Cardinals repeated as pennant winners, their first repeat since they won three in a row in 1942-1944. Many out-of-towners attending the World Series against the Detroit Tigers got their first look at the statue of Musial with its inscription, "Here stands baseball's perfect warrior; here stands baseball's perfect knight."[37] The Tigers rallied from a three-games-to-one deficit to win the Series in seven games, denying the Cardinals back-to-back World Series titles.

The Cardinals appeared in three World Series in the 1980s. The first was in 1982, when Musial was approaching his 62nd birthday. The Cardinals beat the Milwaukee Brewers in seven games. The team gave Musial a World Series ring.

The Cardinals won pennants in 1985, 1987, and 2004, but lost all three World Series. They extracted some level of revenge for 1968 by defeating the Tigers in five games in 2006. As the Cardinals' senior ambassador, Musial earned a seventh World Series ring.

On January 15, 2011, already suffering from Alzheimer's, Musial was awarded the Medal of Freedom, the highest civilian honor in the country, by President Barack Obama.[38] That season the Cardinals made their final appearance in the World Series during Musial's lifetime. The Cardinals beat the Texas Rangers in seven games, capturing the franchise's 11th title – the eighth during Musial's affiliation with the team. As in 1982 and 2006, the Cardinals awarded Musial a World Series ring.

Musial died on January 13, 2013, from complications associated with his battle with Alzheimer's. He was 92 years old.

SOURCES

In addition to the sources cited in the Notes, the author relied on Baseball-reference.com, Retrosheet.org, and Baseball-Almanac.com.

NOTES

1. 1942 World Series. Retrieved on September 11, 2023, from www.baseball-almanac.com/ws/yr1942ws.shtml.
2. James N. Giglio, *Musial: From Stash to Stan the Man* (Columbia; University of Missouri Press, 2001), 78.
3. 1942 World Series.
4. Giglio, 78-79.
5. Giglio, 79. Multiple players have had two hits in one inning in a World Series game. Babe Ruth was the first to achieve this feat, in Game Four of the 1926 World Series between the Yankees and Cardinals. As of 2025, J.D. Martinez of the Boston Red Sox was the last player to have two hits in one inning during a World Series

game. He did it in Game Four of the 2018 World Series against the Los Angeles Dodgers.

6. Giglio, 80.
7. Mark Malinowski, "Biofile Stan Musial Interview." Retrieved on December 3, 2024, from https://mrbiofile.com/2024/01/04/biofile-stan-musial-interview.
8. Malinowski.
9. "The Kids," *Time,* October 12, 1942: 77-79, as cited by Giglio. 77-79.
10. Jan Finkel, "Stan Musial," SABR BioProject. https://sabr.org/bioproj/person/stan-musial/.
11. OPS and WAR did not exist at the time and are retrospectively calculated.
12. Howie Pollet missed the 1943 World Series after leaving the team in August to serve in the military, and did not qualify for the ERA title.
13. Joseph Stanton, *Stan Musial: A Biography* (Westport, Connecticut: Greenwood Press, 2007), 38.
14. Surprisingly, Musial finished fourth in the MVP voting. The award went to teammate Marty Marion, whose play at shortstop was instrumental in the Cardinals winning the pennant going away. The Cardinals finished with a record of 105-49, 14½ games ahead of the second-place Pittsburgh Pirates.
15. "The undisputed underdog, the Brownies barely managed to win the league championship on the last day of the season. The Browns captured the pennant by wining only 89 games for a winning percentage of .578, the lowest for an American League champion to that point." Giglio, 92. One year later the Detroit Tigers won the 1945 American League pennant with a winning percentage of .575.
16. Galehouse, who had earned a deferment for military service was working six days a week at the Goodyear Aircraft plant in Akron, Ohio. From mid-May until the end of the season, Galehouse would leave Akron after his Saturday shift, travel all night by train to wherever the Browns were playing, pitch the first game of the Sunday doubleheader, then immediately returned to Akron and put in another six-day week at the factory before repeating the process the following weekend. Glenn Stout, "Denny Galehouse," SABR BioProject, retrieved on September 14, 2024, from https://sabr.org/bioproj/person/denny-galehouse/.
17. "In the 11th inning, with George McQuinn on second, [Mark] Christman laid a bunt down the third-base line that [reliever] Donnelly fielded with his bare hand and tossed to third to get the runner. The play was heralded as the defensive play of the World Series and one of the better defensive plays in World Series history." Greg Omoth, "Blix Donnelly," SABR BioProject, retrieved on July 13, 2024, from https://sabr.org/bioproj/person/blix-donnelly/.
18. For a good summary of Musial's 1945 season in military service, see "Stan Musial," Gary Bedingfield's Baseball in Wartime, retrieved on May 15, 2024 from https://www.baseballinwartime.com/player_biographies/musial_stan.htm.
19. oWAR measures a player's offensive achievements.
20. In 1946 the Cardinals and the Brooklyn Dodgers finished the regular season tied for first place. The winner was decided by a best-of-three playoff. The Cardinals won, two games to none, and advanced to the World Series. All statistics were included in the regular season.
21. The 27-year-old two-time batting champion (1941 and 1942), hit .346 with 38 home runs and 123 RBIs while leading the American League in runs scored (142), bases on balls (156), on-base percentage (.497), slugging average (.667), OPS (1.164), and total bases (343). There have been few World Series that rivaled the star power of the 1946 fall classic.
22. Stan Baumgartner, "Stan Musial a Better Hitter Than Williams – Durocher," *The Sporting News*, October 9, 1946: 25.
23. Musial had 7 stolen bases and 9 caught-stealing during the 1946 season.
24. "A Brief History: Here's Every World Series Game 7," retrieved on August 17, 2024, from https:// www.mlb.com/news/history-of-world-series-game-7-c39984458?msockid=014d-8d273707667a354299cb36ff6727.
25. Williams played the Series with a severely bruised elbow, sustained when he was hit by a pitch during an exhibition game staged to keep Red Sox players in shape as they awaited the resolution of Cardinals-Dodgers playoff.
26. For a summary of the game, see Gregory H. Wolf's article for SABR's Games Project at https://sabr.org/gamesproj/game/october-15-1946-countrys-mad-dash-enos-slaughter-scores-winning-run-for-cardinals-in-game-7/.
27. Giglio, 143.
28. Stanton, 39-40.
29. Stanton, 103.
30. Stanton, 105.
31. Stanton, 111.
32. Stan Musial as told to Bob Broeg, *The Man's Own Story* (New York: Doubleday, 1964), 229-230.
33. Jan Finkel.
34. Lowell Reidenbaugh, "Gibson, Cards – Second to None," *The Sporting News*. October 14, 1967: 5.
35. Stanton, 119.
36. Giglio, 287.
37. Bob Addie, "Addie's Atoms," *The Sporting News*, October 19, 1968: 14.
38. Basketball legend Bill Russell also received a Medal of Freedom that day.

MUSIAL ARRANGED A MASTERPIECE IN 1948

BY MIKE EISENBATH

Every renowned artist has his or her most famous creation, their *pièce de résistance*, that singularly most remarkable composition that stands out in an already impressive body of work.

For the baseball virtuoso known as Stan Musial, that was the season of 1948.

One of the most accomplished batsmen in big-league history, during a 22-season career that saw him set dozens of records, Musial composed no other 154-game schedule better than that of the Summer of '48. It marked the closest he ever ever came to winning a Triple Crown:

- He led the National League with a .376 batting average, his highest single-season mark and the third of his seven batting titles.
- He led the NL with 131 runs batted in, the most he ever drove in during one season – this from the player who had the league record for career RBIs until 1971.
- He finished third in the league with 39 home runs; Pittsburgh's Ralph Kiner and New York's Johnny Mize tied for the NL top honor with 40 homers apiece. Musial hit 475 home runs in his career, but his 1948 total marked his single-season best and was 20 more than his previous season high.

One more home run would have made Musial the first NL Triple Crown winner since Joe Medwick turned the feat with the Cardinals in 1937.

"Why be greedy?" Musial said of missing that achievement. "I had a pretty good year, so why wish for more than I had coming to me? My only regret is the Cardinals didn't win the pennant."[1]

Musial's 1948 display still holds up as one of the game's greatest seasons. His 11.3 WAR is tied with Ty Cobb's 1917 season and Mickey Mantle's 1957 season for number 14 all-time. With that, Musial picked up his third NL Most Valuable Player honor.

"I think he's the best hitter in baseball," said Cardinals President Bob Hannegan after signing Musial to a new two-year contract at the end of the season.[2]

Wrote Jimmy Cannon of the *New York Post*: "Musial was the greatest player in Organized Ball this year, and there is no way this claim can be challenged. Stan is younger than Joe DiMaggio and sounder. He can do more than Ted Williams on a ball field and is faster than Lou Boudreau. ... Musial is the only great ball player in this period who is not changed by circumstances."[3]

Quite a contrast to the ballplayer described just a year earlier as "smug" with a "swelled noggin" who could do little more than flail at pitches. Indeed, Musial sported a stunningly paltry .196 batting mark 44 games into the 1947 season. He didn't get that average above .300 for good until September 3.[4]

Even though Musial dealt with an inflamed appendix all season, that subnormal hitting display had baseball fans around the country questioning whether Musial really was as good as Ted Williams – or any of the game's other top hitters, for that matter.

St. Louis writer Bob Broeg called out the most vocal national critic in a September 1947 article in *The Sporting News*, in which he referenced a recent *Collier's* magazine article that had writer Kyle Crichton blaming the Cardinals' slow start on what he described as Musial's "smugness and contentedness."[5]

Broeg went on to quote the magazine piece:

"Chief among the deflated personages was Mr. Stanley Musial of Donora, Pa., who led the league in hitting [in 1946], but was now making motions at the plate like a spinster repulsing a wasp with a towel. There were rumors that Stanley was suffering from expanso largesso cerebello, meaning a swelled noggin. After a spring holdout that had brought him a reputed salary of $27,000 – entirely merited by his record – he had taken on the airs of a lesser lama and not available for press interviews."[6]

Crichton then opined that Musial's early-season slump and appendicitis turned him into "a very chastened young man" and "gave him a new mental state that was an improvement."[7]

Cardinals manager Eddie Dyer took great exception to any criticism of his star player and told Broeg: "In my 25 years in baseball, Stan is as fine a boy as I've ever seen or managed. He's never been swell-headed. This season that poisonous appendix deprived him of his strength and timing. He pleaded to stay in the lineup, and I never saw a fellow try harder. Eventually he became more his old self, but day in and day out he still won't be the old Musial until his system is rid of that chronic trouble."[8]

Team captain Terry Moore noted that Musial remained as level-headed as ever as a player. Writers who covered the team, both in St. Louis and on the road, took exception to the report of Musial's poor availability for interviews. And Musial acknowledged that he never had talked with Crichton; he said he was too ill when the writer called his hotel room one day asking for an interview but said he could talk the following day. Apparently, Crichton never took Musial up on that offer.[9]

Musial responded to the criticism by going 14-for-32 during the final nine games in September 1947, pushing his average to .312 and finishing fifth in the NL batting race.

On October 15, 1947, the Cardinals' team surgeon, Dr. Robert F. Hyland, removed Musial's appendix at St. John's Hospital in St. Louis.[10]

Baseball Magazine put Musial on its cover in September 1948. The Cardinals superstar was putting the finishing touches on his greatest season in the big leagues.

A generally healthy Musial went into 1948 rejuvenated, and perhaps with a sharpened competitive edge and something to prove. Dyer decided to move him from first base, where he had played all 149 games the previous season, back to the outfield. He ended up playing all his team's 155 games in 1948, with at least 42 appearances in each of the three outfield spots.

The Cardinals opened the campaign on April 20 with a three-game series against the Reds at Sportsman's Park. Musial, playing right field and batting third in the order, had an RBI double in five plate appearances in a 4-0 victory, then went hitless with two walks and a run scored in a 5-2 triumph the next day.

His first multihit game of the season came in a 4-3 loss on April 22, when he stroked a single, double, and triple with a pair of RBIs.

The Cardinals embarked on a three-game trip to Chicago – Musial was held hitless in two of those contests – then finished the road trip with a couple of games in Cincinnati. That's where his season began to take on a sparkling luster.

The Cardinals fell to the Reds 4-3 in 14 innings on April 29, but Musial went 3-for-5 with a walk, his first home run of the season and four RBIs. He closed out the road trip April 30 by going 5-for-6, including two doubles and a homer, with another four runs batted in to lead the assault in a 13-7 win.

"I'm supposed to help the club with my hitting, so I feel like I'm doing my duty this year," Musial said. "It seems to come easy to me this year. I've picked up the 12 pounds I lost last spring. … Besides that, I'm more relaxed at my new position – in the outfield."

Still, the Cardinals lugged just a 4-4 record when they returned home for what would be a 12-game homestand against six of the NL's seven other teams. The Cardinals won nine of them, and Musial had at least one hit in 10 of them. By the time they boarded an eastbound train after a 6-5, 10-inning win over the Pittsburgh Pirates on May 16, Musial was sporting a .350 batting mark and 18 RBIs through 20 games.

And, of course, it was destined to get even better immediately. The Cardinals were headed for Brooklyn's Ebbets Field – The Man's home away from home.

- May 18: 2-for-4, one double, two runs scored in a 4-3 Cardinals win.
- May 19: 5-for-5 with a walk in six plate appearances, a double and a triple with two RBIs in a 14-7 win.
- May 20: 4-for-6, with two doubles, a homer, three runs scored, and two more RBIs, as the Cardinals swept the series with a 13-4 victory

Sometimes numbers really do tell key parts of a story. Here are more from Musial's 1948 season:

- He batted .411 with a 1.321 OPS in 237 plate appearances against left-handed pitchers – and Musial batted from the left side.
- He drew a total of 83 walks and struck out only 33 times.
- His longest hitting streak was 13 games, his longest on-base streak 21 games. Musial never went more than four straight games without a hit or more than five consecutive games without an RBI.
- Bolstered by a .412 batting average in June – during which he reached base in more than half his plate appearances – Musial wrapped up the season's first half with a .403 batting mark.

On July 9, four days before he had a single and home run in the NL's 5-2 All-Star Game loss, Musial lashed a single and a home run in a 6-4 Cardinals victory over the Reds at Sportsman's Park. That lifted his season batting average to .412, along with 20 home runs and 64 runs batted in – through 74 games played.

Compare that to Ted Williams's showing for the Red Sox in 1941, when his .406 average still stands as the last time anyone topped the .400 mark for a full season. Williams had a .405 average, 16 homers, and 61 RBIs after 74 games.

St. Louis proceeded to drop three consecutive games as Musial went hitless in 12 plate appearances, and he never sniffed the .400 level again. Nonetheless, he didn't exactly slack off, as the Cardinals battled back into the pennant race in August, when much of the country was mired in a heat wave but Musial refused to wilt. He compiled a .348 average with 14 doubles, 4 triples, 10 homers, and 30 RBIs – 100 total bases – in 33 games that month.

On August 21, Musial started in center field against Pittsburgh starter Tiny Bonham at Sportsman's Park. It was a sweltering Saturday evening in St. Louis, with a game-time temperature of almost 92 degrees. Batting third in the lineup, between Marty Marion and Enos Slaughter, Musial singled and scored in the first inning. He singled again in the third but was wiped out in a double play. In the fourth, Musial doubled Erv Dusak home and then scored on Ron Northey's homer. The Cardinals moved into second place with their 9-2 win, tied with the Dodgers and one game behind the Braves.

Musial produced a .415 batting average and 1.257 OPS on the road. He absolutely feasted on the Phillies, against whom he batted .407 and reached base in 52 percent of his plate appearances. He especially enjoyed hitting at Philadelphia's Shibe Park, where he posted a .500 batting average.

Musial managed a mere .313 batting average against New York Giants pitching, but he clubbed 11 home runs in 22 games against them. That included eight homers at New York's Polo Grounds.

He saved his best for when he faced the Brooklyn Dodgers, who finished third that season. Musial slugged .851 with 74 total bases in his 22 games against a pitching staff that included Preacher Roe, Rex Barney, and Ralph Branca. Most impressively, he batted .522 in 11 games at Ebbets Field.

Frankly, no team discerned how to get Musial out. For instance, he drove in 27 runs in 22 games against the Cincinnati Reds. And he batted .443 and posted a .510 on-base percentage against the Boston Braves – whose pitching staff featured Warren Spahn and Johnny Sain en route to the NL pennant.

The Braves, guided by Musial's old manager, Billy Southworth, finished 6½ games ahead of the second-place Cardinals. Boston went 21-7 after August 31; that enabled the Braves to pull away from the Cardinals, who went 17-12 in that final stretch of games.

Still, Musial finished strong. He batted .368 and drove in 22 runs during the Cardinals' 29 games after August 31. Though he continued to amass hits and RBIs in bunches to easily best the NL field in those categories, the home-run race proved most interesting.

Musial hit only five homers in September, the same as Kiner but three fewer than Mize. Homer number 39 for Musial came in the first game of a September 30 doubleheader against the Pirates. That pulled him into a tie with Mize. Kiner had hit his 40th homer two days earlier.

Mize walloped his 40th on the season's final day. Alas, Musial failed to find his power in any of his final 20 plate appearances.

Musial earned $36,000 in 1948. His new contract secured a $50,000 salary for each of the next two seasons, making him one of the highest-paid players in the game.[12]

"They say a player's peak ranges between (ages) 28 to 32," said 27-year-old Musial at season's end. "That means my next five years should be my best, and I think I'm getting better as I go along."[13]

Team President Hannegan concurred.

"Let's put it this way," he said. "I'd say the only untouchable man on the Cardinal roster is Stan Musial. Why? Because I don't think any club in the National League would give up its franchise to pay for him. That's what he means to us."[14]

Baseball fans in 1948 hoped to add this Bowman card of Stan Musial to their collection.

SOURCES

The author accessed Retrosheet.org and Baseball-Reference.com for pertinent information, including box scores, play-by-play, and other statistical data.

NOTES

1   Ray Gillespie, "Stan Decides He's Bird Fixture, So He'll Buy St. Louis Home," *The Sporting News*, October 13, 1948: 13.
2   "Musial Signs Two-Year Contract With Cardinals," *St. Louis Post-Dispatch*, October 4, 1948.
3   Jimmy Cannon. "Stan the '48 Standout – Including Temperament," *The Sporting News*, December 8, 1948: 10.
4   Bob Broeg. "Cards Crack Back at Writer of Musial Blast in Magazine," *The Sporting News*, September 17, 1947: 7.
5   Broeg.

6. Broeg.
7. Broeg.
8. Broeg.
9. Broeg.
10. Edgar Brands. "Ruel Thumbs Out One-Handed Catching for Brown Backstops," *The Sporting News*, October 22, 1947: 9.
11. Ray Gillespie. "Stronger Stan Steps Up Hits, Cards Follow Him Upstairs," *The Sporting News*, May 12, 1948: 2.
12. "Musial Signs Two-Year Contract With Cardinals."
13. "Musial Signs Two-Year Contract With Cardinals."
14. Ray Gillespie. "Highest St. Louis Brass to Be at Draft Meeting," *The Sporting News*, November 10, 1948: 15.

1949: AFTER HIS GREATEST SEASON, THE MAN FACES CHALLENGES

BY JOE SCHUSTER

Stan Musial came into 1949 after what would turn out to be the best season in his Hall of Fame career. In 1948 he won his third (and, as it turned out, final) Most Valuable Player Award after leading the league in nearly every significant offensive category, including batting average (.376) and RBIs (131), and falling one homer shy of the Triple Crown as his 39 round-trippers ranked second, behind Johnny Mize's and Ralph Kiner's 40. In the statistical categories where Musial came out on top, many were by significant margins. His batting average was 43 points higher than that of runner-up Richie Ashburn; his .702 slugging average bested runner-up Johnny Mize by nearly 140 points, while his 1.152 OPS was nearly 200 points above that of runner-up Mize.

The historical significance of Musial's season becomes even clearer if we consider Wins Above Replacement, as Musial's 11.3 WAR was the 11th-best of any player in baseball's Modern Era to that point, a total exceeded only by Babe Ruth (who topped that mark six times), Rogers Hornsby, Lou Gehrig, and Honus Wagner.

Beyond postseason honors, Musial's season earned him a nearly 40 percent raise for 1949, from $36,000 to $50,000, and the Cardinals further rewarded him with a two-year contract, something rare at a time when baseball's reserve clause gave owners no practical reason to strike multiyear deals with their players.

Less than a month later, however, tragedy struck. In the last week of October, a thick chemical fog from zinc factory smokestacks settled over Musial's native Donora, Pennsylvania, resulting in more than 20 deaths and, according to some estimates, sickness in roughly a third of Donora's 15,000 people.[1] Because his mother, Mary, was among those who faced respiratory problems from the smog, Musial moved his parents to St. Louis, but two months later, his father, Lucasz, suffered his second stroke in less than a year and died at the age of 59.[2]

One other event that occurred in the offseason bears reporting simply because of its oddness: In February, as Musial was on his way to Florida for spring training, a 24-year-old Texan named Richard Edward Brame checked himself into a luxury resort in Mississippi under Musial's name, telling everyone he was the star player, giving interviews in which he promised to hit .400 and planned to make a visit to a VA hospital wearing his uniform.[3] When a reporter learned that Musial was then actually in Albany, New York, he alerted police and Brame ended up serving 10 days in jail for vagrancy.[4]

Musial's trials carried over onto the field as he struggled to hit in spring training. While there are no comprehensive statistics for Grapefruit League games, news reports from Florida paint a bleak picture. On April 4, after a loss to the Yankees, the *St. Louis Post-Dispatch* reported, "Stan Musial went hitless again and is in his longest slump of the spring."[5] Two days later, as the Cardinals broke camp and moved north for a series of exhibition games before the season started, the *St. Louis Star and Times* headlined a story: "Musial in Slump as Club Leaves Florida."[6] A little more than a week later, he was still not hitting well; the same newspaper commented, with an allusion to a restaurant business he had recently invested in, "Musial isn't hitting the size of one of his restaurant steaks, although a year ago on the way home 'The Man' was clearing fences."[7]

Musial continued his funk even after the season got underway, going 1-for-7 in the team's first two games in Cincinnati, both losses. It was so bad that when he came to bat for the first time in the Cardinals' home opener on April 22 that fans heckled him for his .143 batting average.[8] He responded with a massive home run that an Associated Press reporter suggested meant he had "found his batting eye" after his "utterly ineffective" start.[9]

The writer, however, was premature as Musial managed only 9 hits in 37 at-bats through the Cardinals' 10 games in April, and he closed out the month hitting .243. There was one bright spot, however, as three of those hits were home runs. Acknowledging that projecting season's totals with such a small sample size was foolish, *St. Louis Post-Dispatch* sports editor J. Roy Stockton nonetheless observed that Musial was on pace for 77 home runs. He went on, "Talking to Musial ... it would make him very happy to hit scads of home runs. He's been the most valuable player ... three times and has led the league in virtually every phase of offensive baseball. ... There aren't many new honors left, but wouldn't it be something to ... lead both leagues in four-baggers?"[10]

Then, even the power vanished. Musial touched .300 with a 3-for-3 day on May 1, but over the next three weeks was 16-for-63 with no homers and only one extra-base hit, a double, closing out May 21 with a .250 batting average and an anemic .380 slugging percentage. During that span, especially with the team also in the doldrums, at 11-16 and sitting in seventh place, Cardinals manager Eddie Dyer contemplated benching Musial but decided against it because, he told reporters, it might not do any good.[11] *Star and Times* writer Sid Keener blamed the two-year contract the team had given Musial, suggesting it was "unsound business … [as] the incentive to get out and hustle for more money on the following year is not there at the start of the first campaign."[12]

Finally, to pull himself out of his funk, Musial, and teammate Enos Slaughter, who was also struggling, hitting only .264 and slugging .403, held a session of private batting practice on May 16. There, Musial seemed to diagnose his own problem. At one point, while Slaughter watched him "hammer ball after ball to faraway places," Musial stepped away from the plate and declared, "I know what's been my trouble. I've been pressing too hard. I want to get going so much that I've been swinging at bad balls instead of picking out the good ones."[13]

The two kept at it for an hour, stopping only when Slaughter's hands started bleeding.[14] Musial came to see that he was overstriding and that, as hurlers figured out his new approach, they were pitching him outside more often and his insistence on pulling the ball was resulting in weak grounders to second. He began making the necessary adjustments and hit .321 with a .429 OBP and .528 slugging average from then until the end of May. In early June, *Post-Dispatch* sportswriter Bob Broeg, declared, "Musial again is Musial. And that means free-swinging, earth shaking destruction."[15]

Musial remained hot at the plate, hitting .339 for the month, briefly flirting with .300 for the season in the last week before going into a brief cold spell. Still, he earned a spot in the starting lineup for the National League All-Star team, in center field; in the balloting, fans gave him the third highest vote total of any player, behind only Jackie Robinson and Ralph Kiner. Musial went 3-for-4 and hit his second All-Star Game home run, though it was not enough to push the NL to a win, as they lost 11-7, in part because of five errors.

When the traditional second half of the season resumed in mid-July, Musial went into a funk for the first eight games, going 10-for-37 with a home run and, unusual for him, zero walks. What cured him was a trip to Ebbets Field in Brooklyn for a four-game set against the Dodgers. It was there, as the story goes, that he had gained his nickname, The Man, three years earlier, and in the series The Man awoke – for good that season. The Cardinals came into town in second place 2½ games behind the Dodgers. In good part because of Musial, when they left town, they were in first by a half-game.

Musial went 2-for-4 in the opener on July 22, including a home run off Preacher Roe in the first inning, as the Cardinals won 3-1. While he went hitless in the second game, he walked twice, including leading off the ninth inning to start a rally that pushed St. Louis to a 5-4 victory. In the third game, he went 4-for-5, hitting for the cycle in a 14-1 romp that moved the team to first place. In the final game, which ended in a 4-4 tie, Musial went 3-for-4 with a double, a triple, and an RBI. When it ended, his average stood at .304 and would never dip below .300 the rest of the year.

Still, by the standards Musial had set for his career since he came into the league in September 1941, his numbers were unimpressive. He was far below his lifetime average of .348 and was only the third-best hitter on his own team, behind Slaughter's .322 and Red Schoendienst's .320. Beyond this, any hopes of repeating as batting champion seemed remote, as he trailed Jackie Robinson's league-leading average by nearly 60 points.

Once the calendar turned over to August, Musial set about trying to close both gaps, as the Cardinals also went to work to widen what was, at the end of July, a 1½-game lead over Brooklyn. By the end of the first week, when Musial went 13-for-27, his average was up to .313, as the Cards went 5-2. While Musial gained slightly on Robinson, who went 12-for-35 that week, the Dodgers were even hotter than St. Louis, going 7-1, moving back into a tie for first. By the end of the month, the Cardinals regained their 1½-game lead and Musial cut the distance between him and Robinson for the batting race nearly in half. Musial's 46-for-120 month had pushed his average to .321, while Robinson stood at .350 after going 37-for-120.

As it turned out, both chases came down to the season's final week, which began with the Cardinals leading the Dodgers by a game and Musial trailing Robinson by only 6 points. Both The Man and his team fell short by time the curtain rang down on the 1949 season. The Cardinals ended up dropping four of their final six games, while Brooklyn went 4-2, clinching the pennant with a 10-inning 9-7 victory over Philadelphia on the final Sunday. As for the Cardinals, their final-game 13-5 shellacking of the Cubs was not enough, after the team had dropped the first two contests against Chicago. If there was one

Musial completes his swing on this 1948-49 Leaf trading card.

key moment that might at least have pushed the club into a playoff with Brooklyn, it came in the fifth inning of the next to last game. With the Cubs leading 3-1, the Cardinals had runners on second and third with no outs after an infield single by Lou Klein, and a double by Musial. After Slaughter popped out to short, Chicago walked Steve Bilko intentionally, loading the bases, but Marty Marion popped to short and Del Rice popped to first, ending the threat.

As for Musial, although he outhit Robinson in the final week – he went 12-for-27 while Robinson collected 6 hits in 18 at-bats – it was still too little, as Robinson ended up winning the only batting title of his Hall of Fame career, with a .342 average, while Musial was runner-up at .338. (Musial's partner in the semiprivate batting practice earlier in the year, Slaughter, ended in third, at .336.) Musial did lead the league in on-base percentage (.438), hits (207), total bases (382), and doubles (41), while finishing second in home runs (36), behind Kiner, who had 54. Robinson also took home the Most Valuable Player Award (the only one in his career), while Musial was runner-up.

Reflecting on the season, and his disappointment in failing to repeat as batting champion – something no one in the league had done since Rogers Hornsby nearly a quarter of a century earlier – Musial focused on his poor start, which he blamed on trying to hit the long ball after just missing out on the Triple Crown the season before.

"There's no doubt I threw myself off stride by swinging for home runs in the spring," he told *The Sporting News* for a November retrospective on his season. "I lost my timing, the pitchers began getting me to nibble at bad pitches and it wasn't until the second half that I got back in the groove."[16] After acknowledging that it was only when he began "meeting the ball on the nose and driving it to all fields," he vowed, "That's the way I'm going to approach this hitting business next year. … I'm not the hottest spring hitter, I know, but I'm hoping to get a good start to build an early average for a big season."[17]

As it turned out, Musial made good on that pledge: No longer striving for home runs, he hit over .400 for the first two months of 1950, flipping the script on Robinson and winning the batting title over the Dodgers great. He went on to repeat in 1951 and 1952, and won his last batting title in 1957. Sadly, however, the 1949 season was the nearest Musial and the Cardinals came to winning the pennant over the last 14 seasons of his career.

SOURCES

In addition to the sources cited in the Notes, the author referred to Baseball-Reference, StatHead, and the SABR BioProject.

NOTES

1. "4218 of Donora's 15,000 Persons Affected by Smog, Survey Shows," *St. Louis Post-Dispatch*, January 7, 1949: 1.
2. "Stan Musial's Father Dies at St. Louis," *Pittsburgh Press*, December 20, 1948: 26.
3. "Texan Charged with Impersonating Musial," *St. Louis Star and Times*, February 10, 1949: 28.
4. "Stan Musial Poseur Released from Jail," *Biloxi* (Mississippi) *Sun Herald*, February 22, 1949: 8.
5. J. Roy Stockton, "Wind Aids Yankees in 3-1 Victory," *St. Louis Post-Dispatch*, April 4, 1949: 3B.
6. W. Vernon Tietjen, "Stan Musial in Slump as Club Leaves Florida," *St. Louis Star and Times*, April 6, 1949: 26.
7. W. Vernon Tietjen, "Cards Appear 'Tired of It All' as Exhibition Tour Ends," *St. Louis Star and Times*, April 14, 1949: 32.
8. W. Vernon Tietjen, "Cardinals in Night Debut Hope to Keep Cubs in the Dark," *St. Louis Star and Times*, April 23, 1949: 6.
9. "Cardinals, Back Home, Win Game," *Mount Vernon* (Ilinois) *Register-News*, April 23, 1949: 8.
10. J. Roy Stockton, "Meet the New Musial, He's the Slugger Type," *St. Louis Post-Dispatch*, April 27, 1949: 18.
11. Bob Broeg, "Cards-Dodgers Game Postponed; Young Players Give Birds a Lift," *St. Louis Post-Dispatch*, May 10, 1949: 12.
12. Sid Keener, "Musial's Slump," *St. Louis Star and Times*, May 18, 1949: 25.
13. Ray J. Gillespie, "Musial and Slaughter, Desperate for Hits, Hold Their First Batting Practice," *St. Louis Star and Times*, May 17, 1949: 20.
14. Gillespie.
15. Bob Broeg, "Musial, Pollett Win One at Midnight," *St. Louis Post-Dispatch*, June 3, 1949: 32.
16. Bob Broeg, "Stan Lost Batting Title in Pennsylvania Parks," *The Sporting News*, November 16, 1949: 4.
17. "Stan Lost Batting Title in Pennsylvania Parks."

STAN MUSIAL, JACKIE ROBINSON, AND THE STRIKE HEARD 'ROUND THE LEAGUE

BY NICK MALIAN

Tensions were high when Jack Roosevelt Robinson took the field on April 15, 1947; the integration of major-league baseball had arrived. For many of the White players, playing with or against a Black player was contrary to their beliefs. So, it was no surprise that rumors had circulated that one team was planning to boycott games against the Brooklyn Dodgers. That team was the St. Louis Cardinals.

The story goes that Cardinals President Sam Breadon had heard rumblings about some of his players planning to strike in defiance of Robinson's ascension to the National League. Upon hearing this, Breadon hastily flew to New York and contacted NL President Ford Frick for fear of reprisal. At the same time, the Cardinals' team doctor, Robert Hyland, got wind of the strike and shared the story with a friend and sportswriter, Rud Rennie, over many libations. Not wanting to out his friend as a source, Rennie gave the tip to his boss, Stanley Woodward, who published the scoop in the *New York Herald Tribune* on May 9, 1947.[1]

Immediately after the story was published, Cardinals manager Eddie Dyer denied the rumors of a boycott. Enos Slaughter, a Southerner from Roxboro, North Carolina, vehemently denied any plans for a strike. Reigning NL MVP Stan Musial said, "There was definitely racist talk, but it wasn't going to amount to nothing."[2]

Whether or not a boycott was planned has been discussed elsewhere.[3] While Cardinals pitcher Freddy Schmidt later recalled a letter being shared around the clubhouse advising players to boycott,[4] other accounts from Cardinals officials and players, including the 26-year-old Musial, suggest that the talk among players could have been interpreted as setting the groundwork for a strike.

After the story was published, Musial's immediate reaction to the boycott allegation is difficult to find.[5] However, he reflected on it later in life, documented in an interview conducted by Roger Kahn in 1993 and later in George Vecsey's biography of Musial, published in 2011.

Vecsey dedicates a chapter to the alleged strike and does a good job of summarizing the accounts and timelines. He includes a 1997 quote from Musial denying the allegations: "We never had a meeting. We never talked about having any organized boycott. ... We'll all tell you; we never had any thoughts in that direction, whatsoever."[6] Musial added that the preconceptions New Yorkers had about St. Louis (they were the closest "Southern" team in the National League) and having Southern players may have led to the assumption that a boycott against a Black player could have been planned by the Cardinals. "I think they felt that we were, you know, we're a Southern town in a way."[7] Musial further said, "You (might have) heard some mumbles before that about playing against Robinson, but when the time came to play, why, everybody played, and it was really nothing. We didn't have any special meeting, or anybody give us any special talk."

In the interview with Kahn, Musial was more open about the alleged strike and admitted that he heard "rough and racist talk" in the clubhouse and justified it as a byproduct of baseball at the time. "First of all, everybody has racial feelings. We don't admit it. We aren't proud of it. But it's there. And this is big league baseball, not an English Tea, and ballplayers make noise. So, I heard the words, and I knew there were some feelings behind the words, but I didn't take it seriously. That was baseball." He went on to say that the thought the racial talk was "just hot air."[8]

Musial and Robinson's relationship seemed to be amicable, despite their bitter National League rivalry.[9] In the Kahn interview, Musial empathized with Robinson about his immigrant father and second-generation American mother who sought after the same economic opportunity in the United States as Robinson did for Black Americans.[10] And despite positing that "everybody has racial feelings," Musial was not considered a

Stan Musial stands with three of his National League teammates in the 1949 All-Star Game at Ebbets Field. Also pictured are Gil Hodges, Jackie Robinson, and Raph Kiner.

racist. "I had no trouble myself with integration," he told Kahn in the interview. Musial grew up playing integrated sports in Donora, Pennsylvania, and was proud of it.[11] According to Vecsey, Ford Frick said that a "prominent player" (read Musial) on the Cardinals told him that "he did not care if Robinson was white, black, green, or yellow."[12]

But when push came to shove, Musial admitted to Kahn that it was out of the question to express to his teammates his feelings on race, Robinson, and integration of baseball being long overdue. "Saying all that would have been a speech, and I didn't know how to make speeches. Saying it to older players, that was beyond me."[13] This suggests that his role in any alleged strike was more nonparticipatory than that of a staunch opposer.

There is a case to be made that the alleged strike by the Cardinals was unsubstantiated and nothing more than vile locker-room threats. If a strike had been really planned and carried out, Musial would have likely opposed it but may not have stopped it. What appears to have been a mix of hasty escalations by the Cardinals brass and claims from eager sportswriters morphed into another stain on major-league baseball's sordid past.

SOURCES

In addition to the sources cited in the Notes, the author consulted Baseball-reference.com.

NOTES

1. Stanley Woodward, "Views of Sport," *New York Herald Tribune*, May 9, 1947, reprinted in *The Sporting News*, May 21, 1947: 4
2. Roger Kahn, *The Era 1947-1957 When the Yankees, the Giants, and the Dodgers Ruled the World* (Lincoln: University of Nebraska Press, 1993), 56
3. Warren Corbett, The 'Strike' Against Jackie Robinson: Truth or Myth?" SABR.org https://sabr.org/journal/article/the-strike-against-jackie-robinson-truth-or-myth/#calibre_link-439, accessed April 2024.
4. George Vecsey, *Stan Musial An American Life* (New York: Ballantine Books, 2011), 155.
5. Musial was being treated for acute appendicitis at the time.
6. Vecsey, 156-157.
7. James Giglio, *Musial: From Stash to Stan the* Man (Columbia: University of Missouri Press, 2001), 154. This argument continued into the 1990s and culminated in an argument between Cardinals beat writer Bob Broeg and Roger Kahn at a dinner with Musial. Kahn believed that Broeg was not sensitive enough to racial matters and that the Cardinals did not do enough to support Robinson. Broeg contended that the situation was not black and white.
8. Kahn, 56.
9. Arnold Rampersad, *Jackie Robinson, A Biography* (New York: Random House, 1997), 178. There is scant documentation about their relationship. In one instance, Robinson once referred to Musial as "a very fine fellow" during an interview with Jack Buck in 1962. And Rampersad in his biography of Robinson wrote that Musial was always friendly with Jackie Robinson. Robinson told Kahn that Musial was a nice guy but when it came to Robinson breaking the color barrier, Musial did not hurt nor help him.
10. Musial's mother was born in New York to Austrian-Hungarian parents and his father was born in Poland.
11. He played against Buddy Griffey, father and grandfather of Ken Griffey Sr. and Jr.
12. Vecsey, 155.
13. Kahn, 56.

STAN THE MAN AND TRADER LANE: HOW MUSIAL ALMOST ENDED UP IN PHILADELPHIA

BY VINCE GUERRIERI

It seems almost unfathomable to think of Stan Musial as anything but a St. Louis Cardinal.

Few players are as completely intertwined with the history and identity of a team as Musial is with the Cardinals. A statue of him in his unique batting stance (White Sox pitcher Ted Lyons, who saw Musial play in the Navy, likened it to "a kid looking around the corner to see if the cops are coming")[1] stands in front of the current iteration of Busch Stadium, with an inscription from Commissioner Ford Frick's remarks on the occasion of Musial's retirement in 1963: "Here stands baseball's perfect warrior; here stands baseball's perfect knight."[2]

Musial's entire career came with the Cardinals, a sign of his popularity and talent as much as a remnant of the days where the reserve clause meant that no player left a team unless the team wanted him gone. And in 1956, at least one person wanted him gone from St. Louis. He happened to be the general manager.

"Except, apparently, for the boldness of my business partner, Biggie Garagnani, and the intervention of August A. Busch Jr., I would have been sent to the Philadelphia Phillies for Robin Roberts at the trading deadline," Musial recalled in his autobiography.[3]

After dominance in the 1940s, when they won three World Series and appeared in another, the Cardinals fell from their perch as one of the National League's top teams in the 1950s. In that decade, the "Boys of Summer" – the Brooklyn Dodgers – were in full ascent, while the New York Giants won two pennants and a World Series as well. After their World Series win over the Boston Red Sox in 1946, the Cardinals finished second in the National League in each of the next three years, and then slid further down into the standings in the 1950s, which also marked a transitional period in the team's ownership.

Sam Breadon, on whose watch the Cardinals had become one of the best teams in the National League, sold his interests in 1947 to Fred Saigh. In turn, Saigh was forced to sell the team in 1953, following a conviction for income-tax evasion. The team's new owner was the Anheuser-Busch brewery, fronted by president August A. "Gussie" Busch Jr. The Cardinals had never had a general manager until Busch installed brewery executive Richard Meyer in the position.

Meyer, who like Busch had considerable business experience but little baseball experience, served in the role for two years before the Cardinals hired Frank Lane, a longtime sports executive who'd gained credit for turning around the Chicago White Sox in his only other stint as a general manager.

Lane was a man of action, described as an indefatigable force of nature. "Frank Lane is as restful as a hurricane," wrote Arthur Daley of the *New York Times*.[4] "Probably the most exciting chapter in the history of St. Louis baseball is about to be enacted," J.G. Taylor Spink of *The Sporting News* said on Lane's arrival.[5]

Lane had played minor-league baseball in his native Ohio (for a Class-D team owned by future President Warren G. Harding) and football for the Dayton Triangles, one of the initial teams in what became the NFL. His physical fitness belied his limitations as an athlete,[6] and he moved into officiating, where he distinguished himself in college football and basketball, and then into the front office. He'd worked for the Reds and the Yankees before being named president of the American Association in 1946. In October 1948 he was named general manager of the White Sox, taking over a job viewed by many as radioactive, as enfant terrible Chuck Comiskey, Charles Comiskey's grandson, tried to wrest control from his sister, Dorothy Comiskey Rigney, who was the team's majority owner.

"It was the one job in baseball nobody wanted, and Frank was warned of the problems: Chicago, then in eighth place, had never drawn a million people in its history; the White Sox were financially impoverished," Mark Kram wrote in a 1968 profile of Lane for *Sports Illustrated*.[7] But Lane took the job, and immediately took action. He waived or traded 38 of the 40 players on the team within a year of taking over and made 253 deals for a total of 341 players – an average of three trades a month by Lane's own calculation. But he laid the groundwork for the Go-Go Sox of the 1950s before his resignation in September 1955 amid rumors of a feud. "I left Chicago because young Chuck was breathing down my neck a little harder than I liked," Lane said in a *Saturday Evening Post* story the following summer.[8] Comiskey, for his part, called stories of a feud overblown and said shortly after Lane's departure for St. Louis, "Believe it or not, I wish Frank had stayed on a couple more years."[9]

Lane was given a three-year contract and started making changes right off the bat – literally, as he redesigned the Cardinals' uniforms, banishing the birds-on-a-bat design seen even today in favor of a script "Cardinals" across the chest. The move was widely excoriated, and lasted only a year.

Again, Lane started wheeling and dealing. He inquired about buying Ernie Banks' contract from the Cubs but was rebuffed.[10] Lane then completed a five-player deal, sending Harvey Haddix, Stu Miller, and Ben Flowers to the Phillies for Murry Dickson and Herm Wehmeier.[11] Solly Hemus also went to Philadelphia, for Bobby Morgan. Bill Virdon, the previous year's rookie of the year, was traded to Pittsburgh for Dick Littlefield and Bobby Del Greco. Then Alex Grammas was traded with Joe Frazier to the Reds for Chuck Harmon.

"I didn't come to St. Louis to raise red roses or tell after-dinner stories or take the tenor lead in Hearts and Flowers," Lane said not long after the trades were made. "I came here to win a pennant, and that's exactly what I intend to do, any way I can."[12]

In the short term, the Cardinals were contending neck-and-neck with the Dodgers as May turned to June on the calendar. The trade deadline loomed on June 15. The Cardinals needed pitching – something Lane had pointed out when he took the job the previous fall – and Lane was ready to make a deal to bring arguably the best pitcher in the major leagues to St. Louis. And all it would cost him was Stan Musial.

Shortly before the trade deadline, Garagnani, a well-known St. Louis restaurateur even before taking on Musial as a partner, heard a rumor from a reputable source that Musial was on the verge of being traded straight up for Phillies pitcher Robin Roberts, who'd been a 20-game winner in each of the previous six seasons, and led the majors in wins in each of the previous four.[13] A call to J.G. Taylor Spink, the editor of *The Sporting News*, confirmed the details. Garagnani then tried to call Busch, who'd previously stated that Musial was untouchable. Unable to reach Busch, Garagnani tried to reach his associates at the brewery, one of whom said, "Lane's moving so fast, we can't keep up with him."[14]

Garagnani took the bold step of telling team officials – before consulting with Musial – that Musial would retire before accepting a trade. (Musial said in his autobiography that Garagnani's read on the situation was correct, but that if he really had to think about it, with his 3,000-hit milestone looming, he might have reported to Philadelphia.)

When word reached Busch about the proposed deal, he felt obligated to step in. "When the Musial trade rumors persisted last year I made up my mind they had to be stopped," he told the *Saturday Evening Post*. "To my way of thinking, Stan was, is and will continue to be a St. Louis institution." Busch then commissioned the brewery's PR firm to draft a statement that said, simply, "At no time has a trade for Stan Musial been considered." Lane suggested he should release the statement. "I don't give a damn who makes it," Busch retorted, "so long as it's made."[15]

The Musial deal was dead,[16] but Lane couldn't be stopped. Three days later, on June 14, the day before the deadline, Red Schoendienst, another fan favorite who'd played with Musial since the 1940s, was traded to the New York Giants.[17] "The telephone receiver had to be taken off the hook at my home," Busch recalled.[18] After the Schoendienst deal, all of Lane's trades were subject to Busch's approval.

The Cardinals finished 76-78-2 in 1956, a distant fourth in the National League (although an eight-win improvement from the previous season). The following February, at a dinner

Cardinals general manager Frank Lane nearly traded Musial to the Philadelphia Phillies in 1956.

for the Knights of the Cauliflower Ear, a St. Louis sportsmen's club started by Busch's father (August Anheuser Busch Sr.), Gussie said, "I expect the Cardinals to come damn close to winning a pennant in 1957, and 1958 is going to be a sure thing, or Frank Lane will be out on his rump."[19] Busch and Lane both said later that the remarks were not made in total seriousness, but contemporary coverage suggested that Busch's patience with Lane was running thin. Lane himself tested the waters by asking for a contract extension but received a three-word telegram from Busch: "Kiss my ass."[20]

The Cardinals again improved, to 87-67, good for second place in the National League. But the pennant (and World Series) was won by the Milwaukee Braves, aided by a midseason acquisition: none other than Red Schoendienst, no longer a Giant. Lane was named *The Sporting News* General Manager of the Year, and his name was linked to a variety of open jobs, including that of the Indians. "I have no interest in the job," he said … a week before being announced as the new Indians general manager, where he remains reviled to this day by fans of a certain age as the man who traded Rocky Colavito. But that was just one of many bad moves Lane made as the Indians slid into mediocrity. Less well-known but every bit as damaging was his trade of Norm Cash to Detroit for Steve Demeter. "Cripes, he didn't make any good deals," Indians pitcher Ray Narleski said.[21]

Lane's departure from St. Louis kept him from consummating one more deal, sending third baseman (and future NL MVP) Ken Boyer to the Phillies for Richie Ashburn – a stroke of good fortune for the Cardinals.[22]

Musial finished out his career with St. Louis, but the idea of his returning to his hometown Pittsburgh Pirates was broached at least once more, in 1960. Benched by Hemus, who'd returned to manage the team, Musial was still looking for a way to prove himself. Before that year's trade deadline, Pirates manager Danny Murtaugh inquired, and was told Musial might be available, but general manager Joe L. Brown said he couldn't make an offer for fear of putting Lane's successor, Bing Devine, in a bad spot. The only way they'd take on Musial was if he was released. Musial said in his autobiography that he considered asking for his release but decided against it.[23]

After retiring as a player in 1963, Musial became the Cardinals vice president but stepped in to become the general manager in 1967. The manager was his old friend and roommate Schoendienst. The two got into the team bus at the hotel to go to the ballpark when Schoendienst heard a familiar voice. It was Lane.

"I never saw Stan move so fast in my life," Schoendienst recalled in his autobiography. "He sprang up from his seat and walked to where Lane was sitting. 'Get the hell out of here,' he ordered Lane. 'Get off our bus.'"[24]

NOTES

1. *The Sporting News*, August 20, 1947: 13. Quoted in Lyons' SABR bio.
2. Larry Schwartz, "Musial Was Gentleman Killer," ESPN. https://www.espn.com/sportscentury/features/00016375.html.
3. Stan Musial, as told to Bob Broeg, *"The Man's" Own Story* (New York: Doubleday, 1964), 177.
4. Arthur Daley, "Sports of the Times: Baseball's Man in Motion," *New York Times*, January 4, 1961: 37.
5. J.G. Taylor Spink. "'Tradin' Man' Will Shake Up St. Louis," *The Sporting News*, October 12, 1955: 1.
6. Famously, he was nearly blind, and well into his old age was too vain to wear glasses, finally opting for prescription sunglasses.
7. Mark Kram, "Would You Trade With This Man?" *Sports Illustrated*, August 26, 1968. https://vault.si.com/vault/1968/08/26/would-you-trade-with-this-man.
8. Frank Lane, as told to Roger Kahn, "I'm Here to Win a Pennant," *Saturday Evening Post*, June 23, 1956.
9. "Feud With Lane Overplayed, Chuck Tells Luncheon Group," *The Sporting News*, October 26, 1955, 2.
10. August A. Busch Jr., as told to Milton Gross, "Baseball's Got Me," *Saturday Evening Post*, May 18, 1957. Busch, who'd made overtures to the Dodgers about Gil Hodges before hiring Lane, said Lane went as high as $500,000 for Banks, but Busch, a multimillionaire, was told, "Mr. Wrigley needs a half a million dollars as much as you do."
11. Dickson had been sold from the Cardinals to the Pirates in 1949, a period when Saigh was attempting to buy out partner Bob Hannegan. A potential sale of Musial to the Pirates was discussed but never consummated. Bob Broeg, "The Man Reveals Near Miss as '48 Bucco," *The Sporting News*, April 6, 1963: 29.
12. Lane, "I'm Here to Win a Pennant."
13. In 1953 he had been tied with Warren Spahn. In 1954 he was tied with Bob Lemon and Early Wynn.
14. Musial, *The Man's Own Story*, 178.
15. Busch, "Baseball's Got Me." Lane, for his part, denied ever attempting to trade Musial, saying in Kram's *Sports Illustrated* story that it was "one of the great myths of baseball."
16. It's an interesting counterfactual to wonder how the Cardinals would have made out had the deal gone down. Roberts led the league in losses in the next two seasons, and never won 20 games in a season again in his career.
17. In his memoirs, Schoendienst said he found out about the deal on the radio.
18. Busch, "Baseball's Got Me."
19. Bob Broeg, "Outfield Gone, Pennant Must Come, Bush Warns Lane," *St. Louis Post-Dispatch*, February 13, 1957: 24. The quote has been variously stated as "out on his ear" or occasionally, "out on his ass."
20. Bob Vandenburg, *Frantic Frank Lane: Baseball's Ultimate Wheeler-Dealer* (Jefferson, North Carolina, McFarland, 2013), 77.
21. Joe Maxse, "The Boys of Past Indian Summers," *Cleveland Plain Dealer*, April 3, 1988: 50.
22. Robert L. Burnes, "The Bench Warmer," *St. Louis Globe-Democrat*, April 4, 1958: 21.
23. Musial, *The Man's Own Story*, 216.
24. Red Schoendienst with Rob Rains, *Red: A Baseball Life* (Champaign, Illinois: Sports Publishing, 1998), 83.

EXAMINING STAN MUSIAL'S BATTING: CONSISTENTLY UNCOILING 'AN EXPLOSION OF POWER'[1]

BY MIKE HUBER

Jan Finkel begins his biography of Stan Musial with a quote from the great broadcaster Vin Scully: "How good was Stan Musial? He was good enough to take your breath away."[2] For more than 20 years, with a bat in his hands, Musial left us gasping for breath again and again and again.

The On-Base Plus Slugging (OPS) statistic combines getting on base with power, offering insights into a batter's offensive potential to help his team win.[3] More recently, Wins Above Replacement (WAR) measures the number of wins the player added to the team above what a replacement player would add.[4] A WAR value can be scaled for a single season or be used to compare players over their entire careers. When analyzing Stan Musial's batting statistics to understand winning, we gain more insight by studying his types of base hits (not just his OPS or WAR).

First, the obvious. A deserved first-ballot Hall of Famer, Musial is sixth in career Offensive Wins Above Replacement (125.1).[5] The Offensive WAR career list names the best of the best batters. The only five batters above Musial on the list are Babe Ruth, Ty Cobb, Barry Bonds, Willie Mays, and Henry Aaron. Great company.

It is easy to admire Musial's career statistics: a .331 batting average, a .417 on-base percentage, and a .559 slugging percentage. He ranks fourth in career base hits (3,630), split amazingly with 1,815 hits at home and 1,815 on the road. That's consistency. His 1,377 extra-base hits,[6] fourth-best of any player in history, reinforce his legacy of power. He led the majors in seven different seasons in extra-base hits.[7] In fact, Musial was in the majors' top 10 of extra-base hits in every season from 1943 to 1957 except one (he did not play in 1945, due to military service). It was precisely his ability to produce extra-base hits that correlates directly with more wins.

Musial is one of only 15 players in the history of the game to have collected 100 or more extra-base hits in a single season.[8] He ranks tied for sixth-most all-time, when he had 103 extra-base hits in 1948. When he accomplished that rare feat, he was only the 10th player in history to have at least 100 extra-base hits in a single season, and he was the first since 1937 (when Hank Greenberg broke the century barrier). Musial missed winning the Triple Crown by one home run,[9] but he did win his third (of three) National League Most Valuable Player Award that season. He also placed second in the NL MVP balloting four more times. In 1950 he was runner-up to a pitcher, indicating that Musial was presumably the best hitter in the National League.

Back to how could Musial influence a game offensively. In 1948 he had 230 hits, giving him a percentage of extra-base hits of 0.4478 (close to one-half). How can we think of this in a practical sense? If Musial was 2-for-4 in a game in 1948, we could expect one of those hits to be for extra bases – a double, triple, or home run. With a runner on base, there is a high chance that the runner could score (maybe from first on a double but much more likely if a runner was on second or third). In addition, Musial would then put himself in scoring position (if he didn't hit a home run), waiting to be driven home by his teammates, leading to another run. We know that in his career he scored 1,949 runs and drove in 1,951, creating a run in every 5.6 at-bats. Again, that's consistency.

Musial had two other seasons with 90 or more extra-base hits. In 1949 he had 90 extra-base hits as part of his 207 total hits (43.49 percent). He also hit for the cycle on July 24, 1949, banging out three different extra-base hits with a single, while scoring three times and adding four RBIs. Four seasons later, in 1953, Musial had 92 extra-base hits in 200 total safeties (46 percent). For his career, Musial's percentage of extra-base hits is 0.3793.[10]

Musial's career slugging percentage of .559 translates roughly into five total bases for every nine at-bats, or, in a simpler way, at least one base in every two at-bats. His career percentage of extra-base hits (0.3793) means he would get at least a double in every third base hit. From a power point of view, Musial drove in a run, or got into a position to be driven in, with every third base hit over his entire career.

When comparing players with a combined batting average of at least .300, an on-base average of at least .400, and a slugging percentage of at least .500 (in the same season), Musial ranks second-most in major-league history, with 15 such seasons.[11] The last time he accomplished this triple-stat mark was in the 1962 season (.330 BA, .416 OBP, .508 SLG), when Musial was 41 years old. For comparison, the 15 seasons stand three behind Ted Williams and one ahead of both Babe Ruth and Lou Gehrig, who each had 14 such seasons. Since Musial's performance spans a 22-season career, interrupted by military service, all we can say is, "Wow! This is consistently impressive!"

We can combine Musial's career batting average, on-base percentage, slugging percentage, and percentage of extra-base hits to define a typical series for him. Hypothetically, if Musial got 15 at-bats in a four-game series, he would reach base at least six times (with at least five hits), with about two extra-base hits,

Musial looks forward to another game at the Polo Grounds. Musial smashed 49 home runs at that ballpark, more than he hit at any other opposition park.

each leading to a potential run or two. He would drive in two to three runs and score two to three himself. In every series. For every season. Obviously, his numbers were higher during his peak seasons. What manager wouldn't want that consistency?

Using a relativity example, in Musial's 1948 MVP season, the average National League team had 384 extra-base hits and a percentage of extra-base hits of 0.2787. The Cardinals' numbers were similar, 401 and 0.2872 respectively. Musial accounted for more than a quarter of his team's extra-base hits. He alone was 60.67 percent better than the average team in producing extra-base hits per hit.

Finally – just imagine! – if we could put nine Stan Musials batting on the same team, that team would win 77.9 percent of its games.[12] Musial's Offensive Win Percentage ranks 15th all-time (tied with Tris Speaker), out of every baseball player who ever swung a bat in the big leagues. The only other players above Musial on this list who played in roughly the same era as he did were Boston's Williams (his career Offensive Win Percentage was 85.7 percent) and New York's Mickey Mantle (80.4 percent). Babe Ruth is first on the list (his 85.8 percent edges out Williams), and Barry Bonds is fourth (81.5 percent), but nine of the top 14 players come from the 1910s-1930s (representing some of the game's greatest hitters – Ruth, Oscar Charleston, Rogers Hornsby, Shoeless Joe Jackson, Turkey Stearnes, Ty Cobb, Mule Suttles, Lou Gehrig, and Jimmie Foxx).[13] That means that for the entirety of his 22-season career, Stan the Consistent Man Musial contributed to his team's winning more games than all but two other players, out of the thousands who played in that stretch of time. That should take your breath away.

NOTES

1. Jan Finkel, "Stan Musial," SABR BioProject, https://sabr.org/bioproj/person/stan-musial/. In his bio, Finkel cites a quotation from a Paul Warburton article that appeared in the 2001 *Baseball Research Journal*. See Paul Warburton, "Stan Musial's Spectacular 1948 Season," *Baseball Research Journal*. 30 (2001), 99-104.
2. Finkel.
3. John Thorn and Pete Palmer, *The Hidden Game of Baseball: A Revolutionary Approach to Baseball and Its Statistics* (New York: Doubleday, 1984).
4. See https://www.baseball-reference.com/leaders/WAR_career.shtml.
5. Musial is tied with Tris Speaker and Ted Williams for sixth place in Offensive WAR. See https://www.baseball-reference.com/leaders/WAR_bat_career.shtml. When fielding statistics are included (giving career Position Player WAR), Musial ranks eighth; Tris Speaker and Honus Wagner move ahead of him. Williams dropped to 11th-best.
6. Of Musial's 475 home runs, 252 came at home while 223 came away, in 12 different ballparks. See Finkel for more details.
7. Musial led the majors in extra-base hits in 1943, 1944, 1946, 1948, 1949, 1950, and 1953.
8. See https://www.baseball-reference.com/leaders/XBH_season.shtml. As of the end of the 2023 season.
9. In 1948 Musial had 46 doubles, 18 triples, and 39 home runs – 103 extra-base hits. His 39 homers were one behind both Ralph Kiner and Johnny Mize, who led the majors.
10. In fairness, the percentage of extra-base hits statistic does not take any pitching or ballpark factors into account.
11. See https://www.statmuse.com/mlb/ask/most-seasons-with.300-batting-average.400-on-base-percentage-and.500-slugging-percentage. Accessed April 2024.
12. See https://www.baseball-reference.com/leaders/offensive_winning_perc_career.shtml. According to Baseball-Reference, this statistic "uses the Pythagorean win pct formula with the player's RC/G for runs scored and the league's R/9 as runs allowed."
13. Dan Brouthers makes the list as the only nineteenth-century player above Musial. As of the first month of the 2024 season, active player Mike Trout jumped to the 13th spot on the list (78.9 percent).

OF (A)SYMMETRY AND (IN)CONSISTENCY: STAN MUSIAL'S HOME/AWAY SPLITS

BY CLEM HAMILTON

One of the most celebrated facets of Cardinals historical lore is Stan Musial's remarkable home/away symmetry of career base hits: 1,815 at home and 1,815 away. In his book *Men at Work: The Craft of Baseball*, George Will found this phenomenon significant: "Stan Musial may have been baseball's most consistent hitter, at least as measured by this stunning statistic."[1] On the perimeter of its current Busch Stadium, the Cardinals placed 3,630 bricks in the ballpark's western boundary sidewalk, evenly divided by the location of Musial's statue (and labeled HOME and AWAY on either side), to invite visitors to draw the same conclusion, that he didn't care where he played: Bat met ball with equally positive results. Lee Allen, then the National Baseball Hall of Fame's historian, contributed a career statistical summary as an appendix to Musial's autobiography, in which he offered a more agnostic interpretation: "Through a fantastic coincidence, Musial made exactly as many hits on the road, 1,815, as he did in St. Louis."[2] Which is it, then, a statistic that provides a window on The Man's remarkable consistency and focus, unwavering in the face of diverse playing environments? Or merely a happy statistical accident?

The question is easily answered, unromantically favoring Allen's prosaic interpretation. The Donora Greyhound recorded a nontrivial home/away difference in batting average: .336 at home and .326 on the road. How was this possible, to produce the same number of hits? Did he sit out more home games, thereby coming to the plate less often? No, actually Musial drew a staggering 14.6 percent more bases on balls at home than away (857 versus 748). As a result, his fairly even division of plate appearances (6,332 home to 6,386 away, the difference likely reflecting fewer ninth-inning plate appearances at home) turned into a significantly uneven split of at-bats: 5,402 versus 5,569. With that difference in the denominator for calculating batting average, 1,815 hits at home produced .336, and the same number on the road .326, for a 3.1 percent advantage.

Other career statistics reveal further home advantages in Musial's performance: on-base proportion .427 versus .407 (4.9 percent better), slugging .582 and .537 (+8.4 percent), and consequently OPS 1.009 versus .944 (+6.9 percent). But he indeed hit very well both at home and on the road. A lifelong Musial fan can understandably feel guilty about drawing attention to these differences, so perhaps there is salvation in discovering that his home/away statistical splits still were more symmetrical and consistent than his contemporaries'. Were they?

MUSIAL'S HOME/AWAY SPLITS COMPARED TO HIS CONTEMPORARIES

To quantify offensive productivity, we employed OPS (on-base plus slugging), an imperfect but useful and universally understood statistic. We used adjusted OPS, written OPS+, to normalize a player's OPS against a season's offensive context and to correct for his home ballpark characteristics, thus enabling more accurate comparisons among players and seasons. (A value of 100 matches the league average.) And when we explore Baseball-Reference.com's splits for each player's career and individual seasons, we find the highly useful tOPS+ (with the catchy name "OPS for split relative to Player's Total OPS") to quantify the magnitude of performance difference between, say, home vs. away, facing right-handed vs. left-handed pitchers, month of the season, batting order position, and so forth. A perfectly symmetrical scenario for a binary split would produce tOPS+ values as 100 and 100, e.g., exactly the same at home as away; whereas a slight difference might be, say, 103 and 97, and a more extreme pair of values 110 and 90. For simplicity's sake I present only Musial's Home tOPS+ values.

Musial's career Home tOPS+ is 107. At first blush, that seems close enough to 100 to suggest that his legendary offensive neutrality regarding a game's location is indeed supported, albeit imperfectly. But testing that premise requires comparing Musial's tOPS+ to overall major leaguers' splits (not including contemporary Jim Crow-era Black ball) for his primary seasons, 1942-1963, omitting 1941 (he played only 12 games) and 1945 (his World War II service). Over that time, baseball's overall Home tOPS+ was 105. That suggests that "The Man," with his Home tOPS+ of 107, actually favored playing at home vs. on the road even somewhat more than did his contemporaries, on average.

Might elite batsmen show home/away splits that are consistently different from ordinary players, and thus serve as an alternative basis for peer comparison? Fifteen elite hitters who overlapped Musial's career by at least six seasons were selected: Henry Aaron, Ernie Banks, Roy Campanella, Joe DiMaggio, Ralph Kiner, Ted Kluszewski, Mickey Mantle, Ed Mathews, Willie Mays, Johnny Mize, Bill Nicholson, Frank Robinson, Jackie Robinson, Duke Snider, and Ted Williams. Remarkably, they too averaged 105 for Home tOPS+, as we found for the majors as a whole. So Musial still appears to have favored his home ballpark more than most players.

Another question to explore is how consistent, from season to season, Musial was in his home/away offensive splits. His

Stan Musial doubled, then scored by sliding past catcher Ernie Lombardi on Walker Cooper's sixth-inning single at Braves Field on September 16, 1942. The Cardinals won, 6-2.

standard deviation in Home tOPS+ over his career, a measure of variation around the mean, was 15.2, with Home tOPS+ values ranging from a low of 83 in 1948 (hitting well better on the road in his finest offensive season) to a high of 148 in 1961.[3] His 15 peer sluggers showed an average standard deviation of 12.9, leaving Musial more variable – i.e., less consistent – in his tOPS+ than most of his contemporaries. Jackie Robinson and Mantle showed the greatest consistency in home/away offensive splits, as evidenced by their standard deviations of 7.2 and 9.4, respectively; both had career tOPS+ values of 104. At the other end of the standard deviation spectrum were the highly inconsistent Duke Snider (17.8) and Bill Nicholson (17.5).

Musial often is compared with Williams, as the two finest hitters in their respective leagues at that time. Their two career Home tOPS+ values are close, 107 vs. 106. But Teddy Ballgame's splits are more "normal," with a 10.1 percent home BA advantage (.361 to .328) and only 4.5 percent for walks (1,031 to 987), resulting in a 12.2 percent home edge in base hits (1,403 to 1,251).

Thus it is clear that Musial actually preferred home cooking even more than did his contemporaries, whether everyday players or his elite peers. He also showed greater than average season-to-season variation in his home/away splits, another mark against his purported offensive consistency.

MUSIAL'S FOUR MOST PECULIAR SEASONS

Four of Stan Musial's seasons stand out as having markedly anomalous Home tOPS+ values: 1948 (tOPS+ of 83), 1957 (84), 1961 (148), and 1963 (134). Plausible explanations are presented for three of those seasons, leaving only 1957 as an unfathomed mystery.

The 1948 campaign was Musial's best offensive season, and one of the best in baseball history, featuring an OPS+ of 200 and an offensive WAR of 10.8, as well as 429 total bases and a near-Triple Crown. He began crouching lower and gripping the bat down to the knob, which contributed to his doubling his previous high in home runs (19) to 39.[4] So why, in such a successful season, would he have performed so much better on the road? In general, Musial was not prone to either marked hot streaks or prolonged slumps, gauged by eyeballing each season's game logs. But from May 19 through May 28, 1948, he went on a remarkable tear: 9 games in four road ballparks, 47 plate appearances, 27 times reached base, and 53 total bases (including walks). Unlike today's schedules, with typically single-digit homestands and road trips, schedules in those days featured very long homestands and road trips: In 1948 the Cardinals had four homestands of 12 to 20 games against 4 to 7 teams each, and four road trips of 12 to 22 games against 5 to 7 teams, plus several shorter stints. Consequently a hot or cold streak of, say, 10 games would very likely fall completely or primarily within one home or away stretch. Therefore even if the streak was caused by factors unrelated to home/away playing environments – such as freedom from injury, seeing the ball well, or locked-in hitting mechanics – it could contribute to a misleadingly high or low home/away split for the season. All that suggests that his tOPS+ of 83 was an artifact of dumb luck regarding the timing of his hot streak, although Musial himself noted in his 1977 autobiography, "If I could have played the 1948 season on the road, I might have hit .400 and ripped the record book apart."[5]

The 1957 season, with another away-favoring tOPS+ of 84, featured no such prolonged streak or slump, except that on August 18 to 21 Musial might have been launching a streak (5 games, 22 PA, 14 OB, and 26 total bases) in Milwaukee (normally a tough offensive ballpark for him) and New York (a typically easy ballpark) before he was injured on August 22 in Philadelphia.[6] So, contrary to 1948, in 1957 we see a season-long overperformance on the road compared with home; but nowhere in his biographies was this pattern recognized, much less a cause suggested.[7]

At the opposite end of the split spectrum were 1961 and 1963, with Home tOPS+ values of 148 and 134, sandwiching a more normal split (tOPS+ 107) and successful 1962, with an OPS+ of 137, fourth in the National League at the age of 41. In 1961 he played 61 games at home, with 15 excellent offensive games, vs. a road record of 62 games with only six outstanding games, and no evident streaks or slumps. The 1963 season showed a similar pattern, with 64 home games, of which 14 were excellent; and 58 road games, of which only four were outstanding.[8] But Musial's two autobiographies indirectly address why 1961 and 1963 were so home-skewed: he noted that his greatest challenge in those later years was concentration, which he often found lagging.[9] He had been so embarrassed by his 1961 performance (OPS+ 119 and offensive WAR 2.1) that he worked especially hard the following offseason on his conditioning and adapting his stance and swing, thereby producing a gratifying comeback in 1962.[10] One may infer that he improved his concentration at the plate throughout the season, both at home and on the road, in order to produce more Musial-like numbers. But it would be natural for concentration to lag again in his final season, especially away from his home fans.[11]

WRAP-UP

Stan Musial's base hit home/away symmetry of 1,815 reflects no deep truth about his consistency, but rather is a statistical accident that distracts from the fact that he actually performed better offensively at home, even more so than most of his hard-hitting peers and major-league batters overall. But two mysteries remain, for future creative hypothesizing and analysis: (1) Why did his home/away offensive splits fluctuate so wildly and apparently so randomly during his career?[12] And (2) why did he walk so much more frequently at home? Was he more selective at the plate? And/or did he have a superior visual hitting environment in his home ballpark?

SOURCES

Musial's statistics and those for his contemporary players, including home-away split statistics, are gleaned from Baseball-Reference.com.

NOTES

1. George F. Will, *Men at Work: The Craft of Baseball* (New York: Macmillan, 1990), 176.
2. Lee Allen's statistical summary appeared first in Stan Musial, *Stan Musial: "The Man's" Own Story as told to Bob Broeg* (Garden City, New York: Doubleday, 1964), 315, and then in Stan Musial, *The Man Stan: Musial, Then and Now ... as Told to Bob Broeg* (St. Louis: Bethany Press, 1977), 244.
3. By season, Musial's Home tOPS+ values are 114 (1942), 99 (1943), 96 (1944), 107 (1946), 100 (1947), 83 (1948), 104 (1949), 113 (1950), 109 (1951), 91 (1952), 121 (1953), 109 (1954), 118 (1955), 121 (1956), 84 (1957), 112 (1958), 104 (1959), 103 (1960), 148 (1961), 107 (1962), and 134 (1963).
4. Musial, *Stan Musial*, 110; George Vecsey, *Stan Musial: An American Life* (New York: Ballantine Books, 2011), 201.
5. Musial, *The Man Stan*, 123. Musial noted also his extraordinary performance at Ebbets Field and the Polo Grounds, but that tendency prevailed most years, not just 1948.
6. Musial's career tOPS+ values were 67 for Milwaukee County Stadium (104 games, 1953-63) and 118 for the Polo Grounds (171 games, 1941-57).
7. Cf. all biographies already cited plus Irv Goodman, *Stan The Man Musial* (New York: Bartholomew House, 1961); James N. Giglio, *Musial: From Stash to Stan the Man* (Columbia: University of Missouri, 2001); Wayne Stewart, *Stan the Man: The Life and Times of Stan Musial* (Chicago: Triumph, 2010); St. Louis Post-Dispatch, *Stan Musial: Baseball's Perfect Knight* (St. Louis: St. Louis Post-Dispatch Books, 2010).
8. Musial's games were evaluated in an ad hoc manner as "excellent" or not in the context of their particular seasons, e.g., (on-base plus total bases) divided by plate appearances greater than or equal to 1.5 in 1961 and 1963, relatively poor seasons; greater than or equal to 1.75 in 1962, a much better season; and greater than or equal to 2.0 in his peak seasons.
9. Cf. Musial, *Stan Musial*, 244-245 regarding the importance of concentration and the challenge to maintain it; Musial, *The Man Stan*, 221 regarding his difficulties particularly in 1963. Cf. also Giglio, *Musial*, 238-239 and Post-Dispatch, *Stan Musial*, 90.
10. Musial, *The Man Stan*, 208; Giglio, *Musial*, 258; and Post-Dispatch, *Stan Musial*, 97.
11. Post-Dispatch, *Stan Musial*, 105.
12. Baseball changed significantly during Musial's career, e.g. the ascent of the slider; as did his approach to hitting, e.g. changing his bat characteristics and swinging more, then less in later years, for power; and his occasional injuries and the effects of aging. Cf. Musial, *Stan Musial*, 247, 301-306; Musial, *The Man Stan*, 115-116, 168-169; Giglio, *Musial*, 252.

STAN MUSIAL, JOHN F. KENNEDY, AND THE PRESIDENT'S COUNCIL ON PHYSICAL FITNESS

BY BILL PRUDEN

While his baseball exploits made Stan Musial a well-known and recognized public figure, for the most part his efforts were limited to baseball and business, especially his restaurant that built upon his baseball renown. However, Musial also made one brief foray into the world of politics, one which led to a little-remembered government position not long after the end of his playing days.

The road to his appointment, as well as the beginning of the relationship between a young senator with presidential aspirations and the aging baseball superstar[1] began with a chance meeting between the St. Louis Cardinals star and the senator from Massachusetts in September 1959 in Milwaukee. John F. Kennedy was in Milwaukee in the early stages of his as-yet-undeclared candidacy for the presidency and, hearing that the Cardinals were outside the hotel waiting to get onto the bus that would take them to County Stadium and their game with the Braves, sought out Musial. Upon finding the Cardinals star, he introduced himself, saying, "You're Stan Musial, aren't you? My name is Jack Kennedy. I'm glad to meet you."[2] The senator then quipped, "They tell me you're too old to play ball and I'm too young to be president, but maybe we'll fool them."[3]

The encounter represented the beginning of an active engagement with the Kennedy campaign as well as a devotion to the young future president. While Musial had supported Dwight Eisenhower in 1952 and 1956, he had not been active in the campaigns, and as the 1960 campaign got underway, Musial found himself attracted by the candidate's energy and vigor, as the saying went. Too, their shared Roman Catholic faith also made for a connection. At the time Kennedy's Catholicism was seen as a political liability, especially in the very Protestant Midwest. But Musial's popularity in that very region, as well as beyond, led Kennedy campaign adviser and one-time pro football star Byron "Whizzer" White to think that the baseball star might be able to help the young senator's electoral prospects.[4]

Although Musial had never previously been actively involved in politics, he agreed to help, and so, in the final week of the 1960 campaign, with the baseball season behind him, Musial became a member of a group of celebrities that included White, author James Michener, historian Arthur Schlesinger Jr., Kennedy sisters-in-law Ethel and Joan Kennedy, and Hollywood stars Jeff Chandler and Angie Dickinson. The group campaigned in Michigan, Nebraska, Oklahoma, Illinois, Indiana, Utah, Colorado, Idaho, and Kentucky.[5] Musial enjoyed the camaraderie of the group – he and Michener became lifelong friends and he would frequently see Angie Dickinson at Dodgers games in Los Angeles – and he had enough experience from appearances at baseball banquets to be a relaxed but effective speaker as he offered a straightforward pitch on behalf of the candidate whose support for a "more just society" had particular appeal to a man who had seen the advances baseball had made in that area.[6] Too, his baseball notoriety made him a big draw, with Michener recalling, "I was constantly astonished at how men in the cities we stopped at would crowd the airports to see Stan Musial."[7] Indeed, as election day neared and with Musial's campaign efforts having clearly identified him with the Democratic nominee, he was named one of the co-chairs of the National Sportsmen for Kennedy Committee, a group that included Johnny Unitas, Bob Cousy, Leo Durocher, and Willie Mays.[8] Kennedy's narrow victory on November 8 made clear that it was a successful alliance.

While the always affable Musial would sometimes refer to JFK as "my buddy," and Kennedy was known to occasionally call Musial on the phone, in fact, beyond the encounter at the hotel in Milwaukee, the pair had only two other meetings, both during the festivities surrounding the All-Star Game played in Washington in 1962.[9] Before the game Musial talked briefly with the president, reminding him of their exchange at the hotel, to which the president replied that he thought they both were doing a good job, a comment that was picked up by the media with one paper's next-day coverage including the headline: "JFK, Musial Both Doing All Right."[10] Meanwhile, as the game unfolded, Kennedy cheered enthusiastically when Musial, pinch-hitting for Juan Marichal, lined a single to right on a two-strike curveball from Camilo Pascual in the sixth inning of the National League's 3-1 win.[11]

The next day Stan, his wife, Lil, and their daughter Janet were treated to a tour arranged by Missouri Senator Stuart Symington. They met first with Attorney General Robert Kennedy, who gave them a tour of the Justice Department before they headed to FBI headquarters for a tour that included the firing range. Later, Bobby Kennedy asked the trio if they would like to visit his brother at the White House.[12] While Musial demurred, saying they did not want to bother the president, he was quickly assured that such invitations were not offered unless they were for real and so the Musials went back to their hotel to change clothes before heading over to the White House.[13] They were greeted by Kennedy aide Dave Powers, who talked baseball with Stan in an office adjoining the Oval Office. Janet happily sat in the president's chair until suddenly "she went bug-eyed as in walked the president."[14] JFK spent about 15 minutes with the family. He gave them all little presidential mementos, while telling Lil and Janet what a great job Stan had done campaigning for him in 1960.[15] Then, as Kennedy said he had to get back to work, he arranged for them to get a tour of the White House's family living quarters. It was by all accounts a memorable experience with the ever-humble Musial later telling a reporter, "Everything I have I owe to baseball. Can you imagine the son of a poor steel worker from Donora being invited to visit the president of the United States in the White House?"[16]

Like all Americans, Musial mourned the loss of the president after Kennedy's assassination on November 22, 1963, the day after Musial's 43rd birthday. Indeed, he took his daughters out of school and they went to pray at the Cathedral Basilica in the Central West End area of St. Louis.[17] He would renew his tie with the Kennedy family the following spring, appearing at Fenway Park in Boston when JFK's brothers, Bobby and Ted, as well as sisters Jean Smith and Patricia Lawford, appeared at the Red Sox season opener in conjunction with a ceremony honoring the late president. Bobby threw out the ceremonial first pitch and in addition to handing out the newly-minted JFK half-dollars to the first 6,000 ticket holders, the Red Sox had pledged to donate the game's proceeds to the JFK Library fund.[18]

Musial was, in fact, there in an official capacity, representing the president, for in early 1964, Kennedy's successor, Lyndon Johnson, had asked the now-retired baseball icon to serve as the presidential adviser to the President's Council on Physical Fitness.[19] The council had its roots in work by Dr. Hans Kraus in the 1950s. Kraus's studies about American physical fitness revealed some disturbing facts, foremost among them that American postwar prosperity and the resulting lifestyle had left the nation's youth, in contrast to their European counterparts, "soft."[20]

In response and in an effort to address the problem, President Dwight Eisenhower, a former college football player and avid golfer, convened a conference on youth fitness that issued a long list of goals aimed at improving the fitness of America's youth. Spurred by the findings, in July 1956, Eisenhower issued an Executive Order establishing the President's Council on Youth Fitness.[21] Over the years, the name has changed slightly as has the focus, but during the Kennedy administration and under the leadership of University of Oklahoma football coach Bud Wilkinson, the council enjoyed a heightened public profile.[22] Consequently, when, not long after Kennedy's death, Wilkinson resigned as both head coach at Oklahoma and chairman of the President's Council on Physical Fitness to run as a Republican for a US Senate seat from Oklahoma, the recently retired Musial, with his ties to Kennedy and his efforts on behalf of the Kennedy-Johnson ticket in 1960, was an ideal successor.[23]

Johnson took advantage of a February 14, 1964, visit to St. Louis as part of the celebration of the city's 200th anniversary to announce his decision to appoint Musial as consultant to the president for physical fitness and chair of the slightly re-named President's Council on Physical Fitness and Sports.[24] In speaking before the St. Louis crowd, he praised their longtime baseball favorite, saying of Musial, "There are a few men who have served as American heroes with such dignity. I am proud to have 'Stan the Man.'"[25]

Stan Musial visits the JFK White House in 1962, along with wife, Lilian, and daughter Janet.

The appointment was formally announced at a ceremony in Washington on February 26. There, President Johnson called the former Cardinals superstar "a hero to the youth of this country," a man who had shown that "being a champ means a good deal more than just winning."[26] Saying that Musial was eminently qualified for the job, he highlighted the "good sportsmanship and good citizenship" that had characterized his long career, adding that the former slugger had embodied the values of "decency, honor and fair play."[27] Indeed, the choice of Musial was well received and while Musial admitted to being nervous, he was also gratified by the large crowd in the White House Cabinet Room that witnessed the announcement, a reception that led Musial to joke, "If I'd known I had so many friends in Washington, I might have run for office."[28] In addition to Lil and the couple's daughters, Janet and Gerry, the onlookers included two of his 1960 campaign partners, Ethel Kennedy, the wife of Attorney General Robert Kennedy, and historian and former Kennedy aide Arthur Schlesinger Jr.[29]

At the ceremony Musial made clear that his approach to the new post was based on more than just his baseball career. In talking about the importance of physical fitness, Musial harked back to his youthful days as a member of the Donora branch of the Polish Falcons, a club that offered training and competition in gymnastics and track and field, while also engaging in charitable activities that supported causes in Poland.[30] Musial sought to paint a vision asserting that physical fitness involved more than just calisthenics and other forms of exercise. He affirmed its value but asserted that "games and other forms of recreation [were] important too."³¹ Musial also declared that his effort would be aimed at both adults and children.³²

The job was only loosely defined – indeed, at various times he was referred to as an adviser, an ambassador and on the day of the announcement, the "director of President Johnson's physical fitness program."³³ Too, given that Musial was compensated on a per-diem basis, at a rate of $75 a day, he was often left having to choose between making real money with his various businesses or serving the public.³⁴ But in typical fashion, outside pressures aside, what Musial did, he did fully, throwing himself into his new duties, traveling widely in an effort to raise awareness of the importance of physical fitness for American of all ages.

Upon assuming the office, Musial appointed former Washington University in St. Louis athletic director Bob Stewart as the council's executive director.³⁵ Under Stewart's direction and with Musial beating the drum for both the council and fitness at large, the council was able to increase its budget, one that enabled it to expand its advertising, part of its effort to encourage citizens of all ages to exercise more.³⁶ It was also able to expand its reach into schools, where it advocated for more physical education classes as well as greater encouragement of more exercise for all.³⁷ While critics argued that some of the money was being wasted on excessive travel, including at least one major overseas trip, Stewart pointed to the continued success of the council's effort to raise awareness and expand formal programing, especially as seen in the increased number of state laws mandating physical education in elementary schools, as well as better student performances on basic fitness tests. He said the council was determined to build upon the improved foundation.³⁸

Central to Musial's efforts was travel. He went to all sorts of gatherings in his effort to spread his message about the importance of physical fitness. In mid-March 1964, just weeks after his appointment, he was in Albany, New York, where he addressed the participants at the Northeastern Regional Fitness Clinic, a gathering of fitness educators from the region who were looking to share information to better enable them to increase awareness about the importance of greater fitness in citizens of all ages, while also working to develop programs to help people achieve it.³⁹

The month of May saw Musial in a different setting when he attended a lunchtime event in Wahington for over 600 government workers. In his folksy way, Musial introduced a do-it-at-home fitness program, noting that they were "really starting our fitness program right here by having you all miss lunch."⁴⁰ Musial said he hoped that everyone would begin a fitness program but that only 100 individuals would be chosen to participate in the pilot program that would seek to publicize the newly developed Council on Physical Fitness for Adults, a product of the pledge Musial had made in his introductory press conference when he made clear that his efforts would be aimed at young and old alike.⁴¹

Further evidence of the breadth and range of his efforts was a visit in mid-September to Pocatello, Idaho, for a conference with state physical education leaders, recreation directors and coaches in an effort to support and boost their efforts. Reflective of Musial's star power, Pocatello's mayor had formally proclaimed the week of his visit "Physical Fitness Week."⁴² Musial's dedication to the cause was evident in the fact that in early September, attending a Cardinals-Braves game, he "collapsed from complete exhaustion brought on by his heavy schedule as director of the President's Council on Physical Fitness" and had to be hospitalized in St. Louis.⁴³

Despite his reputation for fitness and durability, details emerged of his "break-neck schedule" – in what Musial told one person was "not an unusually heavy schedule for the day" – he had started the day on August 25 in Little Rock, Arkansas, where he dedicated a hospital, then stopped in his office in St. Louis before heading to the Connie Mack World Series in Springfield, Illinois. He returned to St. Louis that night before taking an early morning flight to Philadelphia for an event – his collapse became understandable, if not overdue.⁴⁴ Happily, he bounced back and was able to do the Pocatello event, although Bob Feller pinch hit for him at a luncheon combining his physical fitness work with the opening of the Stan Musial World Series of the American Amateur Baseball Congress. Musial's colleague, Fitness Council administrator Bob Stewart, was also on the program to share Musial's message.⁴⁵

Another less arduous way that Musial got the word out was through newspaper columns and news articles. During a busy September 1964, he penned a column titled "Your Child and Physical Fitness," in which he emphasized the lifetime benefits of physical fitness in children. As he often did, he wrote of his own nonbaseball experiences growing up in Donora.⁴⁶ No less typical were the newspaper articles that would appear after one of the many interviews he did in the course of his travels. An April 1965 syndicated piece had Musial talking about the combined impact of diet and exercise on a person's fitness, with the reporter also including some research in the article that reaffirmed Musial's advice.⁴⁷

Similarly, as he had as a player, Musial's leadership by example was no small part of his efforts to encourage the American people to make caring for their physical fitness a regular part of their life. An article in the nationally circulated Sunday newspaper supplement *Parade* in April 1966 showcased the way the whole family stayed fit. Titled "How the Stan Musial Family Stays Fit," in addition to a photo of Stan working out as well as a description of the workouts he did in a hotel room on the road, it also talked about what the rest of the family – from his wife, Lil, a golfer, to his 3-year old grandson and the others in between – did to stay fit and healthy.⁴⁸ The article also noted that the family was about to move to a new home that included a miniature gym that would make it even easier for Musial and other family members.⁴⁹ The article on the Musials was accompanied by a coupon that readers could use to purchase for $1, *Parade*'s "Fitness Is a Family Affair" booklet.⁵⁰

Through it all, Musial tried to get people to understand that attending to their physical fitness should be part of their daily life, something that would have long-term benefits. It need not, he would often say, be an arduous regimen of exercises, but could be as simple as regular walking or as enjoyable as swimming. As he told one writer, "When I talked to President Johnson about his physical shape I recommended he do more walking and more swimming. I don't mention straight exercise once."[51] And in that same vein, Musial urged companies to give employees exercise breaks rather than coffee breaks arguing that fitter workers were better workers.[52]

In the end, despite his best intentions, Musial never really took to the job, in part because he never established the kind of rapport with Johnson that he had with Kennedy. Too, while the job offer may in fact have had its roots in his 1960 campaign efforts, Musial did not see the job as a political one. As a result, when the ever-political Johnson and his administration not only asked Musial to lobby a Polish congressman, but also vetoed a joint appearance with a local baseball official in Rochester, New York, because the official was a Republican, Musial became increasingly uncomfortable in the post.[53] In addition, with Johnson actively in the midst of his push for greater civil rights protections as well as the Great Society, while at the same time expanding the war in Vietnam, physical fitness was not a top priority.[54] Consequently, there was little fanfare when, in January 1967, Musial resigned the position, with White House press secretary George Christian explaining that Musial's recent appointment as Cardinals general manager made continuation impossible.[55]

NOTES

1 Actually Kennedy (born in 1917) was older than Musial (b. 1920).
2 Stan Musial and Bob Broeg, *Stan Musial: "The Man's" Own Story as Told to Bob Broeg* (Garden City, New York: Doubleday & Company, 1964), 3.
3 Musial and Broeg, 3.
4 George Vecsey, *Stan Musial: An American Life* (New York: Ballantine Books, 2011), 234.
5 Vecsey, 233-234.
6 Vecsey, 235, 240.
7 Jack Doyle, "Jack & Stan, Kennedy/Musial: 1959-64," PopHistoryDig.com, March 25, 2016; https://pophistorydig.com/topics/jack-kennedy-stan-musial/
8 Doyle.
9 "Stan Musial Shared a Special Bond with JFK," Retrosimba: Cardinals History Beyond the Box Score, November 19, 2019; https://retrosimba.com/2010/11/19/musial-shared-special-bond-with-jfk/; Doyle.
10 "Stan Musial shared a special bond with JFK"; Doyle.
11 "Stan Musial shared a special bond with JFK."
12 Vecsey, 255.
13 Vecsey, 255.
14 Vecsey, 255.
15 Doyle; Vecsey, 256.
16 Vecsey, 256.
17 Doyle.
18 Doyle.
19 Doyle.
20 *President's Council on Physical Fitness and Sports The First 50 Years: 1956-2006*, 17.
21 *President's Council on Physical Fitness and Sports The First 50 Years: 1956-2006*, 17.
22 "Stan Musial shared a special bond with JFK."
23 "Musial Is Sworn In as Physical-Fitness Director," *New York Times*, February 27, 1964.
24 "Stan Musial Heads Physical Fitness Program," *Springfield* (Ohio) *News-Sun*, February 15, 1964; "Musial Is Sworn In as Physical-Fitness Director."
25 "Stan Musial Heads Physical Fitness Program."
26 "Musial Is Sworn In as Physical-Fitness Director."
27 "Musial Is Sworn In as Physical-Fitness Director."
28 "Musial Is Sworn In as Physical-Fitness Director."
29 "Musial Is Sworn In as Physical-Fitness Director."
30 Vecsey, 263.
31 Vecsey, 263.
32 Vecsey, 263.
33 "Musial Is Sworn In as Physical-Fitness Director."
34 Vecsey, 263.
35 Vecsey, 263.
36 Philip Meyer, "LBJ's Physical Fitness Council Goes Budget Happy," *Tallahassee Democrat*, August 28, 1966.
37 Meyer.
38 Meyer.
39 "18 Vermonters Attend Physical Fitness Clinic," *Burlington Free Press*, March 14, 1964.
40 "Musial Addresses Workers on Physical-Fitness Plans," *New York Times*, May 14, 1964.
41 "Musial Addresses Workers on Physical-Fitness Plans."
42 Tom Morrison, "Pocatello Welcomes Stan Musial Monday," *Idaho Sunday Journal* (Pocatello), September 13, 1964.
43 "Bob Feller Offers to Hit for Musial," *Battle Creek* (Michigan) *Enquirer*, September 3, 1964.
44 Bill Frank, "Frankly Speaking," *Battle Creek Enquirer*, September 6, 1964.
45 Frank; "Lakewood Wraps Up Musial Regional Title on Two Wins," *Battle Creek Enquirer*, September 16, 1964.
46 Stan Musial, "Your Child – Physical Fitness," *Zanesville* (Ohio) *Times Recorder*, September 20, 1964.
47 Gaynor Maddox, "Moderate Exercise Essential," *Alexandria* (Louisiana) *Daily Town Talk*, April 22, 1965.
48 "How the Stan Musial Family Stays Fit," *Parade Magazine*, April 17, 1966.
49 "How the Stan Musial Family Stays Fit."
50 "For You and Your Family: How to Look Better and Feel Better," *Parade Magazine*, April 17, 1966.

51 "Fewer Coffee Breaks, More Exercise," *Lancaster* (Pennsylvania) *New Era,* March 27, 1965.
52 "Fewer Coffee Breaks, More Exercise."
53 Vecsey, 263-264.
54 Vecsey, 264.
55 "Musial Submits His Resignation," *Columbia* (South Carolina) *State,* January 26, 1967.

STAN AND ST. LOUIS

BY DANNY SPEWAK

Stan Musial arrived rather anonymously at Sportsman's Park on the afternoon of September 17, 1941, the day he slipped into the St. Louis Cardinals lineup for the first time as the starting right fielder during the second game of a doubleheader against the Boston Braves. The clean-shaven, skinny rookie, weighing just shy of 160 pounds and a few months short of his 21st birthday, made his major-league debut that afternoon on the north side of St. Louis in front of roughly 8,000 fans, most of whom had likely never heard of him and could only guess at the pronunciation of his unusual last name. Musial himself seemed surprised by his own ascendance to the majors, following his call-up from Double-A Rochester, along with teammate Erv Dusak. "Both of us started out in small leagues this year with no idea of moving up to the majors so soon," Musial said. "You can imagine how thrilled we are."[1]

The native of Donora, Pennsylvania, a faraway industrial town located 600 miles to the east, quickly introduced himself to the people of St. Louis. After collecting two hits in his first game, Musial batted .426 through the rest of September 1941 with a brilliant performance that demanded the attention of baseball fans across the city. He was anonymous no more. "Stanley Frank Musial, who won't be 21 until Nov. 21," W.J. McGoogan of the *St. Louis Post-Dispatch* wrote, "is the name."[2]

From that point forward, Musial proceeded to build a Hall of Fame legacy over the course of 22 seasons with the Cardinals and, in the process, forged an unbreakable bond with his adopted hometown that would last the rest of his life. After surfacing in this unfamiliar city three months before Pearl Harbor, Musial spent the next seven decades until his death in 2013 as one of St. Louis's most beloved and commanding presences, known as much for his accessibility to the public and easygoing nature as he was for his 3,360 hits in a Cardinals uniform. "He loved St. Louis," said Brian Schwarze, Musial's grandson and longtime caretaker, "and St. Louis always loved him back."[3]

Although he would always be from Donora, there was no better career or personality fit for Musial than St. Louis, an unwaveringly loyal and humble Mississippi River town where folks embraced him unconditionally as one of their own. "I have never seen anyone in all my life who was revered the way Stan was in St. Louis. He was an icon's icon," St. Louis native Ken Makovsky wrote for *Forbes*. "He was also my boyhood hero, as I grew up a Cardinal fan in my hometown city; he could do no wrong, and he was the personification of glamour and decency."[4]

As a devout Catholic who regularly attended Mass, Musial particularly appealed to the city's large and vibrant Catholic community, which still makes up a quarter of the region's population.[5] In January 1999 Musial played a prominent role in hosting Pope John Paul II during his visit to St. Louis (the pope, a longtime friend and contemporary who was born just six months before Musial, referred to him as "America's great athlete").[6]

Musial was also held in high regard by the Jewish community, where *St. Louis Jewish Light* editor-in-chief emeritus Robert A. Cohn described him as having "transcended *all* religious, ethnic, national, racial and other barriers as a unifying force."[7] Meanwhile, one of the city's leading Black newspapers, the *Argus*, wrote during Musial's playing days that he "will always be remembered for his fine sportsmanship and cooperativeness on and off the field and also as a gentleman."[8]

The beauty of Musial's relationship with St. Louis stemmed in part from his longevity, given that his playing career with the Cardinals spanned portions of three different decades and endeared him to multiple generations of St. Louisans. He won three World Series titles and three Most Valuable Player Awards during the 1940s, notched four of his seven National League batting championships during the 1950s, and appeared in four All-Star Games in the early 1960s.[9] He played his first game during the Roosevelt administration and played his last game a few months before the Kennedy assassination. "Stanley Frank Musial was part of that magnificent class of post-World War II baseball geniuses every child of the late 1940s, '50s and '60s fell hard for," *Post-Dispatch* columnist Bryan Burwell once wrote. "He smiled at us from the cover of those color portraits in old *Sport* and *Sports Illustrated* magazines, and he marveled us as he uncoiled from his distinctive lefty batting stance in so many of those black and white action shots on the daily sports pages."[10]

Through the everyday rhythms of baseball, Musial developed into an omnipresent figure in St. Louis each spring until autumn, fueled in part by the 50,000-watt strength of KMOX Radio. "Growing up in a suburb of St. Louis some of my best childhood memories were listening to Cardinals games on KMOX and sometimes actually getting to go to a ballgame [at Sportsman's Park/Busch Stadium]," Sherry Graehling wrote in a fan tribute to Musial. "I still remember watching Stan play and my father telling me that I was watching history in the making as Stan was probably the greatest player I would ever see."[11]

For his entire adult life, Larry Dorsey reminisced about listening with his father to Musial's five-homer performance against the New York Giants in a 1954 doubleheader. "Those front porch days and the miracle of becoming a Cardinal fan for life at my dad's knee," Dorsey wrote in his own tribute, "are simply the best memories of all."[12]

The attachment to Musial only grew stronger after his retirement in 1963. Even as he transitioned out of the spotlight,

Musial held several business interests, including a popular restaurant in St. Louis.

Musial planted roots in St. Louis and stitched himself into the fabric of the city in a way that no modern athlete ever could, by mingling with adoring supporters during lunches at the Missouri Athletic Club or by engaging with autograph seekers of any age at any time. "He was able to have a normal life here," Schwarze, his grandson, said. "I used to take him to dinner all the time, and yes, people would come up every once in a while, but at least he got to go out to dinner and go out in public and be a normal person. So, I think that says something for the city, to let a celebrity be."[13]

At the same time, Musial remained highly visible with the Cardinals and eventually established an organization known as Stan the Man, Inc. to help him keep up with the dozens of publicity requests and fan letters he received each day. Musial intimately understood the connection he enjoyed with the fan base in St. Louis. "It's a special game because the season lasts so long. People grow up with it the way they don't in other sports," he said in 1994 during a 50th-anniversary commemoration of the Cardinals' 1944 World Series victory over the St. Louis Browns. "Like, people remember that 1944 season. They have lived with it all these years, even people who weren't born then. … Baseball, it's part of our life."[14]

As he got older, Musial's frequent appearances at Busch Memorial Stadium exposed him to a younger generation of Cardinals fans, whether he was playing the harmonica during Opening Day festivities or throwing the ceremonial first pitch to Bob Gibson prior to Game Three of the 2004 World Series against the Boston Red Sox. Decades removed from his playing days, Musial was untouchable in St. Louis, so revered that even Albert Pujols rejected using the nickname El Hombre (The Man in Spanish). "I don't want to be called that. There is one man that gets that respect, and that's Stan Musial. He's the Man," Pujols said. "He's the Man in St. Louis."[15]

Despite his unquestioned status in St. Louis, there is still a lingering perception in the city that Musial's accomplishments have been overlooked on a national level, a sentiment driven by some infamous events such as his initial omission from the All-Century Team in 1999 by way of a fan vote. "Did he deserve to be there? Are you kidding me? That to me was the biggest shock of the whole thing," Commissioner Bud Selig told the author George Vecsey. "I felt an incredible sadness. I said, 'this is impossible.'"[16] Under Selig's direction, a special panel moved quickly to correct the error and added Musial to the All-Century list, but the damage had been done. "He probably doesn't get the recognition that he might have gotten had he played for a major-market team," former Cardinals vice president of communications Ron Watermon said, "but he truly is one of the greatest players to have ever worn a uniform."[17]

Starting in the mid-to-late 2000s, Watermon and other team officials vowed to give Musial the credit he deserved. Toward the end of the George W. Bush administration, they began a lobbying effort to have Musial receive the Presidential Medal of Freedom, the highest honor an American civilian can receive. It did not happen overnight. After an unsuccessful attempt at the end of the Bush years, the team tried again when President Obama took office and even hired a writer to craft a 10-page essay laying out the arguments for Musial as a Medal of Freedom recipient. Players, coaches, and federal lawmakers in Missouri all sent letters to the president.

In 2009 the stars seemed to align when Obama visited St. Louis for the All-Star Game at Busch Stadium III. "I remember at the time thinking that the president is coming because he's going to make this big announcement," Watermon said. "When that didn't happen, I remember being really disappointed the day after the All-Star Game, feeling like we had failed Stan."[18]

That feeling of failure kept Watermon persistent. One year later, in 2010, he devised a campaign dubbed Stand for Stan that made creative use of technology and the nascent social media platform Twitter. Inspired by the Canadian educational figure known as Flat Stanley, Watermon decided to produce a Stan Musial-themed Flat Stanley paper doll that fans could download and print directly from their computers. The Cardinals encouraged fans to post pictures of their Flat Stanleys and sign a petition asking President Obama to give Musial the Presidential Medal of Freedom. Thousands obliged, and each individual post told a story. Some fans uploaded pictures with their dogs and Flat Stanley,[19] while others tweeted heartfelt messages about Musial with the hashtag #StandForStan.[20] The movement arguably reached its peak on October 2, 2010, during the Cardinals' final home series of the season, against the Colorado Rockies, when more than 39,000 fans sent a clear message to the White House by waving their Flat Stanleys from every corner of Busch Stadium – all while Musial paraded around the field in a cart driven by a team staffer. "That was a special moment," manager Tony La Russa said. "I looked around and there were a lot of guys choking up."[21]

Musial embraced the campaign and even posed for a photograph with his own Flat Stanley outside Stan the Man, Inc.'s headquarters, surrounded by his grandchildren. "I remember welling up with tears as I looked at that picture and thinking to myself, 'Oh my gosh, this campaign is not really about the Medal of Freedom,'" Watermon said. "What was so beautiful about that campaign was that it really did sort of link generations. There were older folks that said, 'How do I log on to get this thing?' And they're having to ask their grandkids to help them. It was just a cool experience."[22]

The Stand for Stan idea worked. Weeks after the season, the White House announced Musial as one of 15 Medal of Freedom recipients, and on February 15, 2011, President Obama officially awarded Musial his Presidential Medal of Freedom. "Stan remains, to this day, an icon," Obama said, "untarnished, a beloved pillar of the community, a gentleman you'd want your kids to emulate."[23] Brian Schwarze said his grandfather cherished the Medal of Freedom more than his induction into the National Baseball Hall of Fame. "When he came back with the Medal of Freedom, he didn't take it off for 30 days," Schwarze said. "He always said that the Hall of Fame ring, that was about baseball. The Medal of Freedom, that was about his life."[24]

By then Musial's health had started to deteriorate. In 2012 he mustered the energy to wave to fans from a cart before Game Four of the National League Championship series, which was his final appearance at Busch Stadium.[25]

Musial's death on January 19, 2013, at the age of 92, prompted a citywide period of mourning. One week later, during the doldrums of winter, television stations across St. Louis carried his funeral service live from the packed Cathedral Basilica of St. Louis as broadcaster Bob Costas delivered the eulogy. "No one in St. Louis ever had to wonder where Stan Musial had gone. He was right here, right here at home," Costas said. "Our greatest ballplayer, sure, but also our friend, our neighbor. And that is why the bond and attachment between this player and this city is unique and lasting."[26]

At the conclusion of the service, the funeral procession traveled four miles to the western entrance of Busch Stadium, where hundreds of fans in bright red sweatshirts and winter jackets jammed the sidewalks to catch a glimpse of the hearse. As a color guard consisting of local law enforcement and first responders greeted the procession, members of the Musial family emerged to bring flowers to the base of Musial's statue outside the ballpark, a moment so powerful that it led the crowd to begin singing, "Take Me Out to the Ballgame."[27] The older fans felt as though they had lost a member of their own family. "I was finishing college when Stan retired and I cried then," Sam Richards said earlier that week. "I am now 67 and when I heard the news last night, I sat down and cried again."[28]

The younger fans, like 7-year-old Bryce Beyers, mourned the loss of a figure they never watched but knew from stories passed through generations. "Dear Stan, you are the best Cardinal ever," Bryce hand wrote in a letter to Musial. "Every Cardinal misses you. Love, Bryce Beyers."[29]

More than a decade after his death, the Musial name remains a part of daily life in St. Louis. The road outside Busch Stadium is named Stan Musial Drive; Urban Chestnut Brewing Company introduced the #6 Classic American Lager in honor of Musial's uniform number; and the Stan Musial Veterans Memorial Bridge connects Missouri and Illinois over the Mississippi River. "I miss him every day, so to see reminders of him, and just what he was able to accomplish, I love seeing that all the time," grandson Brian Schwarze said. "Especially the bridge. I always thought he was a bridge. He was able to bring people together. It kind of encompasses who he was as a person."[30]

In St. Louis, though, there is perhaps no more recognizable Musial landmark than his statue near the front gate of Busch Stadium – the one that, despite looking nothing like his trademark crouched batting stance, hovers 18 feet above the sidewalk and has long served as the universal gathering point for fans attending a Cardinals home game. "Meet me at the Musial statue," the phrase goes. The Musial name, so new and mysterious when he played his first game at Sportsman's Park in September 1941, has transformed over time to become practically inseparable from the city itself. "They're synonymous with each other," Schwarze said. "Stan and St. Louis."[31]

SOURCES

In addition to the sources cited in the Notes, the author consulted Baseball-Reference.com, *The Sporting News*, and the following:

Tomasik, Mark. "The Story of the Stan Musial Statue in St. Louis," August 3, 2018, https://retrosimba.com/2018/08/03/the-story-of-the-stan-musial-statue-in-st-louis/ (accessed November 24, 2023).

NOTES

1. Associated Press, "Stan Musial Joins Cards in St. Louis," *Springfield* (Massachusetts) *Daily News*, September 17, 1941: 7.
2. W.J. McGoogan, "Dodgers Win, Boost Lead Over Idle Cards to 1½ Games," *St. Louis Post-Dispatch*, September 22, 1941: 1B.
3. Author interview with Brian Musial Schwarze, August 16, 2023.
4. Ken Makovsky, "My 'Thing' for Stan Musial," *Forbes*, January 28, 2013, https://www.forbes.com/sites/kenmakovsky/2013/01/28/my-thing-for-stan-musial/?sh=158708d659e0 (accessed December 8, 2023).
5. "Adults in the St. Louis Metro Area," Pew Research Center, https://www.pewresearch.org/religion/religious-landscape-study/metro-area/st-louis-metro-area/ (accessed December 8, 2023).
6. Patricia Rice, "Add Another Cardinal to the Pope's Greeters: Stan Musial," *St. Louis Post-Dispatch*, January 24, 1999: P10.
7. Robert A. Cohn, "Musial's Lasting Legacy: Stan the Mensch," *St. Louis Jewish Light*, January 23, 2013, https://stljewishlight.org/opinion/musials-lasting-legacy-stan-the-mensch/ (accessed December 8, 2023).
8. Photo caption, *St. Louis Argus*, August 16, 1963: 7.
9. Musial appeared in 24 All-Star Games.

10. Bryan Burwell, "Saying Goodbye," *St. Louis Post-Dispatch*, January 27, 2013: S11.
11. "Stan Musial – 1920-2013," https://www.mlb.com/cardinals/fans/tribute/stan-musial/fan-tributes (accessed November 24, 2023).
12. "Stan Musial – 1920-2013,"
13. Author interview with Brian Schwarze.
14. Mike Eisenbath, "The Man: At 73, Musial Remains St. Louis' Baseball Icon," *St. Louis Post-Dispatch*, April 10, 1994: 3F.
15. Bernie Miklasz, "Cards' Pujols Is a Happy Man," *St. Louis Post-Dispatch*, February 27, 2010, https://www.stltoday.com/sports/columns/bernie-miklasz/article_263620fc-1810-5d5c-9c29-bd5bd6757d19.html (accessed December 6, 2023).
16. George Vecsey, *Stan Musial: An American Life* (New York: Ballantine Books, 2011), 6.
17. Author interview with Ron Watermon, August 15, 2023.
18. Author interview with Ron Watermon.
19. https://www.facebook.com/photo/?fbid=1420976937999&set=a.1491237894479 (accessed December 1, 2023).
20. https://twitter.com/JRadloff/status/26206335414 (accessed December 1, 2023).
21. Rick Hummel, "Win-Win with Musial Visit," *St. Louis Post-Dispatch*, October 3, 2010: E9.
22. Author interview with Ron Watermon.
23. Obama White House Archives, https://obamawhitehouse.archives.gov/videos/2011/February/021511_MOF_StanMusial.mp4 (Accessed October 21, 2023).
24. Author interview with Brian Schwarze.
25. "Gallery: Stan Musial's Surprise Appearance at Busch," *St. Louis Post-Dispatch*, January 19, 2013, https://www.stltoday.com/news/local/metro/gallery-stan-musials-surprise-appearance-at-busch/collection_933c45e3-9b5e-5cd0-a761-9b790a47727c.html#2 (accessed November 20, 2023).
26. "Musial Celebrated During Funeral Service," Fox Sports, January 26, 2013, https://www.foxsports.com/stories/other/musial-celebrated-during-funeral-service (accessed October 20, 2023).
27. Joe Millitzer, "Fans Serenade Musial Family With 'Take Me Out to the Ballgame,'" Fox 2 News, https://fox2now.com/news/fans-serenade-musial-family-with-take-me-out-to-the-ballgame/ (accessed December 6, 2023).
28. "Fans Pay Tribute to Stan Musial," *St. Louis Post-Dispatch*, January 20, 2013, https://www.stltoday.com/news/fans-pay-tribute-to-stan-musial/collection_7377a206-3b4a-5da0-8060-c7ae632107c3.html#4 (accessed November 24, 2023).
29. "Fans Pay Tribute to Stan Musial."
30. Author interview with Brian Schwarze.
31. Author interview with Brian Schwarze.

BASEBALL, THE POPE AND POLITICS: STAN MUSIAL AND POLAND

BY JOSH CHETWYND

Stan Musial's father, Łukasz, believed in the American dream. Work hard, get an education, and succeed. In fact, he was so committed to that ethos that when Stan, the fifth of six children, was offered a basketball scholarship at the University of Pittsburgh, he famously tried to push his son in that direction, because he believed that education came first. Thankfully, for baseball fans everywhere, Stan's mother, Mary, was there to intercede, ensuring that what became a Hall of Fame career remained on track.

But as much as Łukasz fit the striving immigrant role, the native of Przemyśl, Poland, was deeply proud of his roots and imbued that love of his ancestral home in Stan. This affection would last a lifetime and lead to both the important development of baseball in Europe and the start of a long friendship between Musial, a devout Catholic, and Pope John Paul II. This primarily happened through the prism of the Cold War, which colored much of the early work that the three-time National League MVP did in Poland.

Musial's connection to his Polish heritage began at a young age. In his preteen years, he started going to the Polish Falcons' Alliance of America in his hometown of Donora, Pennsylvania. The Polish Falcons were a movement that began after an 1863 uprising. Its purpose was to improve the Polish spirit through physical fitness, and eventually it became an international organization. In 1934, Lukasz formally signed him up for classes.

"We marched and trained [in] military drills, and then we exercised on machines and mats," Musial later said. "We swung on gymnastic handrails, jumped over the horse and performed acrobatic exercises, which helped me avoid any injuries in my professional career. In the spring, our instructors took us outside to compete in athletic tournaments against other cities. I have no words to describe how much these three years of gymnastics with the Falcons have given me."[1]

Musial would hold to close to his heart both those experiences and the importance of Poland to his father, And while Poland was still under the sway of a Communist government when Musial's career came to an end in the early 1960s, he made it a priority to visit the country and make a difference to its people.

According to the *St. Louis Beacon*, Musial and his wife, Lillian, made a trip to to Poland during this period "with a small group of prosperous Polish-Americans to see what they could do to help its people."[2]

While not much is known about that reported journey, Musial's next sojourn to Poland proved to be particularly memorable.

While planning a trip in 1970, Musial asked St. Louis's archbishop, John Carberry, for a letter of introduction to Cardinal Primate Stefan Wyszynski, who was based in Warsaw and someone Musial had admired for his anti-communist stances.[3] Carberry wrote the letter, but also recommended that the retired baseball star meet another Polish cardinal, who was around Musial's age. His name: Cardinal Karol Wojtyla. While Wojtyla didn't speak great English and Musial had just a rudimentary ability in Polish, the pair got along, which would start a relationship between baseball's greatest Cardinal and the man who later became Pope John Paul II.

Two years later, Musial returned to Poland for the first time in a more public capacity. In what was dubbed the "Stan Musial Sportsman Tour,"[4] a group of 22 "distinguished" business and political leaders traveled with the stated goal being an opportunity for Musial to hand out trophies and some baseballs at various sporting events. Considering the time – the Cold War was in full bloom – Musial's appearance in Poland was quite notable. This was particularly true because Musial became the first foreigner to receive Poland's Merited Champions Medal from Communist Poland. No doubt such an act by the Communist government toward an American showed bravery on the part of the Polish government.

"It is an honor to award this medal to one of the greatest American athletes of Polish descent," said Dr. Wlodzimietz Reczek, who was the chief of the Polish Olympic Committee. "It is a measure of the high regard with which we view our links with the Poles of America."[5]

This was just the first of many times that Musial's work in Poland would be used by politicians and pundits in discussing the role of Americans in a country on the western border of the Soviet Union's sphere of influence. Musial seemed to be fine with this attention as he made visiting Poland a regular occurrence for much of the rest of his life.

In 1976 Musial traveled through Poland and wowed Philadelphia Inquirer columnist Tom Fox with his abilities on the harmonica. In a restaurant in Warsaw, Musial played with a polka band of which Fox wrote: "None of the Poles were aware that the guy playing the harmonica was Stan Musial, the American baseball legend, one of the most famous Polish-Americans of all time, but that didn't stop the dancing."[6] Three

Stan Musial Stadium opened in Kutno, Poland, in August 2000. Musial was the son of Polish immigrants.

years later, Musial visited Krakow to spend time with his friend, Pope John Paul II, who had assumed leadership of the Catholic Church the previous year.[7]

The friendship endured. In 1999, when the pope paid a pastoral visit to St. Louis, Stan Musial was named honorary co-chair.[8]

But it was his trip in 1987 that really kicked off his role as a baseball ambassador in his father's homeland. That year, Commissioner Peter Ueberroth asked Musial and fellow major-league veteran Moe Drabowsky, who was born in Ozanna, Poland, to be "goodwill ambassadors" on behalf of baseball. Baseball was just starting to get a toehold in Poland at the time. With baseball receiving recognition as an Olympic sport, the Polish Baseball Federation was registered as an official discipline within the country's Ministry of Sport. Baseball had existed in Rybnik for some time and other areas of the country like Kutno and Warsaw were also seeing growth.[9]

Musial and Drabowsky provided clinics, offered media interviews, and met with teams throughout the country. They also served as the face for $25,000 in equipment donations from the United States to Poland's relatively nascent baseball efforts. Clearly, Musial showed great charm during the tour. At one point on the trip, he met Gary Gildner, an American expat teacher and baseball coach, and his team, which was called the Warsaw Sparks.

The retired Cardinals star was so warm with Gildner that after he left, one of his players was sure that the two previously knew each other and had played together. Gildner assured the player he had never met the 24-time All-Star, but on reflection of the importance of Musial to the baseball world (and his baseball experience), he conceded: "Musial and I never played baseball together, but you're absolutely right, we're old friends."[10]

Communism was on the wane in Poland by this point, but hardline media still couldn't help but talk about the trip through the lens of capitalism. Articles referenced the local bat-and-ball sport of palant as an antecedent to baseball. (A common claim in communist countries during this era was to take credit for baseball by suggesting baseball was a copy of their regional game.)

One Polish sports magazine made the wry comment that "Coca-Cola and the potato beetle have lost their imperialistic sting over time, but somehow baseball couldn't get through."[11] Grzegorz Stabeusz, a Polish native who played baseball in Warsaw during this era, explained the reference to the potato beetle: "During the 1950s, when there was a potato harvest failure, communist propaganda said it was due to the fact, that Americans were dropping the potato beetle on crop fields in Poland, and Coca-Cola as a symbol of the American lifestyle was used as an example of American 'nouveau riche,' which contrasted with hard-working labor class in the Eastern Bloc," he said.[12]

Also biting was *Walka Mlodych*, a weekly publication of the Polish Communist Party PZPR, which was geared toward young adults. That publication wrote: "If you ask a random American who is [famed Polish athletes] Irena Szewińska, Ryszard Szurkowski or Zbigniew Boniek, they'll flip their eyes and say they've never heard these names. That's because America is such a backwater place, where the interest in sports by the fans is very limited and focused mainly on professional types of sports practiced on that continent."[13]

But Musial's upbeat tone received positive reviews from the American media. The seven-time batting champ diplomatically described the level of play – and its relative importance at that juncture: "[I] reckoned that an American high school team could probably handle Kutno easily. … But that's not important. … We're here to help get them going, and maybe we can invite some of their coaches to the U.S. next year to see how we train so they can come home and teach the kids more."[14]

The trip was an overall success and got the attention of Little League Baseball, which was looking for a permanent home for conducting baseball tournaments in the European region. While the premier youth baseball organization considered many locales, the willingness of the city of Kutno to donate 40 acres of land appeared to jump-start it as the top location to build.

In 1989 President George H.W. Bush gave a speech in Warsaw to celebrate Polish baseball receiving a Little League charter. That year, Poland had established itself as a democratic republic and Bush's words seemed to hold Musial up as an exemplar of the American – and Polish – spirit.

"As the son of Polish immigrants in Donora, Pennsylvania, Stan Musial had a dream – to make the big leagues," Bush said. "Like so many Poles, hard work made his dream come true. Stan the Man was already climbing toward the majors when Little League began. He never played it, but he embodied its qualities. For he was a humble winner and a gracious loser. A man of self-discipline and pride."[15]

From there, the effort was on to build a massive complex in Kutno – an endeavor Musial didn't shy away from helping. According to one estimate, the facility cost $6 million to build.[16] Among Musial's work on this front: He would lend his name and time to fundraisers, like one he did in 1996 in St. Louis at $100 a ticket.[17]

It took some time, but the funds were eventually raised – in part thanks to the help of Edward Piszek, a longtime friend of Musial's who was the co-founder of Mrs. Paul's frozen food brands. When the Kutno complex had its official opening in August 2000, Musial was in attendance. The main field at the complex was named the Stan Musial Stadium[18] and it featured an electronic scoreboard draped by the likeness of the Cardinals legend. (Another diamond was named after Piszek.)

Musial's legacy looms large in St. Louis but the continued development of the sport in Poland – and in all of Europe, since the Kutno facility is the home for Little League tournaments for teams across the continent – also deserves a big tip of the cap for the Cardinals great.[19]

In 1987, Stan Musial traveled to Poland. He is shown here during a baseball clinic in Kutno (wearing a Boston Red Sox cap borrowed from another American) with Waldemar Goralski and Moe Drabowsky. For more about the visit, see Paula Butturini, "Stars coach Poles in basics of baseball," *Chicago Tribune*, September 27, 1987: 1-3. Photograph courtesy of Slawomir Podemski, with thanks to Josh Chetwynd.

ACKNOWLEDGMENT

Special thanks to Grzegorz Stabeusz for his assistance on this article.

NOTES

1. Justyna Staroń, "'Stan the Man.' A Baseball Player with Poland in His Heart," *Przystanek Historia*, May 5, 2024, https://przystanekhistoria.pl/pa2/tematy/english-content/104568,Stan-the-Man-A-baseball-player-with-Poland-in-his-heart.html.

2. Patricia Rice, "The Man, the Pope and Poland," St. Louis Public Radio, January 20, 2013, https://www.stlpr.org/arts/2013-01-20/the-man-the-pope-and-poland. (The article first appeared in the St. Louis Beacon.)

3. Musial appears to have had strong anti-communist feeling. According to one source, he was partially driven to develop baseball in Poland because he heard that Cuba was planning to send coaches to Poland and that didn't sit well with him. See Robert Strybel, "Pol-Am Baseball Great Stan Musial Dies," *Am-Pol Eagle*, February 2013, https://ampoleagle.com/polam-baseball-great-stan-musial-dies-p6441-1.htm.

4. Associated Press, "Stan Musial to Visit Poland Next Month," *Jersey Journal* (Jersey City, New Jersey), January 21, 1972: 19.

5. Associated Press, "Poland Honors Stan Musial," *Hartford Courant*, February 12, 1972: 26.

6. Tom Fox, "Stan Musial Still Hitting," *Philadelphia Inquirer*, June 3, 1976: 3.

7. "Former Cardinal, Musial Impressed in Poland," *Belleville* (Illinois) *Messenger*, June 6, 1979: 8.

8. Patricia Rice, St. Louis Public Radio, January 20, 2013, https://www.stlpr.org/arts/2013-01-20/the-man-the-pope-and-poland).

9. Information from this paragraph comes from Josh Chetwynd, *Baseball in Europe: A Country by Country History* (2nd edition), (Jefferson, North Carolina: McFarland & Co., 2019), 229-233.

10. Gary Gildner, *The Warsaw Sparks* (Iowa City: University of Iowa Press, 1990), 148.

11. Andrzej Person, "A Batter's Visit," *Wiadomości Sportowe*, October 13, 1987: NR 41. (Translated from original Polish by Grzegorz Stabeusz).

12. Correspondence with the author, August 26, 2024.

13. "To the Olympics With a Bat," *Walka Mlodych*, November 1, 1987. (Translated from original Polish by Grzegorz Stabeusz).

14. Paula Butturini, "Stars Coach Poles in Basics of Baseball," *Chicago Tribune*, September 27, 1987: 3.

15. Lawrence M. O'Rourke, "Bush Pitches Musial Story to Young Poles," *St. Louis Post-Dispatch*, July 11, 1989: 10-A.

16. "Braun," *Newark Star Ledger*, July 4, 2001: 8.

17. "Miklasz," *St. Louis Post-Dispatch*, March 2, 1996: 6-C.

18. It's worth noting that this wasn't the first time Musial had a field named after him in Poland. In 1990 the city of Wroclaw in Silesia built a monument in Musial's honor at that city's first Little League field that included a 6-foot-high gray granite marker and a bronze plaque with the name and likeness dubbing the diamond the Stan Musial Little League Field. See Theresa Tighe, "Stan the Man: Musial a Hero in Poland, Too," *St Louis Post-Dispatch*, September 9, 1990: 42.

19. As of 2024, former major-league pitcher Dennis Cook was named manager of the Poland national team. Cook enlisted the help of former Seattle Mariners manager John McLaren to serve as bench coach. Michael Clair, "Poland Hires Former MLBer Dennis Cook with Hopes for Future Success," MLB.com, April 11, 2024. https://www.mlb.com/news/poland-hires-former-mlb-player-dennis-cook-to-manage-team.

MUSIAL BREATHES JOY INTO A SOMBER NIGHT

BY MIKE EISENBATH

On a bitterly cold winter's night, almost 30 years after his last swing of a bat in a meaningful baseball game, Stan Musial again came through in the clutch for St. Louis Cardinals fans. In doing so, The Man sent everyone home with a smile and warm heart on what could have been remembered only as a tragic night.

The daytime high temperature was a mere 32 degrees on January 19, 1993. That plunged to 17 overnight. So hundreds of Cardinals faithful had to bundle up as they trekked to a downtown hotel for the 35th annual awards dinner hosted by the St. Louis chapter of the Baseball Writers' Association of America.

Not much to toast about the 1992 Cardinals. The ballclub had finished four games over .500, in third third place in the six-team NL East and 13 games behind the first-place Pirates.

Catcher Tom Pagnozzi, pitcher Bob Tewksbury, and shortstop Ozzie Smith were All-Stars; the Wizard of Oz won another Gold Glove, and Tewksbury – with less than one walk for every nine innings pitched – landed number 3 in the Cy Young Award voting. Left-handed hurler Donovan Osborne came in fifth in Rookie of the Year balloting. Center fielder Ray Lankford finished among the top 20 in MVP voting with a team-high 20 homers and 86 RBIs; he also led the league in strikeouts and times caught stealing.

Lee Smith led the league in saves. Cris Carpenter was a Cardinals pitcher. No, not THAT Chris Carpenter, who didn't wear the uniform for another 12 years. Andres Galarraga, Pedro Guerrero, Ozzie Canseco, Juan Agosto, and Bob McClure also were Cardinals in 1992.

Overall, the Cardinals had begun their second 100 years as members of the National League in mostly forgettable fashion.

That didn't matter to several hundred fans who packed the grand ballroom of the Adam's Mark hotel. They seemed to do it every winter: Look hopefully toward the next summer and – maybe more importantly – celebrate memories of a rich baseball history.

As a recap in the next day's St. Louis Post-Dispatch said: "They heard Cardinals manager Joe Torre give his first pep talk of the season. They heard Ozzie Smith, the night's principal drawing card, talk of his love affair with St. Louis and the Cardinals' fans."[1]

A group of us sat around a table just to the front-right of the long head table. The mood was festive. Once Christmas decorations come down in St. Louis, most folks in the region look with great anticipation to that date when pitchers and catchers report for spring-training camp.

Our table – with friends, family and co-workers – brimmed with that kind of excitement.

The most prominent guest at the head table, seemingly as usual, was Stan Musial. The St. Louis writers' group had decided to give him their "Nostalgia Award" – for the fourth time. "That must be a record," wisecracked Musial, certainly no stranger to setting records.[2]

Sometime after dinner and before the speeches – these moments of my memory are understandably hazy – the unthinkable happened.

One of our dining partners suffered a heart attack.

The event, so close to the front of the room, put an immediate pause on the program. Paramedics rushed to the man's aid while the rest of the room filled with hushed whispers. Concern for the gentleman teetered against impatient curiosity about whether the rest of the night's plans would be canceled.

After an ambulance took the man to a nearby hospital, the writers' committee decided to move ahead. But how to lift the somber mood?

Musial stepped up and took center stage.

Musial, 72 years old, appeared to have some vim and vigor as he greeted the crowd. That proved a welcome sight, as there had been reports he had faced some recent health issues.

At that moment, Musial pulled out his harmonica, which always seemed to be inside one of his pockets, and immediately broke into a rollicking rendition of "The Wabash Cannonball." By the second verse, everyone in the room was clapping along, then Musial enticed the crowd to sing along as he played "It's a Small World."

And the rest of the night moved along according to plan.

Yes, those of us at that table remember it as the night our friend, who loved baseball and the Cardinals, passed away. But the rest of the fans in attendance have good memories of the evening, and there always has been certain solace in that.

Thanks to Stan the Man, ever the hit of the party.

Mike Eisenbath was a longtime member of the St. Louis BBWAA during his 25-plus years as a professional sportswriter, including 18 years at the St. Louis Post-Dispatch.

NOTES

1 Cathie Burnes Beebe, "Stan the Harmonica Man Tunes Up the Baseball Writers Dinner," *St. Louis Post-Dispatch*, January 20, 1993.
2 Beebe.

WHEN HEROES BECOME FRIENDS

BY EVERETT "EV" COPE

Back in 1985, while I was living on a 5,000-acre cattle ranch 15 miles of unpaved, rocky road from the nearest town (Three Forks, Montana), the phone rang one cold February morning. After I answered with my standard greeting, the man on the line introduced himself as "Stan the Man in St. Louis." The call was initiated by this all-time great major leaguer due to our mutual friendship with Paul MacFarlane, the historian at *The Sporting News*. Mac and I had been trading information I uncovered in my research that would help him as editor of *Daguerreotypes*, which was a great publication of player career records, and me with my endeavor to create the most complete player record ever compiled going back to when I was a kid.

That passion began in the early 1950s on the desert 10 miles north of downtown Phoenix in a working-class area known as Sunnyslope. Then, in the early 1980s, with encouragement and friendships of Harmon Killebrew and Ted Williams, I used my printing background and produced their limited-edition career record art prints that eventually became a total of 21 players with Rod Carew the last in 1986. MacFarlane is the one who named the growing list *The Cope Collection*. In the 1990s, with some major changes affecting the hobby and new technology making it possible to do smaller quantities, we began using that technology to produce smaller quantities. This allowed us to react to those families and friends of lesser-known players. It kept it more personable and enjoyable as it all originally began.

Stan Musial grew to be a baseball hero for me primarily in that I began collecting baseball books and studying records in 1949 right after his great 1948 season. Living in Phoenix then, it seemed great to have an idol in the most Western major-league city of the time. In addition, everything you read, or heard, about this great player indicated he was also a great person and family man.

The phone conversation with Stan lasted a glorious 30 minutes or so and began a friendship that would last until his and Mrs. Musial's health began to fail. Some of the findings on his career that I shared with him brought out memories and that famous "Stan the Man" laugh. Some were news to him. The one that seemed to please him most was that he was the third batter in professional baseball history to make 4,000 or more career hits in their career, counting minors and majors. Stan finished with 4,001 in 1963 and joined Ty Cobb and Arnold "Jigger" Statz. (The latter had 3,356 of his 4,093+ overall hits in the Pacific Coasf League with the Los Angeles Angels.)

Over the years there were many phone calls that are often referred to letters I still have and cherish. My favorite is the June 1990 handwritten letter (shown here) that reflects on his mention of President George H.W. Bush's influence and Stan's trip to Poland, where Stan was being honored. In a visit to Warsaw on September 10, 1989, President Bush talked about famous Polish-born Americans. He and Stan had just been together the week before at a ceremony honoring the 50th anniversary of Little League Baseball, so Stan was a major topic. That presidential speech in 1989 led to Stan's trip and his letter to me in 1990. Stan told me later that he had taken one of his career record prints to Poland in conjunction with the park being named after him. The next time we were on the phone, I had to tease him about his P.S. that mentioned him going into the Brooklyn Hall of Fame. I said, "Stan, you know you stole Mel Allen's famous 'How About That!!!'" I still remember his laugh.

Speaking of President Bush, this brings back a memory of another Hero That Became a Friend. One time I called Ted Williams down in Florida and his longtime secretary, Stacia Gerow, answered the phone. She said Ted couldn't come to the phone as he was playing tennis with then Vice President Bush! So when Ted called back, I had to tease him about getting into politics.

Stanley Frank Musial, Stan the Man, Stash … whatever you want to call him, here was a man who earned the respect and adoration of young boys on the playgrounds in the 1940s and on to at least seven United States presidents by 2010. Broadcasting great Bob Costas put it this way at Stan's funeral in 2013: "It seems that all Stan had going for him was more than two decades of sustained excellence as a ballplayer and more than nine decades as a thoroughly decent human being."

This writer was so fortunate to become part of *both* of the Stan Musials that Bob mentioned. Over the past few decades, my friends have come to hear me refer to such as "Cope Luck!" A term I have coined to explain how this, and other friendships with baseball heroes, happened over the years.

HOW IT ALL BEGAN AND EVOLVED

From This…..

1949 - In my room

To This…..

1954 – Mother's old Underwood

To This....

1986 – My personal #2/1000 with Stan's comment
(Stan said his personal #1/1000 was displayed in his St. Louis restaurant)

RECEIVED JUN - 2 1990

Stan Musial

Dear Ev —

Nice talking with you last week. Received the golf invite from the Thompson people & committee. Maybe can kill two birds with a card show at that time.

President Bush sang my praises while in Poland last year they decided to name a field & sports complex after me — Feel highly honored.

Lil & I and a few friends are heading there around the 21 of June.

Enclosed are a few copies of the activities —

Regards
Stan Musial

P.S. going in Brooklyn Hall Fame June 10 How about that...!!!

1990

Stan Musial Stadium • Completed & Dedicated • Kutno, Poland - 2000

Note: More information is available about Stan Musial Stadium in Kunto, Poland on:

- https://retrosimba.com/2018/05/10/moe-drabowsky-stan-musial-special-connection/
- Polish-American newspaper the *Am-Pol Eagle* of February 12, 2013
- https://www.littleleague.org/region/europe-africa-region/history/
- https://przystanekhistoria.pl/pa2/tematy/english-content

STAN MUSIAL'S RECORD

Number of Records Held by Stan Musial at His Retirement
15 – Major League Batting and Fielding Records
31 – National League Batting Records
31 – St. Louis Cardinal Batting Records
15 – All-Star Game Batting, Baserunning and Fielding Records
 5 – World Series Batting and Fielding Records

| CAREER BATTING RECORDS |||||||||||||||
| MINOR, MAJOR LEAGUES, ALL-STAR AND WORLD SERIES GAMES |||||||||||||||
	G	AB	R	H	1B	2B	3B	HR	TB	RBI	BB	BA	SA
MINORS	303	1107	213	371	252	60	27	32	581	200	82	.335	.525
MAJORS	3026	10972	1949	3630	2253	725	177	475	6134	1951	1599	.331	.559
ALLSTAR	**24**	63	11	20	12	2	0	**6**	**40**	10	7	.317	.635
W SERIES	23	86	9	22	13	7	1	1	34	8	12	.256	.395

Bold - Major League and National League records held by Stan at the time of his retirement at the end of the 1963 season.

STAN MUSIAL VS. HALL OF FAME PITCHERS

PITCHER	PA	AB	H	2B	3B	HR	RBI	BB	SO	BA	OBP	SLG	OPS	SH	SF	IBB	HBP	GDP
Spahn	353	302	96	21	6	14	45	48	30	.318	.415	.566	.981	1	0	0	2	3
Roberts	220	203	78	25	4	9	31	16	12	.384	.432	.680	1.112	0	0	2	1	4
Drysdale	75	68	22	4	0	1	5	5	6	.324	.360	.427	.787	0	2	0	0	2
Koufax	44	38	13	2	0	2	7	6	5	.342	.432	.553	.984	0	0	0	0	0
Marichal	40	35	11	3	0	2	4	5	2	.314	.400	.571	.971	0	0	2	0	1
Wilhelm	28	24	9	1	0	4	8	4	2	.375	.464	.917	1.381	0	0	2	0	0
Lasorda	3	1	0	0	0	0	1	1	1	.000	.333	.000	.333	0	1	0	0	0
Perry	1	1	0	0	0	0	0	0	0	.000	.000	.000	.000	0	0	0	0	0
TOTALS	764	672	229	56	10	32	101	85	58	.341	.415	.597	1.012	1	3	6	3	10

STAN MUSIAL GRANDSLAM HOME RUNS

GS HR	CAREER HR	YR HR	DATE	INN	OPP	LOC	PITCHER	T	FINAL SCORE
1	11	10	9/22/42	5	PIT	H	Rip Sewell	R	9-3
2	67	15	8/21/47	6	PHI	A	Charley Schanz	R	13-3
3	92	21	7/17/48	2	PHI	H	Blix Donnelly	R	10-11
4	271	14	5/21/54	7	CIN	H	Frank Smith	R	8-7
5	310	18	7/9/55	6	CHC	H	Warren Hacker	R	4-2
6	328	3	4/22/56	6	MLN	H	Warren Spahn	L	10-4
7	329	4	5/2/56	5	PIT	H	Jack McMahan	L	10-9
8	360	8	5/26/57	8	CIN	A	Hal Jeffcoat	R	6-7
9	438	9	6/23/61	7	SFG	H	Bobby Bolin	R	10-5

Thank you, Stan, for your kindness and memories.

STAN MUSIAL DEBUTS

September 17, 1941: St. Louis Cardinals 3, Boston Braves 2 (second game of doubleheader), at Sportsman's Park, St. Louis

BY JOE SCHUSTER

In spring training before the 1941 season, the St. Louis Cardinals listed Stan Musial on the roster as a pitcher.[1] His numbers from the previous year would suggest this was sensible. Although he also played the outfield on days he was not on the mound and had finished among the top 10 hitters in the Florida State League with his .311 average, he also ranked among the best hurlers in the circuit, leading the league in won-loss percentage with an 18-5 record and ranking in the top 10 in victories and ERA (2.62) among pitchers with at least 100 innings on the mound.[2]

Hidden in those statistics, however, was an arm injury Musial suffered diving for a fly ball in August that kept him out of 20 games.[3] Early in the 1941 preseason, the injury's effect was evident in several abysmal outings that made Musial a candidate for release.[4]

However, Ollie Vanek, manager of the Cardinals' Class-C Western Association team in Springfield, Missouri, had once managed a Redbirds farm team near Musial's hometown of Donora, Pennsylvania, and had seen him work out for scouts before the Cardinals signed him. Mindful of his performance at the plate in 1940, Vanek asked the organization if it would allow him to add Musial to his roster.[5]

Given that second chance, Musial caught fire immediately. For the first two months of the season his batting average hovered around .400.[6] By late July he was running away from the rest of the league in nearly every offensive category, hitting .379 with 26 home runs, 94 RBIs, and a .739 slugging average. The Cardinals promoted him to Double-A Rochester in the International League, where he batted .326 over the last six weeks of their season, helping the team run off a streak of 16 wins in its final 20 games that put the team in the International League playoffs.

Once the playoffs ended, St. Louis called Musial up to the big leagues. The news received relatively modest attention in the press. The *St. Louis Post-Dispatch*, for example, reported that the team had added Musial to the roster, summarizing his season's statistics, but giving considerably more attention in the article to first baseman Ray Sanders, who had finished second in the American Association in RBIs and among the leaders in batting average and home runs.[7] St. Louis's other major daily paper, the *Globe-Democrat*, gave Musial even less ink, merely listing his name along with four other players the team had brought up.[8]

As it turned out, Sanders did not play for the Cardinals until the next season, while a week after the press reported his recall, Musial found himself in the starting lineup for a team fighting for the pennant.

* * *

When Musial joined the club, it was in second place, 1½ games behind Brooklyn, and struggling through an offensive dry spell: Over the previous 15 games, the team had hit a combined .218 and had managed to go 8-6-1 over that stretch largely on the strength of its pitching.[9]

It was because of this slump and Billy Southworth's desire for outfield reinforcement through the last two weeks of the pennant chase that the Cardinals decided to bring Musial up in September rather than wait until the next spring.[10]

Musial reported to Sportsman's Park on Tuesday, September 16. His arrival was marked by a photo session, for which he and fellow call-up Erv Dusak posed for an AP photographer admiring each other's new Cardinals white home uniforms.[11] Musial already wore what would become one of the most iconic numbers in baseball history, 6, which clubhouse attendant Butch Yatkeman had given him simply because the number was available and the jersey fit.[12]

He made his major-league debut the next day, in the second game of a doubleheader against the lowly Boston Braves, who were in seventh place among eight teams, 32 games out of first. The Cardinals had taken the opener, 6-1, thanks to five unearned runs in the eighth, to keep pace with Brooklyn, which had won its game against the Pittsburgh Pirates to hold onto a 1½-game lead over St. Louis.

For the nightcap, Southworth shuffled his outfield. He rested center fielder Terry Moore, who had returned to the team only three days earlier from a month's layoff after being hit in the head by a pitch; moved Johnny Hopp from left field to center, shifted Estel Crabtree from right field to left, and started Musial in right and batted him third.[13] He sent southpaw Max Lanier, 8-8, against the Braves' Jim Tobin, a right-handed knuckleballer who had the misfortune of being a good pitcher on a bad team: he ended the year among the top 10 in several key statistical categories and, despite finishing 12-12, earned a handful of votes for MVP.

It was a pleasant afternoon, in the high 80 degrees and the sky clear as a ladies-day special drew 7,713 fans to the park. After Lanier set down the Braves in order in the top of the first, the Cards put their leadoff hitter on base when Jimmy Brown singled, but he was doubled off when Braves center fielder Gene

Moore made a spectacular catch on a Hopp line drive to the wall and Brown couldn't get back to first before the throw.[14] That brought Musial to the plate for his first major-league at-bat.

In his 1964 autobiography, *Stan Musial: The Man's Own Story*, which he wrote with sportswriter Bob Broeg the year after he retired as a player, Musial described his debut: "[The] first knuckleball I'd ever seen. It fluttered up the plate, big as a grapefruit but dancing like a dust devil. Off-stride, fooled, I popped up weakly to Sibby Sisti, playing third base for Boston."[15]

Although he'd been flummoxed in the first, by the time Musial came to the plate again, in the bottom of the third of a still-scoreless game, with two outs and runners on first and second thanks to an infield single by Lanier and a walk to Hopp, he'd figured out how to hit the pitch. As he said in his autobiography: "I learned to delay my stride, cut down on my swing and just stroke the ball."[16]

Fittingly for the player who, when he retired 22 years later, held the National League record for doubles, Musial laced the ball to the wall in right-center for a two-base hit, driving in the first two of what would eventually be 1,951 career RBIs and giving the Cardinals a 2-0 lead.[17]

Tobin settled in after that and held the Cards to only one hit – a single by Musial – between the fourth inning and the eighth. Lanier, meanwhile, was limiting the Braves to two hits through the first six.

In the top of the seventh, however, two defensive lapses by St. Louis allowed Boston to tie the score. With one out, second baseman Frank Crespi misplayed a groundball and Eddie Miller followed it with a drive to right that Musial, "who appeared nervous … didn't play too well," allowing the Braves to get on the board.[18] Boston added its second run on a single by Moore.

In the ninth Boston threatened. Carvel Rowell led off with a double and first baseman John Dudra bunted along the first-base line but rather than advance, Rowell stayed put. The *Globe-Democrat* account of the game said Rowell's decision likely cost his team a run because shortstop Marty Marion had to range far to his left to snag a groundball by Frank Demaree that would have plated Rowe had he advanced.[19] Marion's play effectively ended the threat as Lanier retired the side on a groundout by Johnny Cooney.

That set up a sudden and dramatic finish in the bottom of the inning. Leading off, Crabtree watched the first pitch go by for a ball and then drove the second, a low knuckler, to the pavilion roof "with the ease of Ben Hogan lofting a No. 9 iron."[20] The win moved the Cards to within a game of Brooklyn.

In the aftermath, the headlines went, rightly so, to Crabtree, a 37-year-old reclamation project for St. Louis that year; the team had plucked him out of the minors, where he had played the last seven-plus seasons after spending three years in the major leagues. Not only had he hit the walk-off winner in the second game of the afternoon, he had also homered in the opener.

But Musial, too, earned ink. Southworth told reporters he was "impressed" by his performance.[21] The *Post-Dispatch* noted

MUSIAL GETS THRILL IN CARD UNIFORM

The *Joplin Globe* welcomed Stan Musial to the big leagues. Graphic from the *Joplin Globe*, September 17, 1941.

that, without his play, Lanier would have been saddled with a disappointing loss.[22]

In the end, the Cardinals fell short of the pennant, finishing 2½ games behind Brooklyn, but Musial made plain through his play that he would be a force in the game. That September he appeared in a dozen games, hitting .426 and driving in seven runs. It was impressive enough that, despite his limited résumé that season, he earned votes for the Rookie of the Year award.[23]

NOTES

1 "East Coast Breezes," *The Sporting News*, March 13, 1941: 8.

2 Unless otherwise noted, all statistics are from Baseball Reference: baseball-reference.com/players/m/musiasto1.shtml.

3 Jan Finkel, "Stan Musial," Society for American Baseball Research Biography Project. sabr.org/bioproj/person/2142e2e5. Accessed September 19, 2016.

4 James Giglio, *Musial from Stash to Stan the Man* (Columbia: University of Missouri Press, 2001), 39.

5 George Vecsey, *Stan Musial: An American Life* (New York: Ballantine Books, 2011), 77

6 "Latest Batting and Pitching Averages," *The Sporting News*, July 3, 1941: 12.

7 "Cardinals Buy Sanders from Columbus Farm," *St. Louis Post-Dispatch*, September 10, 1941: 15.

8 "Pollet and Lanier Face Braves Today," *St. Louis Globe-Democrat*, September 17, 1941: 4B.

9 "Good Pitching Helps Birds Win Twin Bill from Braves," *St. Louis Post-Dispatch*, September 18, 1941: 15.

10 "Cards Send Hurry Call for Musial and George Kurowski," *Dunkirk (New York) Evening Observer*, September 16, 1941: 12.

11 "They're Redbirds Now," *St. Louis Post-Dispatch*, September 17, 1941: 11.

12 Vecsey, 84.

13 "Lanier and Tobin Hurl Nightcap," *St. Louis Post-Dispatch*, September 17, 1941: 11.

14 Martin J. Haley, "Birds One Game Behind After 6-1, 3-2 Triumphs," *St. Louis Globe-Democrat*, September 18, 1941: 3B.

15 Stan Musial and Bob Broeg, *Stan Musial: "The Man's" Own Story, as Told to Bob Broeg* (Garden City, New York: Doubleday & Company, 1964), 49.

16 Musial and Broeg, 49.

17 James P. Dawson, "Cardinals Subdue Braves, 6-1, 3-2; Crabtree's Homer Takes Nightcap," *New York Times*, September 18, 1941: 32.
18 W. Vernon Tietjen, "Cards, Game Behind, to Start Cooper Today," *St. Louis Star-Times*, September 18, 1941: 22.
19 Haley.
20 Haley.
21 Haley,
22 "Good Pitching Helps Birds Win Twin Bill from Braves,"
23 "Pete Gets Big Pat from 'Chi' Writers," *The Sporting News*, December 25, 1941: 5.

MUSIAL ENJOYS ONE OF HIS "FINEST DAYS" IN SEPTEMBER 1941 CALL-UP

September 21, 1941: St. Louis Cardinals 6, Chicago Cubs 5 (first game of doubleheader), at Sportsman's Park, St. Louis

BY RICHARD CUICCHI

At the start of the 1941 season, 20-year-old Stan Musial was playing at the Class-C level of the minors. By the end of the season, he was playing for the St. Louis Cardinals. He was thrust into a starting role after his mid-September call-up and helped the Cardinals contend for first place with the Brooklyn Dodgers. His outstanding performance against the Chicago Cubs in the first game of a doubleheader on September 21, together with his all-around play in the second game, made for one of many red-letter days in his career. In his 1977 autobiography co-written with sportswriter Bob Broeg, Musial said about that doubleheader, "I enjoyed one of the finest days I'd ever have in the majors."[1]

For Musial, 1941 was a transition year. He had originally been signed by the Cardinals as a 17-year-old pitcher in 1938 and spent his first three seasons as a pitcher with Class-D teams. He became a full-time outfielder for the first time in 1941. As an outfielder with Class-C Springfield of the Western Association, he wasted no time in proving he could hit, as he batted .379 with 26 home runs in 87 games.

Musial's performance with Springfield earned him a promotion on July 22 to Rochester of the International League, one of two highest-level minor-league affiliates in the Cardinals' organization. He continued to hit well, batting .326 in 54 games.

With the Cardinals only 1½ games out of first place, Musial was promoted on September 15 by GM Branch Rickey to help fill a void in the outfield created by Enos Slaughter's injury in August.

Manager Billy Southworth didn't waste any time using Musial. He was in the lineup of the second game of a doubleheader against the Boston Braves on September 17, since Southworth needed a left-handed hitter in the lineup. Musial was impressive during his first three starts, going 6-for-11 with three RBIs.

After a pinch-hit appearance against the Cubs on September 20, Musial was back in the starting lineup for a doubleheader the next day.

A crowd of 26,210 attended the Sunday twin bill at Sportsman's Park. In the first game, Southworth went with lefty Ernie White as his starter. In only his second major-league season, White had a 17-6 record coming into the game. Cubs manager Jimmie Wilson countered with veteran right-hander Claude Passeau, a 1941 All-Star selection with a current 14-14 record.

The Cardinals got on the scoreboard first with two runs in the bottom of the second. After Estel Crabtree walked and Walker Cooper singled, Marty Marion's single scored Crabtree. White bunted safely, moving Cooper to third and Marion to second. Cooper scored on Jimmy Brown's grounder that forced an out at second.[2]

St. Louis struck again in the third inning. Johnny Hopp led off with an infield single but was erased at second on a groundball force out by Walter Sessi. In his second at-bat, Musial's double advanced Sessi to third. Crabtree's fly ball scored Sessi for a 3-0 lead.

White had faced only nine batters before starting the fourth inning, yielding only a first-inning leadoff single to Stan Hack, who was later retired on a double play. Hack delivered another leadoff single in the fourth. After he stole second, Barney Olsen's single sent him to third. Lou Novikoff's double tied the score, 3-3, when a relay throw from second baseman Frank Crespi went into the dugout, allowing Novikoff to also score, following Hack and Olsen.[3]

The Cardinals broke the tie in the fifth inning. Hopp singled and advanced to third on Musial's second hit of the game. With two outs, Hopp stole home on a play that was hotly contested by the Cubs.[4] Musial stole second on the same play but was stranded on Crabtree's out.

In the sixth inning, Hack led off with a single for the third time. Novikoff followed with a groundball to Brown that was overthrown to first. Bill Nicholson walked to load the bases. Lou Stringer's double scored Hack and Novikoff. With runners on second and third, Ira Hutchinson relieved White and prevented further scoring, as Clyde McCullough popped out to shortstop Marion.[5] The Cubs took the lead, 5-4.

The Cardinals stymied a Cubs opportunity to score again in the seventh. Bobby Sturgeon led off with a double against Bill Crouch, who had relieved Hutchinson. Passeau laid down a sacrifice bunt, and first baseman Hopp threw late to third in an attempt to put out Sturgeon. Hack's groundout forced Passeau at second. Charlie Gilbert, pinch-hitting for Olsen, struck out on a play in which the Cubs attempted a double steal. But Sturgeon was thrown out at home on an exchange between shortstop Marion and catcher Cooper.[6]

In the Cardinals' half of the seventh, three doubles yielded only one run to tie the score, 5-5. With Passeau still on the mound, Hopp led off the inning with a double, but was thrown out at third on a fielder's choice. Musial delivered his second double of the game, moving Sessi to third. Crabtree's double scored Sessi. After Passeau walked Crespi to load the bases, Cubs manager Wilson went to the bullpen for Ken Raffensberger, who was successful in shutting down the rally.

In addition to Musial's offensive display, he made a running catch of Stringer's line drive in the eighth.[7]

But it was Musial's daring sprint in the ninth that won the game for the Cardinals. With one out in the ninth, he singled, his fourth straight safety. Crabtree's groundout to second advanced Musial one base. With two outs, Wilson ordered an intentional walk to Crespi. The next batter, Coaker Triplett, swung hard on a pitch from Raffensberger and squibbed a weak groundball in front of the plate. Cubs catcher McCullough fielded the ball and threw to first base for an out that should have ended the game. But umpire Lee Ballanfant signaled that Triplett was safe. First baseman Babe Dahlgren began to argue with Ballanfant, while McCullough headed down the line to lend vocal support. Noticing that home plate was not covered, Musial, who had taken off from second on the groundball, never broke stride at third and raced home ahead of Dahlgren's rushed attempt to throw him out.[8] Upon Musial's return to the dugout, Southworth turned to one of coaches and said, "That kid was born to play baseball."[9]

Musial collected four of the Cardinals' 14 hits. Crouch got his third win of the season, while Raffensberger took the loss.

In the second game of the doubleheader, Musial's defensive plays were instrumental in shutting out the Cubs, 7-0. Playing right field, he raced a long way to prevent a fly ball from turning into a double in the third inning. In the fifth, Musial fielded Hack's single and threw Olsen out at the plate. Musial wasn't finished yet in the field, as he made a somersaulting catch of Emil Kush's line drive in right-center in the eighth inning. Cardinals fans gave Musial a rousing hand at his next turn at bat.[10] Musial recorded two hits, with one coming on a successful bunt, for a combined 6-for-10 day at the plate.

Musial's all-around play prompted Cubs manager Wilson to proclaim, "Nobody can be that good."[11]

The Cardinals ended the season 2½ games behind Brooklyn. But it was no fault of Musial's. In 12 games, he slashed .426/.449/.574, with four doubles, one home run, and seven RBIs. It was an early indicator of the type of impact he would have during his 22 years with the Cardinals.

Musial was convinced his play at the end of the 1941 season was a significant factor in his making the Cardinals squad coming out of spring training the next year. He said in his autobiography, "Because of my spectacular climb from Class C to the majors the previous year, I was the rookie most talked about in spring training, but frankly I was a lemon in the Grapefruit League." He was referring to his concern that he had not hit the ball hard in spring games.[12]

Yet Musial proved the Cardinals' front-office decision to put him on the major-league roster in 1942 was correct. As the primary starter in left field, he finished second on the team, behind Slaughter, in batting average (.315), home runs (10), and RBIs (72). The Cardinals won the pennant with 106 wins and defeated the New York Yankees in five games in the World Series.

SOURCES

In addition to the sources listed in the Notes, the author consulted:

https://www.baseball-reference.com/boxes/SLN/SLN194109211.shtml.

https://www.retrosheet.org/boxesetc/1941/B09211SLN1941.htm.

"Stan Musial Leaves for Rochester as Club Ponders Seven Game Lead," *Springfield* (Missouri) *Leader and Press*, July 22, 1941: 6.

Hassett, Don. "Kurowski, Musial Due to Join Cards Today," *Rochester Democrat and Chronicle*, September 15, 1941: 18.

NOTES

1   Stan Musial and Bob Broeg, *The Man Stan Musial ... Then and Now* (St. Louis: Bethany Press, 1977), 67.

2   Martin Haley, "Birds Trail by Only One Game," *St. Louis Globe-Democrat*, September 22, 1941: 8B.

3   Haley.

4   Haley.

5   Haley.

6   Haley. It should be noted that the account of the seventh inning in the newspaper differs from the play-by-play account in Baseball-Reference, which records Sturgeon being thrown out at home on Hack's groundball. The newspaper account describes Sturgeon's out at home as coming an attempted steal as Gilbert struck out.

7   Haley.

8   Musial and Broeg, 68.

9   Jerry Lansche, *Stan the Man Musial: Born to Be a Ballplayer* (Dallas: Taylor Publishing Company, 1994), 26.

10 Haley.

11 Musial and Broeg, 68.

12 Musial and Broeg, 71

STAN MUSIAL SMASHES FIRST CAREER MAJOR LEAGUE HOME RUN

September 23, 1941: St. Louis Cardinals 9, Pittsburgh Pirates 0, at Forbes Field, Pittsburgh

BY ANDREW HECKROTH

After he turned heads with 12 hits in his first 22 major-league at-bats as a late-season call-up to the St. Louis Cardinals in 1941, rookie Stan Musial achieved a career milestone in front of family and friends at Pittsburgh's Forbes Field on September 23.[1] The 20-year-old native of nearby Donora, Pennsylvania, hit the first of his 475 big-league home runs in a 9-0 Cardinals victory over the Pittsburgh Pirates.

Musial, who signed with the Cardinals as a left-handed pitcher from Donora High School in 1938, struggled with control in his first professional season with Class-D Williamson (West Virginia). He walked 80 batters, struck out 66, and finished with a won-lost record of 6-6.[2] In his second season with Williamson, Musial increased his strikeout total to 86 but walked 85. In 1940 Musial was sent to Class-D Daytona Beach, where manager Dickey Kerr gave Musial outfield shifts when he saw how good a hitter Musial was.[3]

A shoulder injury on a dive for a fly ball in August 1940 all but ended Musial's pitching career. When Musial arrived at Double-A Columbus (Ohio) in 1941, manager Burt Shotton noticed Musial did not appear loose when he warmed up.[4] In his autobiography, Musial quoted Shotton as saying, "[T]here's something wrong with your arm. At least, I know you're not throwing hard enough to pitch here. I think you CAN make it as a hitter. I'm going to send you to another camp with the recommendation that you be tried as an outfielder."[5]

Musial was sent to Albany, Georgia, and later Columbus, Georgia, where Cardinals veterans Terry Moore[6] and Johnny Mize both blasted long home runs against him.[7] While in Georgia, Musial met with Class-C Springfield (Missouri) player-manager Ollie Vanek, who along with business manager Andy French had to persuade Stan's father, Lucasz, to let him sign with St. Louis. Musial had one question for Vanek: "Will you give me a chance with your ball club?"[8]

Vanek agreed, and the rest was history. In 87 games with Springfield, Musial hit .379 with 26 homers and 94 RBIs.[9] In July the Cardinals' general manager, Branch Rickey, asked Vanek if Musial was ready for Double-A Rochester, and Vanek said yes. In 54 games with Rochester, Musial batted .326. Rickey, impressed with Musial when he saw him play that July, decided to promote Musial to the Cardinals in September.[10]

On the morning of September 23, 1941, the Cardinals were 94-53 and in second place, 1½ games behind the Brooklyn Dodgers. Manager Billy Southworth's team dropped the first game of a doubleheader that day, 4-0. Pittsburgh lefty Ken Heintzelman pitched nine innings and allowed six hits. It was a frustrating game for the Cardinals, who made five errors and had only one baserunner reach third. Musial, batting fifth and playing right field, was hitless in four at-bats.[11]

Max Lanier took the mound for St. Louis in the second game. The left-hander had a record of 9-8 with a 3.01 ERA. Lanier looked to build off his last game, a 3-2 complete-game victory over the Boston Braves in Musial's major-league debut on September 17.

Opposing Lanier was right-hander Truett "Rip" Sewell, with a record of 14 wins and 16 losses. Sewell, who later became famous for throwing the "eephus" pitch to Ted Williams in the 1946 All Star Game,[12] had most recently thrown 1⅓ innings in relief of Johnny Lanning on September 18 against the Brooklyn Dodgers. While Sewell blew the save, the Pirates came back to defeat the Dodgers.[13] This was Sewell's first win since September 4, when he pitched five shutout innings in a 4-0 victory over the Cincinnati Reds.

The Cardinals scored the first run against Pittsburgh when Jimmy Brown led off with a triple to the deepest part of left field and came home on Terry Moore's groundout.[14] Musial, hitless in his four at-bats against Heintzelman earlier in the day, reached on an infield single to first base, but later overran second base on Estel Crabtree's single and was thrown out for the third out of the inning.[15]

St. Louis scored three runs in the fourth inning. Musial led off with a walk and advanced to third on Crabtree's second single of the game. Frank Crespi grounded into a fielder's choice to rookie shortstop Billy Cox, who planned to turn the double play until he heard someone shout "Home!"[16] Cox, though, threw too late to catcher Vinnie Smith and Musial scored.

Marty Marion laid down a sacrifice bunt and reached safely when third baseman Frankie Gustine made a wild throw to

Not only did Musial shine at the plate. He also made a fine catch in the ninth inning to help Lanier finish off the shutout.[23] It was Lanier's 10th and final win of the 1941 season. After the game, when the entire clubhouse was nearly vacated, Musial introduced his father, Lucasz, to manager Southworth and coaches Mike González and Buzzy Wares.[24]

Western Pennsylvania was proud to see one of its own succeed at such a high level of competition. The headline in the *Pittsburgh Press* after the game was "Local Boy Makes Good … with the Cardinals."[25] The story by Edward F. Balinger of the *Pittsburgh Post-Gazette*, "Donora Boy Stars," highlighted Musial's rise from the minor leagues to the Cardinals and his home run.[26]

According to Musial, the city of Donora was mighty proud of him. Forbes Field celebrated Stan Musial Day two days after his first home run. For the first time since Bob Coulson played for Cincinnati in the 1908 National League season, a man from Donora took the field in the big leagues. Musial later claimed that grade-school classes were canceled in celebration of his hometown debut.[27]

St. Louis finished the season with 97 wins, second behind the 100-win Dodgers. For Musial, his abbreviated 1941 season was the start of a brilliant career that ended with him as the Cardinals' all-time franchise leader in hits, home runs, total bases, and games played.

SOURCES

The author accessed Retrosheet.org and Baseball-Reference.com for pertinent information including box scores, play-by-play, and other statistical data. He also consulted player biographies in the SABR BioProject.

https://www.retrosheet.org/boxesetc/1941/B09232PIT1941.htm

https://www.baseball-reference.com/boxes/PIT/PIT194109232.shtml

Musial hit his first big-league home run off Rip Sewell on September 23, 1941, at Forbes Field in Pittsburgh.

second. Crabtree scored.[17] With one out, Pirates second baseman Stu Martin handled a grounder hit by Lanier and threw to first baseman Elbie Fletcher, nabbing Lanier as Crespi broke for home. Fletcher, who tried to pick Marion off second,[18] threw to Cox, who threw home to Smith. The throw beat Crespi, but Smith dropped the ball and Crespi was safe. The Cardinals were now up by four runs.[19]

St. Louis sent seven batters to the plate in the fourth and Musial got another at-bat the next half-inning. With Moore at first, Musial crushed a line drive well over the short right-field wall for his first major-league home run.[20] A Donora man caught the ball in the stands and exchanged it for another baseball as a souvenir.[21]

Left-hander Joe Sullivan relieved Sewell in the top of the sixth. With two outs in the seventh, Moore reached on Gustine's second throwing error of the day. Musial singled for his third and final hit of the game. Crabtree put the game out of reach with a three-run homer to deep right field.[22]

NOTES

1. Jack Sher, "The Stan Musial No One Knows." *Sport*, March 1949: 66.
2. Sher, 64.
3. Stan Musial and Bob Broeg, *Stan Musial: "The Man's" Own Story, as Told to Bob Broeg* (Garden City, New York: Doubleday & Company, 1964), 31-32.
4. Musial and Broeg, 37.
5. Musial and Broeg, 37-38.
6. During the final regular-season road trip, Musial recounted this home run with Moore on the train. Moore was surprised he was talking to the pitcher that gave up those big home runs: "'It can't be,' Moore blurted, 'you're not that kid lefthander.' Moore called to Mize, the big soft-spoken Georgian known as the 'Big Cat,' and said. 'Hey, John, you won't believe this! Musial is the lefthander who threw us those long home-run balls at Columbus this spring." George Vecsey, *Stan Musial: An American Life*, (New York: Random House Publishing Group, 2012), 87.
7. Musial and Broeg, 38.

8   Sher, 65.
9   Musial and Broeg, 42.
10 Sher, 66.
11 J. Roy Stockton, "Musial Gets Home Run in No. 2; Heintzelman Scatters 6 Hits," *St. Louis Post Dispatch*, September 23, 1941: 1B.
12 Associated Press, "Rip Sewell, 'Eephus Ball' Pitcher for Pittsburgh Pirates, Dies at 82," *New York Times*, September 5, 1989: B6.
13 Edward F. Balinger, "Pirates Beat Dodgers in Wild Tilt, 6-5; Arguments Mark Bitter Battle; Durocher Chased by Magerkurth Late in Game." *Pittsburgh Post-Gazette*, September 19, 1941: 18.
14 Lester Biederman, "Cardinals Need Miracle to Win Flag: Split with Pirates Enables Dodgers to Keep 1½ Game Lead," *Pittsburgh Press*, September 24, 1941: 22.
15 W. Vernon Tietjen, "Cardinals Lead Pirates in Second Contest After Losing Opener, 4-0; Birds Two Games Behind," *St. Louis Star-Times*, September 23, 1941: 13.
16 Biederman, "Cardinals Need Miracle to Win Flag."
17 Biederman.
18 Tietjen.
19 Crespi, according to Biederman in the *Pittsburgh Press*, kicked the ball out of Smith's glove.
20 Biederman, "Cardinals Need Miracle to Win Flag: Split with Pirates Enables Dodgers to Keep 1½ Game Lead."
21 Musial and Broeg, 51.
22 Tietjen.
23 Lester Biederman, "Local Boy Makes Good ... With the Cardinals," *Pittsburgh Press*, September 24, 1941: 22.
24 Bob Broeg, *The Man Stan: Musial, Then and Now* (St. Louis: Bethany Press, 1977), 69.
25 "Local Boy Makes Good ... With the Cardinals."
26 Edward F. Balinger, "Cards Lose Ground, Split with Pirates," *Pittsburgh Post-Gazette*, September 24, 1941: 16.
27 Musial and Broeg, 51.

STAN MUSIAL'S FIRST CAREER MULTIHOMER GAME

May 1, 1942: St. Louis Cardinals 8, Boston Braves 7, at Sportsman's Park, St. Louis

BY ANDREW HECKROTH

In the words of Stan Musial, "If I hadn't come up to the Cardinals in the fall of 1941 and hit so hard, I'm convinced I would have been sent down in the spring of 1942 because I hit so softly."[1] Musial, the rookie most discussed in baseball circles, started slowly in spring training in Florida. Despite Musial's struggles, Boston Braves manager Casey Stengel predicted, "You'll be looking at [Musial] a long, long while … 10 … 15 … maybe 20 years. He's up to stay."[2]

Fittingly, it was Stengel and his Braves who witnessed the first of Musial's many multihomer games. In a tight back-and-forth battle between the Braves and Cardinals on May 1, 1942, Musial's home runs propelled the Cardinals to an 8-7 victory.[3]

St. Louis, considered the favorite to win the National League pennant,[4] entered May with a record of 7-7. The starter for the Cardinals on May 1 was the veteran right-hander Lon Warneke. Warneke, a 1941 All-Star pitcher who won 17 games that season, was searching for his first victory of the season. He had lost his previous two starts, both against the Pittsburgh Pirates, but pitched seven innings each time and allowed a combined four runs.

The Braves, winners of five straight games, opened the scoring on the second pitch of the game with a line drive hit by Tommy Holmes that bounced past Terry Moore for an inside-the-park home run. Johnny Cooney singled and Eddie Miller hit an RBI double to center field that gave Boston a 2-0 lead with no outs recorded.[5]

The Cardinals got both runs back in the bottom of the second against third-year Brave Manny Salvo. Enos Slaughter doubled and Ray Sanders walked to bring up catcher Ken O'Dea. O'Dea, acquired over the offseason in the Johnny Mize trade with the New York Giants, doubled to right-center field, scoring Slaughter and moving Sanders to third base. After Frank Crespi grounded out to third baseman Nanny Fernandez, Marty Marion grounded to shortstop Miller, and Sanders raced home to even the score.[6]

In the bottom of the third, Musial hit a drive off the right-center-field roof for a double.[7] Or was it?

The ball had bounced back to the field of play. First-base umpire Lee Ballanfant ruled that it had landed on the roof for a home run. The Braves protested the call; Stengel argued that the ball had hit against the screen on the roof for a double instead of over the roof. So outraged by the call was left fielder Max West that he fired the ball over the left-field stands in disgust. Despite these protests, Ballanfant, along with fellow umpires Babe Pinelli and Al Barlick, stuck with their call and the Cardinals now led 3-2. Sanders belted a home run to right field to make it 4-2.[8]

Musial hit a two-out double in the fifth but was left stranded. The Braves regained the lead in the top of the sixth. Consecutive singles by Fernandez, Ernie Lombardi, and Max West made it 4-3. With Lombardi at third, Sibby Sisti grounded to Marion between third and short and Marion, surprised to see the lumbering Lombardi take off for home, booted the ball. Everyone was safe, and the score was tied, 4-4.[9]

Manager Billy Southworth brought in right-hander Bill Lohrman to face Buddy Gremp. Gremp bunted back to Lohrman, who attempted to nab West at third but threw late. The bases were now loaded for pinch-hitter Paul Waner, who batted for Salvo.[10]

Waner, a noted thorn in the Cardinals' side for many years,[11] had the righty-on-lefty matchup advantage and drove a bases-clearing double that gave Boston a 7-4 lead. As W. Vernon Tietjen noted in the *St. Louis Star-Times*, "Paul Waner can apply for voluntary retirement anytime so far as the Cardinals are concerned."[12]

Bill Donovan relieved Salvo in the bottom of the sixth. Sanders walked with one out and O'Dea singled to right field, moving Sanders to third. Crespi grounded to short and Eddie Miller fumbled the ball, allowing Sanders to score. Stengel summoned right-hander Dick Errickson to take over for Donovan. Errickson got pinch-hitter Coaker Triplett, batting for Marion, to ground into a rally-ending double play.

The score remained 7-5 until the bottom of the ninth inning, when Errickson gave up a leadoff double to Walker Cooper. Estel Crabtree pinch-hit for Murry Dickson, who had thrown two shutout innings of relief in the eighth and ninth. Crabtree fouled out to catcher Lombardi, while Brown grounded out to second, moving Cooper to third.

When the game appeared all but over, Stan Musial stepped into the left-handed batter's box. Musial drove a pitch from Errickson to the right-field pavilion roof to tie the game at 7-7. In the 10th inning, rookie Johnny Sain got the first two Cardinals out before Ken O'Dea stepped into the left-handed box. O'Dea homered for the second time that season, and the

Cardinals captured victory from the jaws of defeat with an 8-7 extra-inning triumph.[13] St. Louis went on to win a franchise-record 106 games, and Musial played on the first of his three World Series championship teams.

SOURCES

In addition to the sources cited in the Notes, the author consulted Baseball-Reference.com and Retrosheet.org for pertinent information, including the box score and play-by-play. He also consulted player biographies in the SABR BioProject.

https://www.baseball-reference.com/boxes/SLN/SLN194205010.shtml

https://www.retrosheet.org/boxesetc/1942/B05010SLN1942.htm

NOTES

1. Stan Musial and Bob Broeg, *Stan Musial: "The Man's" Own Story, as Told to Bob Broeg* (Garden City, New York: Doubleday & Company, 1964), 53.
2. Musial and Broeg, 54.
3. "Birds 8, Braves 7: Musial's Second Homer Ties Score; O'Dea Wins Game," *St. Louis Post-Dispatch*, May 2, 1942: 1B.
4. Musial and Broeg, 53.
5. Glen L. Wallar, "Browns Outslug Red Sox, 10-6; Cards Nip Braves in Tenth, 8-7," *St. Louis Globe-Democrat*, May 2, 1942: 3B.
6. Waller, 3B, 5B.
7. Gerry Moore, "Cards Show They Still Have Power," *Boston Globe*, May 2, 1942: 8.
8. Moore.
9. Moore.
10. Waller, 5B.
11. Throughout his career, Paul Waner batted .345 at Sportsman's Park.
12. W. Vernon Tietjen, "Musial and O'Dea Twin Heroes in Cards' 10th Inning Victory," *St. Louis Star-Times*, May 2, 1942: 4.
13. Waller.

FIVE HITS, THE FIRST TIME FOR THE MAN

July 21, 1943: St. Louis Cardinals 14, New York Giants 6 (second game of doubleheader), at Sportsman's Park, St. Louis

BY KEVIN LARKIN

The St. Louis Cardinals defeated the New York Giants, 3-1, in the first game of a doubleheader on Wednesday afternoon, July 21, 1943, at Sportsman's Park III in St. Louis. Martin J. Haley of the *St. Louis Globe-Democrat* noted the attendance: "The day's activities were attended by 5,755 paid customers, 668 military men, 165 blood donors, 2,138 boys and 288 girls."[1]

"The Cardinals made only three hits while winning the first game for recruit George Munger who got the mound assignment in place of Mort Cooper," Haley wrote.[2] The Giants' Rube Fischer got the loss, the winning hit a two-run double in the bottom of the second by shortstop Marty Marion.

The second game of the twin bill was the polar opposite of the first game as the two teams combined for 29 hits and 20 runs, and the Cardinals completed the sweep with a 14-6 victory. "Victims of the Card fury in the nightcap were Cliff Melton, Bill Sayles, Harry Feldman, Van Mungo and Hugh East – in that disorder," noted the *New York Daily News*.[3]

Howie Krist, in his fifth major-league season, was the St. Louis starting pitcher. Krist, who was 13-3 (league-leading .833 winning percentage) in 1942. He entered this game with a record of 6-3 and a 3.68 ERA. Cliff Melton, a seven-year veteran, started for the Giants. He had a record of 4-4 with a 3.35 ERA.

The Giants took a 1-0 lead in the first inning on a single by Joe Medwick and a triple off the bat of player-manager Mel Ott. In the Cardinals' half of the first, Cardinals, Lou Klein and Harry Walker both singled, putting runners at first and second for Stan Musial.[4]

Musial, a native of Donora, Pennsylvania, was in just his third season of major-league baseball. He entered the day's second game with a .331 batting average, which was helped by a 22-game hitting streak that began on May 16 and ended on June 5.

Musial singled, scoring Klein and sending Walker to third. A fly ball by Walker Cooper (brother of Cardinals pitcher Mort Cooper) scored Walker. Musial stole second base and Ray Sanders' two-out single scored Musial as the inning ended with the Cardinals leading 3-1.

With one out in the bottom of the second inning, pitcher Krist singled and went to second base on a sacrifice by Klein. Walker's single advanced Krist to third base and Musial followed with his second single of the game to drive in Krist, making the score 4-1, Cardinals.

Neither team scored for the next inning and a half. Musial came to bat in the fourth inning with two outs. In his third plate appearance of the day, he stroked a double to left field that brought home Klein who had walked. "Despite the lopsidedness of the score, the nightcap was a close tussle half the way," the *New York Daily News* observed.[5]

The Giants sent eight men to the plate in the top of the fifth inning and scored three runs. Consecutive doubles by pitcher Bill Sayles, Johnny Rucker, and Mickey Witek gave them two runs. Murry Dickson replaced Krist on the mound and retired the first two batters he faced. He then gave up a single to Buster Maynard that scored Witek. The inning ended with the Cardinals ahead 5-4.

The Cardinals exploded for nine runs in the bottom of the inning. Whitey Kurowski drew a leadoff walk from Sayles and went to second base on a single by Johnny Hopp. Harry Feldman replaced Sayles and gave up a single to Ray Sanders that scored Kurowski and sent Hopp to second base. Debs Garms, pinch-hitting for Marty Marion, singled to score Hopp and send Sanders to third base. Sanders scored when Dickson singled. Garms went to third.

Van Mungo replaced Feldman on the mound for the Giants, and he induced Klein to ground into a force out at second base as Garms scored the fourth Cardinals run of the inning. After Harry Walker grounded out, Musial tripled (his fourth hit of the game), driving in Klein. Doubles by Cooper and Kurowski scored the Cardinals' sixth and seventh runs of the inning.

Hopp was hit by a pitch. Sanders singled to right, scoring Kurowski, and Hopp tallied when right fielder Ott booted Sanders' hit. Debs Garms walked, but pitcher Dickson's fly out ended the inning with the Cardinals holding a 14-4 advantage.

Dick Bartell, pinch-hitting for Mungo, walked with one out in the Giants' sixth inning. A single by Rucker sent Bartell to second, and he scored on a hit by Witek with Rucker motoring around to third base. Joe Medwick's groundout scored Rucker and the inning ended with the Giants trailing by eight runs, 14-6.

Neither team scored again. Musial came to bat twice more. In the sixth inning, he doubled for his fifth hit of the game in five at-bats. Musial came to bat for the last time in the bottom of the eighth inning, in search of his sixth hit and maybe a home run that would complete the batting cycle for him.

However, Hugh East, the fifth and final pitcher of the game for the Giants, was able to do something that Cliff Melton, Bill Sayles, Harry Feldman, and Van Mungo had all failed to do, keep Musial off the basepaths. Musial popped up to Giants shortstop Billy Jurges.

Haley summarized: "Twelve of the Cards' 19 hits were delivered by three men. Stanley Musial gathered five straight, including two doubles and a triple in six times at bat; Harry Walker had four singles and Sanders three more."[6]

This was Musial's first five-hit game. He and the Cardinals hoped it would not be the last.[7]

The 1943 campaign turned out to be the first great season of Musial's playing career. He led the National League in batting average (.357), games played (156), plate appearances (701), hits (228), doubles (50), triples (20), on-base percentage (.425), slugging percentage (.562), and total bases (347). He also won the first of his three Most Valuable Player awards.

SOURCES

In addition to the sources cited in the Notes, the author consulted Baseball-Reference.com and Retrosheet.org,

https://www.baseball-reference.com/boxes/SLN/SLN194307212.shtml

lhttps://www.retrosheet.org/boxesetc/1943/B07212SLN1943.htm

NOTES

1   Martin J. Haley, "Musial Paces 19-Hit Attack in Nightcap," *St. Louis Globe-Democrat*, July 22, 1943: 19.

2   Haley.

3   Dick McCann, "Cardinals Blast Giants in 2d, 14-6, After Winning, 3-1," *New York Daily News*, July 22, 1943: 48.

4   Musial was 0-for-4 in the first game.

5   McCann.

6   Haley.

7   Musial had five hits in one game eight times in all, including four times in 1948. After this game, he also had five-hit games on September 19, 1946; September 3, 1947; April 30, 1948; May 19, 1948; June 22, 1948; September 22, 1948; and September 27, 1962.

Stan Musial appeared on this cover of *Baseball Magazine* in March 1943. The young Cardinals star went on to win his first NL MVP award that season.

MUSIAL HITS TWO HOME RUNS, HAS FIVE RBIS AGAINST DODGERS

August 15, 1943: St. Louis Cardinals 11, Brooklyn Dodgers 3, at Ebbets Field, Brooklyn

BY GLEN SPARKS

On August 15, 1943, Stan Musial was not yet The Man. That would come later.

Even so, the 22-year-old already had established himself as one of the game's bright stars. He was now in his second full big-league season. The Cardinals promoted him to the majors in mid-September 1941, and he hit .426 in 47 at-bats. Chicago Cubs manager Jimmie Wilson watched the lefty batter go 6-for-10 and make some impressive defensive plays in a doubleheader at Sportsman's Park. He decided, "Nobody can be that good."[1]

The following year, Musial hit .315 with a .397 on-base percentage and a .490 slugging percentage. The Cardinals won the National League pennant and beat the New York Yankees in the World Series. Musial finished 12th in the NL Most Valuable Player voting.

The precocious outfielder briefly held out in the spring of 1943. From his home in Donora, Pennsylvania, he asked Cardinals owner Sam Breadon for a $10,000 contract, a raise from $4,250 in 1942. Later, he amended that request to $7,500. Breadon, though, was offering just a $1,000 pay bump from the previous season and refused to budge. He wanted Musial to sign a contract in St. Louis. "And," Breadon wrote, "if you do not sign a contract and want to stay out of baseball in 1943, we will pay your round-trip expenses" back to Donora.[2]

Musial thought about it, and "I knew that once I sat across from that square-jawed, white-haired Irishman whose blue eyes could warm you or chill you, I'd succumb."[3] Musial reported to Cairo, Illinois, about 150 miles from downtown St. Louis, where the team was training as World War II raged. Breadon had acknowledged in one of his letters that Musial was a "good player" who had the chance to be a "great player."[4]

In the high summer of 1943, Breadon's prediction looked solid. Musial's batting average stood at .354 through August 14, with a .554 slugging percentage. He had just knocked New York Giants pitching around, going 10-for-17 over a four-game series at the Polo Grounds.

From upper Manhattan, the Cardinals took the short trip to Ebbets Field in Brooklyn. The Cardinals were 69-34 and in first place by 14 games over the Cincinnati Reds. The Dodgers sat in fourth place with a mark of 54-53, 17 games behind St. Louis.

The starting pitchers for the opener of this Sunday doubleheader were Max Lanier of the Cardinals and Curt Davis of the Dodgers. The 27-year-old Lanier had an 8-5 won-lost record, a 2.08 ERA, and a tender left elbow.

Davis, a 39-year-old right-hander, was 6-7 with a 3.24 ERA. A former top pitcher with the San Francisco Seals of the Pacific Coast League, Davis was on his fourth big-league team and had made two All-Star squads, including in 1939 when he won 22 games for the Cardinals. Brooklyn acquired Davis, along with slugger Ducky Medwick, on June 12, 1940, for four Dodgers and $125,000 cash.

Several fans who filed into Ebbets Field brought pointed signs directed at team president Branch Rickey, the former Cardinals executive known to some by the pejorative nickname of El Cheapo. Donald H. Dreese wrote how "irate Flatbushers," upset about the recent sale of players such as Dolph Camilli, "have drawn and quartered the mental effigy Prexy Branch Rickey because of his recent Brooklyn players manipulations." Placards asked, "Why don't you cut your own salary?" or insisted, "We know you're going to collect your share from St. Louis when you go back to them."[5]

Amid the hubbub, Brooklyn took an early 1-0 lead. Frenchy Bordagaray led off the bottom of the first inning with a base hit but was forced at second by Arky Vaughan. Luis Olmo, from Arecibo, Puerto Rico, reached first base on an error and Vaughan scooted to second. Billy Herman singled the run home.

Ray Sanders hit a two-out solo home run for St. Louis in the top of the second inning. Johnny Hopp's triple kept the rally going; Marty Marion walked and stole second. Lanier then lifted a lazy fly to right field.

After the Dodgers went down one-two-three in the bottom of the second, St. Louis struck again in the third inning. Lou Klein singled and came home on Harry Walker's triple. That brought up Musial, who had flied out in his first at-bat. This time around, he belted a two-run homer into the center-field bleachers. It was just the second home run hit to that spot at Ebbets Field in 1943.[6]

Musial had recently switched from a 35-ounce bat to a 34½-ounce model "to get more speed into my swing." He also had moved his hands farther down on the bat handle. "This increased the power of my drive," he explained. Musial added, "I figure that these changes – along with a bit more confidence this season – helped my batting a lot."⁷ Thus far in August, he was hitting .512 (22-for-43) with a .791 slugging percentage.

Following Musial's homer, the next three Cardinals hitters made outs. Brooklyn got back one run in the fourth. Herman led off with a walk and was forced out on an Augie Galan groundball. Gene Hermanski followed with an RBI double.

Both starting pitchers cruised along over the next few innings. The game took a final tilt the Cardinals' way in the seventh. Lanier hit a one-out single but was erased when Klein hit into a force play. Walker singled, and the Cardinals had runners at first and second with Musial, "the league's top slugger,"⁸ stepping to the plate. In his previous at-bat, in the fifth inning, he lined out,

Musial unraveled from his famous corkscrew batting stance and belted a three-run homer, giving him five RBIs in the game and 10 home runs for the season. It was the fourth time in Musial's young career that he had homered twice in one game, the second time against the Dodgers. St. Louis now led 7-2.

The Cardinals added two more runs in the eighth inning, with lefty Max Macon now pitching for the Dodgers. Macon, a one-time top prospect in the Cardinals organization, got into trouble right away. He allowed a leadoff single to Whitey Kurowski before Sanders homered again.

Hopp flied out, while Marion walked and made it to second base on Lanier's sacrifice. Klein, enjoying a solid season as a 24-year-old rookie second baseman (a .283 batting average entering the game and a .346 on-base percentage), hit an RBI double. Walker flied out to end the frame.

Brooklyn scored its final run in the eighth inning. Olmo hit a one-out single and, after Herman flied out, Galan reached on a fielder's choice, Olmo taking second. Hermanski's single drove Olmo home.

St. Louis scored again in the ninth. Musial led off with a single and took off for second base on a passed ball with Walker Cooper at bat. Cooper doubled Musial home but was out trying to stretch the hit into a triple. Kurowski flied out and Sanders struck out.

Lanier retired the Dodgers in order in the bottom of the ninth. Al Glossop popped out and Mickey Owen, pinch-hitting for Macon, struck out. Bordagaray's fly out to Hopp in left field ended the game at 11-3, St. Louis.

A reporter asked Musial about his big day. The ballplayer offered a surprising response. "Homers are all right," he told the *Star and Times*. "I'll certainly never refuse them, but I like triples better. Triples are almost as effective as homers, and they give you a chance to run. I like to run."⁹

Brooklyn won the second half of the doubleheader, 4-3, in 10 innings. Musial went 0-for-4 with a walk. The Cardinals ended the day at 70-35, 13 games in front of the Reds in the National League pennant race. The Dodgers were now 55-54, still stuck in fourth place.

After holding out in the spring of 1943, Stan Musial went on to win NL MVP honors.

Musial completed the 1943 campaign with an NL-leading .357 batting average. He also topped the circuit in hits (220), on-base percentage (.425), slugging percentage (.562), and several other categories. He won the first of his three Most Valuable Player Awards. The Cardinals took the pennant with a 105-49 record but lost to the Yankees in a World Series rematch.

Musial, who batted .347 in 1944 before missing the 1945 season while serving in the Navy, always loved hitting at Ebbets Field. He averaged .359 lifetime at the cozy ballpark, with a .660 slugging percentage and a 1.108 OPS. Dodgers fans dubbed him Stan the Man in 1946. The story goes that *St. Louis Post-Dispatch* writer Bob Broeg listened one afternoon as fans throughout the ballpark exclaimed – grumbled? – "Here comes The Man" as Musial stepped into the batter's box to take his hacks. Broeg wrote in his memoir, "So I began to refer to him as Stan (The Man) Musial. As you have noticed, it caught on."¹⁰

SOURCES

In addition to the sources cited in the Notes, the author used Baseball Reference for more information on the August 15, 1943, contest.

https://www.baseball-reference.com/boxes/BRO/BRO194308151.shtml

https://www.retrosheet.org/boxesetc/1943/B08151BRO1943.htm

NOTES

1. Stan Musial as told to Bob Broeg, *Musial: The Man's Own Story* (New York: Doubleday & Company. 1964), 50.
2. Musial, 75.
3. Musial, 75.
4. Musial, 75.
5. Donald H. Drees, "Cards in Twilight Game after Splitting with Dodgers," *St. Louis Star and Times*, August 16, 1943: 14.
6. Jack Smith, "Cards Slug Dodgers in First Game," *New York Daily News*, August 16, 1943: 56.

7   Jack Cuddy (United Press), "Stan Musial, Majors' Best Hitter, Tells Secrets of His Latest Success," *St. Louis Star and Times*, August 16, 1943: 14.

8   Lee Scott, "Dodgers' New First Sacker, Howard Schultz, to Play This Evening," *Brooklyn Citizen*, August 16, 1943: 6.

9   Cuddy, 14.

10 Bob Broeg, *Bob Broeg: Memories of a Hall of Fame Sportswriter* (Champaign, Illinois: Sagamore Publishing, 1995), 156.

MUSIAL'S FOUR HITS OVER THE FIRST FOUR INNINGS HELP CRUISING CARDS CRUSH BRAVES

August 20, 1944: St. Louis Cardinals 15, Boston Braves 5 (first game of doubleheader), at Sportsman's Park, St. Louis

BY MARK S. STERNMAN

St. Louis had won nine straight games from July 23 to July 29, 1944, and looked to win nine in a row again going into an August 20 doubleheader opener against the visitors from Boston. Although star outfielder Stan Musial "had gone hitless in his last ten times at bat[,]"[1] the Cardinals had continued to pull away from the rest of the National League. The pitching matchup heavily favored the home team as 28-year-old rookie phenom Ted Wilks (11-1) faced Johnny Hutchings (0-1), who earlier in 1944 had a six-game losing streak in the minor leagues.[2]

The Braves threatened immediately with the first three batters reaching base. Whitey Wietelmann singled, Tommy Holmes doubled, and Butch Nieman walked. Wilks wiggled out of the jam thanks to two groundballs. The first resulted in a force at the plate, and the second ended the inning on a 6-4-3 double play started by eventual 1944 MVP Marty Marion.

The failure to turn a groundball into an out started the beginning of the end for Hutchings. Third baseman Dee Phillips made an error on a grounder by St. Louis leadoff hitter Emil Verban, the first of a career-worst three errors Phillips would make in this game. Boston suffered through poor third-base play all season. In his history of the team, Harold Kaese noted in recapping 1944, "Personnel changed so often that the Braves tried ten different men at third base during the season."[3]

The Cardinals capitalized on the miscue. Johnny Hopp singled Verban to second. Musial ended his hitless streak with an RBI single to put St. Louis up 1-0. Walker Cooper walked, loading the bases. Ray Sanders' single made it 2-0. Hutchings finally got an out by fanning Whitey Kurowski, but Danny Litwhiler singled in two runs to make the score 4-0 and put a swift end to Hutchings' afternoon.

Of the seven starts Hutchings made in 1944, this was the worst. While giving up less than one hit per inning for the season, he had a few games where the hits just kept on coming. In his return to Boston nine days earlier against Cincinnati, Hutchings retired four of the first five Reds batters before yielding a startling seven straight hits.

Ira Hutchinson came on in relief. He got one out before RBI singles by Wilks and Verban extended the lead to 6-0. Hopp's fly out finally ended the frame for St. Louis.

Wilks set down the Braves in order in the top of the second. In the bottom of the inning, Musial singled before Walker Cooper's homer put the Cardinals up 8-0.

Pitcher-first baseman-outfielder Max Macon batted for Hutchinson and singled to start the third. Another DP allowed Wilks to face the minimum again.

The *Boston Post* wrote of the bottom of the third, "Macon took over [the pitching] … and it appeared to be little more than batting practice as Musial hit for the circuit with one on and Sanders also connected with a mate aboard in the same inning."[4] Thanks to the two homers, the Cardinals led 12-0.

The Cardinals had "felt safe" in trading [the mighty Johnny] Mize to open the position for Sanders, a "great defensive first baseman. …"[5] Unlike his predecessor (359 career round-trippers), and teammates Musial and Cooper (who had 475 and 173 respectively), Sanders generally hit with little power, finishing with 42 home runs in 630 games. Through this game, however, Sanders had 10 homers, two more than Musial and three more than Cooper. Sanders had three RBIs in this game and tacked on another in the nightcap to give him 89 for the season. He finished 1944 tied for fourth in the NL with a career-high 102 RBIs.

The fourth inning mirrored the earlier innings. Boston failed to score, and St. Louis increased its lead. With two outs, Verban singled, Hopp doubled the leadoff hitter to third, and Musial knocked in both with a double to put the Cardinals up 14-0. Musial was now 4-for-4 with five RBIs.

In the fifth, the Braves had a harmless single, and St. Louis piled on against Macon. With one out, Kurowski doubled and Litwhiler walked. Marion had an RBI single to make the score 15-0. With runners on first and second and one out, Wilks sacrificed, but Macon retired Verban. For the first time in the game, St. Louis had completed an inning without a Musial hit.

By pulling Musial and three other starters as the game went to the sixth, St. Louis manager Billy Southworth "used football tactics to keep down his own score and avoid further humiliation of Bob Quinn's All-Stars from Boston," noted the *Boston Globe*. "He yanked his varsity and threw in second and third-stringers like Knute Rockne trying to keep from running up a score on Slippery Rock."[6]

With that, the contest settled down into the rhythm of a regular rout until the eighth, when Wilks yielded a handful of runs due to disinterest, weakness, or both. With one out Warren Huston, who had replaced Wietelmann at shortstop in the seventh, singled. Holmes also singled, and Nieman doubled to get Boston on the board at 15-1. Ab Wright smacked a three-run homer to make the score 15-4. Stew Hofferth singled, the fifth consecutive hit by the Braves, and after an out, Phillips hit an RBI double for a fifth run.

Ben Cardoni finished the game for Boston with three scoreless innings. The outing represented the only contest in Cardoni's 36-game career in which he gave up no runs while pitching at least three innings.

Seven outs later, the "whipping" ended 15-5. Wilks went all the way. Giving up 13 hits – the most he would yield in any of his 385 games – and five runs to a Boston team that finished sixth in the NL in runs scored made Wilks' pitching line looked less effective on paper than in the context of the game.

The Braves went on to win the second game, 5-3, with Woody Rich beating Freddy Schmidt, and Musial had two more hits, pulling ahead of Dixie Walker of the Brooklyn Dodgers, Hopp, and Ducky Medwick of the New York Giants.[8] These four ended the season as the top hitters by batting average in the NL, albeit in a different order as Walker batted .357, Musial .347, Medwick .337, and Hopp .336.

Musial finished the season as the league leader in on-base percentage (.440), slugging percentage (.549), doubles (51), and extra-base hits (77). Clearly the best player in the NL in 1944, Musial still finished a distant fourth in the MVP voting, a result that probably bothered him little given the triumph of the Cardinals in the World Series.

SOURCES

In addition to the sources cited in the Notes, the author consulted Baseball-Reference.com and Retrosheet.org.

https://www.baseball-reference.com/boxes/SLN/SLN194408201.shtml

https://www.retrosheet.org/boxesetc/1944/B08201SLN1944.htm

NOTES

1 Associated Press, "Braves Stop Cards after 15-5 Defeat," *New York Times*, August 21, 1944: 10.

2 "American Association," *The Sporting News*, June 1, 1944: 24.

3 Harold Kaese, *The Boston Braves, 1871-1953* (Boston: Northeastern University Press, 2004), 257.

4 "Rich Cops Nightcap for Tribe," *Boston Post*, August 21, 1944: 9. The game represented Macon's only mound appearance in 1944. He had, however, previously pitched in 79 major-league games dating back to 1938. He finished his pitching career with a 17-19 record and a 4.24 ERA.

5 Frederick G. Lieb, *The St. Louis Cardinals: The Story of a Great Baseball Club* (New York: Van Rees Press, 1947), 195. Ironically given the subject of this essay and the outcome of this game, the Boston Braves in 1950 donated the copy of this book that the author reviewed at the Boston Public Library.

6 "Braves Suffer a 'Football' Defeat at Cards' Hands," *Boston Globe*, August 21, 1944: 11.

7 "Rich Beats Cards, Gives Tribe Split," *Boston Daily Record*, August 21, 1944: 34.

8 "Musial Leads Hit Parade," *The Sporting News*, August 24, 1944: 14.

MUSIAL'S BLAST HELPS CARDINALS LEVEL THE TROLLEY CAR SERIES AT TWO GAMES EACH

October 7, 1944: St. Louis Cardinals 5, St. Louis Browns 1, at Sportsman's Park, St. Louis

Game Four of the World Series

BY KEN CARRANO

Stan Musial's arrival with the St. Louis Cardinals coincided with a resurgence for the franchise, which had not been to the World Series since 1934. In 1942, Musial's first full season, the Cardinals won a team record 106 games,[1] and they won 105 in 1943 and 1944. Musial had a good season in 1942, hitting .315 with 10 home runs and 72 RBIs, enough to finish 12th in National League MVP balloting. His 1943 season was even better: He led the NL in nearly every offensive category and won the MVP vote in a rout. His 1944 season was highlighted with a league-leading 51 doubles and a career-high (to that point) 94 RBIs.

Musial's performance in the Cardinals' 1942 and 1943 World Series, though, could be classified as unremarkable. In the 1942 Series, he hit a pedestrian .222 with only one extra-base hit, a double in Game Four, but the Cardinals took the series from the New York Yankees in five games. Musial hit a bit better in the 1943 series, collecting five hits, all singles, in 18 at-bats (.278), with no RBIs against the Yankees, who captured the Series in five games.

The 1944 baseball season in St. Louis was the same as it had been the last few years, but was remarkably different at the same time. The Cardinals won 105 games for second straight year and captured the pennant by a comfortable 14½ games. That the St. Louis Browns were able to win the 1944 pennant – regardless of the circumstances – shocked the baseball world.[2] The Browns won the AL crown on the season's last day, beating the New York Yankees while the Detroit Tigers lost.

Only the most loyal Browns supporter could have favored the Browns over the juggernaut with which they shared Sportsman's Park. The Cardinals won the "team triple crown" by leading the NL in batting average, home runs, and RBIs, as well as in hits, doubles, and on-base and slugging percentage. The Cardinals also led the league in ERA, fewest runs allowed, and double plays. The Browns relied on their pitching, coming in second in the AL in ERA, but had struggled at the plate, finishing the season seventh (of eight) in team batting average. The comparisons to the 1906 all-Chicago World Series were apt, with the Cardinals playing the role of the Chicago Cubs, winners of 116 games that season, against the "Hitless Wonder" White Sox.[3] Browns fans were hoping for a similar result in the Series.

The momentum that carried the Browns to the pennant carried over into the first three games of the Series. Denny Galehouse scattered seven hits over nine innings as the Browns scraped by with a 2-1 victory in Game One. The Browns notched their runs and only hits in the fourth when George McQuinn homered after Gene Moore got their first hit. The Cardinals tied the Series the next day when Ken O'Dea's walk-off single plated Ray Sanders for a 3-2 win in 11 innings. Game Three saw the Browns prevail, 6-2, thanks in part to a four-run third. Jack Kramer made the runs hold up, scattering seven hits and striking out 10.

The Browns were two games from glory, and if the Cardinals didn't get themselves out of the funk that started in September, they would be on the wrong side of one of baseball's biggest upsets. Cincinnati Reds general manager Warren Giles told NL President Ford Frick, "[I]f they played this kind of ball all season they wouldn't have been in the Series."[4]

No team since 1937 had lost Game Four of the World Series and gone on to win the Series. The Cardinals turned to left-hander Harry Brecheen, who was 16-5 during the season with a 2.85 ERA in 30 appearances (22 starts). Brecheen had the makeup to right the Cardinals' floundering ship. "Deadpanned and apparently nerveless," wrote the United Press's Stan Mockler, "Brecheen has a reputation for having ice water in his veins."[5] The Browns would counter with Sigmund "Sig" Jakucki, 13-9 with a 3.55 ERA in his return to the majors after an eight-year absence. Jakucki was out of Organized Baseball from 1938 through 1943. He worked as a painter and paper hanger, as well as in the shipyards, and played semipro baseball.[6] In March 1944 the 34-year-old Jakucki was surprised to receive a letter from Browns general manager Bill DeWitt inviting him to spring training. Praised for his "fast one," Jakucki made the

The Cardinals and Browns met in the 1944 World Series in St. Louis. Musial batted .304 and hit his lone Series home run.

team.[7] Before Game One Jakucki complained of an abscessed tooth, but by the time he took the mound for Game Four, he said there was no pain.[8]

The Browns were the home team for Game Four, and the largest crowd of the Series so far, 35,455, enjoyed a cool October day. Jakucki struck out leadoff hitter Danny Litwhiler, but then the real 1944 Cardinals showed up. Johnny Hopp singled, bringing up "The Man." Musial had hits in all three games of the Series so far and didn't wait long to get one in the fourth, driving Jakucki's first offering to the far edge of the right-field pavilion for what would be the only World Series home run of his career, giving the Cardinals a 2-0 advantage. Musial said, "It was a fastball just below the belt."[9] After going down in order in the second, the Cardinals doubled their advantage in the third. Brecheen struck out to start the inning. Then Litwhiler singled to left, his first hit in the Series. After Hopp struck out, Musial reached on a slow grounder past the box that was scored a single. Walker Cooper then looped a single to left, scoring Litwhiler. Second baseman Don Gutteridge could not handle Sanders' hot smash, and Musial scored from second to give the Cardinals an unearned run and a 4-0 lead.

While the Cardinals appeared to have awakened, the Browns were frustrated at every turn. With one on and one out in the first, Moore hit a long drive to right-center that Hopp turned into a spectacular grab. "Had that ball been a foot more to Hopp's left, he never could have reached it, we'd have a run in, a man on second or third and one out, but he caught it and it certainly was a great catch," Browns manager Luke Sewell said.[10] The Associated Press described the catch as "first degree robbery."[11] The Browns had another chance in the second, but with runners on first and third, a broken-bat grounder from Red Hayworth turned into an around-the-horn double play, ending the threat.

The Browns had runners in each of the next three innings, but Brecheen's resolve and the Cardinals' glove work kept their lead at four runs. Brecheen's excellent defense was on display in the fourth when he retired Vern Stephens, who tapped a slow roller up the middle, especially important since the next hitter, Chet Laabs, lined a single to center. Hayworth led off the fifth with a high pop foul outside first base that Sanders turned into a great catch – he appeared to overrun the ball but was able to reach back and make the play. After a groundout and a single, Brecheen made another fine play, grabbing a low line drive off the bat of Mike Kreevich.

The Cardinals scored their final run of the contest off Al Hollingsworth, who relieved Jakucki in the fourth. Sanders led off the inning with a single and one out later NL Most Valuable Player Marty Marion doubled to left-center to score Sanders and make it 5-0. The Cardinals squandered a chance to increase their lead in the top of the seventh inning. Litwhiler singled but was thrown out at second trying to stretch the hit to a double. Hopp singled and Musial doubled him to third, Musial's third hit of the game. Hollingsworth walked Cooper to load the bases, but retired Sanders and Whitey Kurowski to end the threat.

The Browns recorded their only run in the bottom of the eighth. Brecheen's third walk of the game to Moore started the frame, and Stephens' single moved Moore to third. With the count 1-and-2 on Laabs, Cardinals skipper Billy Southworth went to the mound to talk to Brecheen after two foul balls. His advice paid off; Laabs hit a sharp grounder that Marion grabbed and turned into a 6-4-3 double play as Moore scored. Another grounder to Marion ended the inning. The Browns had one more chance in the ninth, but with two on and two out Kreevich grounded into a fielder's choice to end the game.

For Musial, his 3-for-4 performance was his best in World Series play. The Cards won Games Five and Six to take the Series, but Musial collected only one double in eight plate appearances in those games. His final fall classic appearance occurred two years later. Musial again hit .222 for the series, collecting four doubles and one triple in St. Louis's win over the Boston Red Sox in seven games. His final postseason line in 23 World Series games was a .256 average, with 7 doubles, one triple, and one home run. Musial did not mention this game, or any other postseason game, among his 10 greatest days in a November 1954 *Sport Magazine* article.[12]

SOURCES

In addition to the sources cited in the Notes, the author accessed *Sport Magazine*, Retrosheet.org, Baseball-Reference.com, SABR's BioProject via SABR.org, *The Sporting News* archive via Paper of Record, the *Cincinnati Enquirer*, *Detroit Free Press*, and *St. Louis Post Dispatch* via newspapers.com, and the *Chicago Tribune* archive.

NOTES

1. As of the end of the 2023 season, the record still stood.
2. Peter Golenbock, *The Spirit of St. Louis – A History of the St. Louis Cardinals and Browns* (New York: Harper Collins ebooks, 2000), 305.
3. Frederick C. Lieb, "Browns Hailed as 'Team of Destiny,'" *The Sporting News*, October 5, 1944: 2.
4. "Cards Play Like Champions for First Time; Cooper, Galehouse to Renew Rivalry Today," *Cincinnati Enquirer*, October 8, 1944: 34.
5. Gregory H. Wolf, "Harry Brecheen," in Bill Nowlin, ed., *Van Lingle Mungo – The Man, The Song, The Players* (Phoenix: Society for American Baseball Research, 2014), 204.
6. Wolf, 94.
7. Wolf, 95.
8. David Allen Heller, *As Good as It Got: The 1944 St. Louis Browns (Images of Baseball)* (Charleston, South Carolina: Arcadia Publishing, 2003).
9. W.J. McGoogan, "Cardinals Win 5 to 1, and Square Series; Brownie Pitchers Yield 12 Hits, Including Homer by Musial," *St. Louis Post Dispatch*, October 8, 1944: 20.
10. McGoogan, 19.
11. W.F. Crawford, "Series Sidelights," *St. Louis Post Dispatch*, October 8, 1944: 20.
12. Joe Reichler, "Stan Musial's Ten Greatest Days," *Sport Magazine*, November 1954: 12.

THIRD STRAIGHT FOUR-HIT GAME RAISES MUSIAL'S BATTING AVERAGE TO .375

August 12, 1946: St. Louis Cardinals 5, Chicago Cubs 0, at Wrigley Field, Chicago

BY TOM SCHOTT

After being instrumental in the St. Louis Cardinals winning the World Series in 1942 and 1944 – with a third National League pennant in between – burgeoning star outfielder Stan Musial enlisted in the US Navy and did not play during the 1945 season.

Musial was honorably discharged on March 1, 1946, and reported to the Cardinals' spring-training camp in St. Petersburg, Florida. The 25-year-old began his fourth full season in the major leagues playing left field.[1] But on June 7, he was moved to first base in place of rookie Dick Sisler, who was off to a slow start offensively and was sidelined with a minor injury.[2]

At the time of the position switch, Musial ranked third in the NL with a .337 batting average and fourth with 27 RBIs.[3] He had turned down overtures from the Mexican League to leave the Cardinals for "luscious cash offerings."[4] The Cardinals, under first-year manager Eddie Dyer, owned a 25-18 record and were in second place, 4½ games behind the Brooklyn Dodgers.

St. Louis spent most of the season in second place and resided there on August 12 for the start of a three-game series with the defending NL champion Chicago Cubs[5] at Wrigley Field that wrapped up a 20-game, 23-day road trip.

Musial was red hot, having gone 4-for-5 in both games of a doubleheader sweep of the Cincinnati Reds (15-4 and 7-3) at Crosley Field the previous day. Among his eight hits were a double, triple, and home run.

In the opener against the Cubs, Musial recorded his third straight four-hit game in a 5-0 Cardinals victory. Batting third in the lineup, the sweet-swinging lefty with the corkscrew stance:

- Singled to left in the first inning against Claude Passeau.
- Doubled to right in the third against Emil Kush, driving in Al Brazle.
- Singled to right in the fifth against Kush, later scoring.
- Singled to right in the seventh against Kush, driving in Harry Walker.

The four-hit performance was Musial's seventh of the season and the 22nd of his young career, to go with a five-hit game against the New York Giants on July 21, 1943.[6]

Musial extended his hitting streak to seven games, during which he got 20 hits in 30 at-bats, including 11 in his past 12. At day's end, he led all NL batters with a .375 batting average, .587 slugging percentage, 158 hits, 33 doubles, 13 triples, and 85 runs. He ranked second with a .439 on-base percentage and third with 74 RBIs.[7]

Sportswriters were comparing Musial with Boston Red Sox star left fielder Ted Williams, who also returned to the majors in 1946 after serving a three-year hitch in the Marine Corps. In his *St. Louis Globe Democrat* column on August 13, Bob Burnes observed: "Williams is completely a pull hitter. ... Musial is not. He can pull one if he wants to but just let the defensive team over-shift on him and he'll punch one to left center or down the left-field foul line."[8]

Fred Lieb wrote in the August 21 issue of *The Sporting News*: "Ted hits a longer ball, but when Stan swivels his famous wrists, hits rattle off the fences like machine-gun bullets."[9]

The win over the Cubs was the Cardinals' fifth in a row and ninth in 11 games after they went 2-5 to begin the excursion that took them completely around the NL: New York, Boston, Brooklyn, Philadelphia, Pittsburgh, Cincinnati, and Chicago. With its 64-41 record, St. Louis trailed the Dodgers (66-42) by a half-game. The Cubs were in third place, nine games out.

"So it can be seen that the Cardinals perform as Musial does," Burnes wrote on August 13. "When he slumped during the first part of the current trip, everyone slumped right along with him and the Birds lost ground. Stan snapped out of it about half way along in the journey and since then the Birds have been winning and picking up ground on the Dodgers."[10]

Against the Cubs, Musial co-starred with Brazle, the Cardinals' starting pitcher, who authored a three-hit shutout to improve his record to 4-8. He walked one batter and induced two double plays while facing just 29 batters and allowing only two runners to reach second base. The left-handed sinkerballer recorded 21 groundball outs. It was Brazle's second whitewash of the road trip (also at Boston on July 28) and began a stretch of eight wins in 10 decisions to finish the season. The 32-year-old left-hander debuted in 1943 and then missed the ensuing two seasons while serving in the US Army.

With 19 putouts and one assist, Musial came close to the record of 22 total chances by a first baseman in a nine-inning game.[11]

The Cardinals scored three runs in the third inning. Marty Marion led off with a single off the glove of Passeau, and the Cubs' starting pitcher aggravated a back ailment on the play and had to leave the game. Kush relieved for Chicago. Brazle singled, advancing Marion to second, and Red Schoendienst sacrificed the runners to second and third. Walker drove in Marion with a single to center, and Musial's double plated Brazle and moved Walker to third. Enos Slaughter was walked intentionally to load the bases, and Whitey Kurowski lined a sacrifice fly to center to bring Walker home.

Musial's fifth-inning single came with two outs and was followed by Slaughter's infield hit. Catcher Mickey Livingston attempted to pick off Musial at second base but his throw missed the mark and second baseman Don Johnson's subsequent throw trying to get Musial at third sailed awry, allowing Musial to score.

A two-out, seventh-inning double by Walker and Musial's RBI single capped the scoring in a game that took 1 hour and 34 minutes to complete before 28,254 Monday afternoon spectators.

In the final two games against the Cubs,[12] Musial went 1-for-4 and 2-for-5, finishing the final nine games of the road trip 23-for-39 (.590 batting average) as the Cardinals won seven games. At this point in his career, he had not yet been christened "The Man." That would come in mid-September by Brooklyn fans at Ebbets Field during Musial's season-long 14-game hitting streak from September 6-19, crowned by a 5-for-5 performance (three singles and two doubles) in Boston against the Braves.[13]

On August 22 the Cardinals moved into a first-place tie with the Dodgers, and the two teams were neck and neck for the rest of the season. Both finished with 96-58 records, necessitating a best-of-three tiebreaker to determine the league champion. St. Louis won the first two games (4-2 and 8-4) to capture its fourth pennant in five seasons. The Cubs finished third at 82-71. From 1942 to 1946, the Cardinals averaged 102 wins per season.

The Cardinals won a thrilling seven-game World Series over Williams[14] and the Red Sox by virtue of Slaughter's famed "Mad Dash" to score the winning run in the deciding game.[15] For Musial, his fourth postseason appearance would be the last of his 22-year playing career. St. Louis next appeared in the fall classic in 1964, the year after Musial retired.[16]

Musial was named the 1946 NL Most Valuable Player after leading the league with a .365 batting average, .587 slugging percentage, 228 hits, 50 doubles, 20 triples, 366 total bases, and 124 runs while playing in all 156 games. He was third with 103 RBIs and tied for fifth with 16 home runs. Musial received 22 of 24 possible first-place votes and amassed 319 points to easily outdistance Brooklyn right fielder Dixie Walker, who had 159 points. Slaughter, the Cardinals' right fielder, received the other two first-place votes and finished third in the balloting with 144 points.

Musial previously was the MVP in 1943 and was honored again in 1948[17] en route to becoming the greatest – and most popular – player in Cardinals history, being called "baseball's perfect warrior" and "baseball's perfect knight" by Commissioner Ford C. Frick,[18] and earning first-ballot election to the National Baseball Hall of Fame in 1969.[19] The 24-time All-Star concluded his career with a .331 batting average and 3,630 hits (1,815 at home and 1,815 on the road).

SOURCES

In addition to the sources cited in the Notes, the author consulted the Baseball-Reference.com and Retrosheet.org websites for pertinent material and the box scores.

https://www.baseball-reference.com/boxes/CHN/CHN194608120.shtml

https://www.retrosheet.org/boxesetc/1946/B08120CHN1946.htm

NOTES

1   Musial played left field in 1942 and primarily right field in 1943 and 1944.

2   Sisler was batting .268 with one home run and 24 RBIs. A hand injury forced him out of the lineup for a few games in early June. Harry Walker played first base from June 2 to 6 before Musial took over the position. Erv Dusak assumed Musial's spot in left field.

3   In the 1946 All-Star Game at Fenway Park in Boston, Musial started in left field.

4   Robert L. Burnes, "Musial Definitely Turns Down Mexican Offer," *St. Louis Globe-Democrat*, June 7, 1946: 17. Musial was offered a five-year, $125,000 contract plus a $50,000 signing bonus from the Mexican League. He initially was making $13,500 with the Cardinals in 1946 and was later given a $5,000 raise. St. Louis pitchers Max Lanier and Fred Martin and infielder Lou Klein did jump to the Mexican League.

5   The Cubs finished three games ahead of the second-place Cardinals.

6   Musial finished his career with 59 four-hit games and eight five-hit games.

7   St. Louis right fielder Enos Slaughter led the NL with 88 RBIs, while Brooklyn right fielder Dixie Walker was second with 84.

8   Robert L. Burnes, "The Bench Warmer," *St. Louis Globe-Democrat*, August 13, 1946: 15.

9   Frederick G. Lieb, "Redbird Flyer Whistling for Flag Stop," *The Sporting News*, August 21, 1946: 7.

10 "The Bench Warmer."

11 The total of 22 chances had been accomplished nine times previously.

12 The Cubs won 1-0 on August 13 and St. Louis won 6-4 on August 14.

13 In a September 20, 1946, article in the *St. Louis Post-Dispatch*, Bob Broeg credited Brooklyn fans with calling Musial "The Man" during the September 12-14 series. Broeg wrote: "[T]he appearance at the plate of the Cardinals' apple-cheeked first baseman frequently brought from several sections of the Ebbets Field stands a distinct: 'O-O-h, here comes The Man again.' Not that man, but THE man."

14 The 28-year-old Williams was the American League Most Valuable Player in 1946 after batting .342 with 37 doubles, 8 triples, 38 home runs, and 123 RBIs – with a .497 on-base percentage and .667 slugging percentage.

15 Musial batted .222 (6-for-27) with four RBIs in the World Series, while Williams batted .200 (5-for-25) with one RBI.

16 Musial was a vice president of the Cardinals from 1963 to 1966, then assumed the role of general manager for one season (1967). The Cardinals were World Series champions in 1964 and 1967.

17 The Cardinals won five MVP awards in seven years from 1942 to 1948: pitcher Mort Cooper (1942); Musial (1943, 1946, and 1948); and shortstop Marty Marion (1944). Over the course of his career, Musial finished second for the award four times (1949, 1950, 1951, and 1957) and in the top 10 a total of 14 times.

18 Frick said these words the day Musial retired: September. 29, 1963.

19 Musial was named on 93.2 percent of the Hall of Fame ballots (317 of 340).

STAN MUSIAL FINDS MOTIVATION IN ATTAINING 1,000-HIT MILESTONE

April 24, 1948: Chicago Cubs 6, St. Louis Cardinals 2, at Wrigley Field, Chicago

BY CHAD MOODY

Battling appendicitis and tonsillitis, Stan Musial got off to a slow start at the plate for the St. Louis Cardinals in 1947. The reigning National League Most Valuable Player was able to avoid missing significant playing time, however, by deciding to undergo a stopgap treatment that involved freezing his appendix.[1] The controversial medical procedure eventually seemed to work as intended with Musial going on a tear to lift a sub-.200 batting average in June to a robust .312 at season's end. "Pretty good, yes, but not good enough," Musial opined when considering that he had hit between .347 and .365 in his three previous years.[2] And with his hit total precipitously declining by 45 from the prior season – leaving him just five short of 1,000 in his career to that point – Musial dubbed his sixth campaign in the big leagues a "lousy year."[3]

"From the moment I picked up a bat in 1948, healthy and strong after offseason surgery [to remove his troublesome appendix and tonsils], I knew this would be it, my big year," Musial wrote in his 1964 autobiography.[4] Now being at his "athletic peak" with more strength than ever, the bat felt lighter to the future Hall of Famer.[5] As such, he stopped choking up on the handle and instead adjusted his hands down to the knob of the bat to generate more leverage and power. "Gripping the bat at the end, I could still control my swing," Musial explained.[6] The slender lefty with the unique crouch at the plate thus evolved from a hitter to a slugger and began his journey to posting one of the most dominant offensive seasons in major-league history.[7] And an important step along the way occurred when Musial collected his 1,000th career hit early in the campaign during a road game against the Chicago Cubs.

After prevailing in the first of three contests in the Windy City, St. Louis under manager Eddie Dyer started veteran lefty moundsman Al Brazle in the second game of the set on April 24. Musial was assigned to right field, his "favorite" position; the 27-year-old had spent his past two years primarily at first base.[8] The Cardinals, winners of four pennants and three World Series since 1942, featured a lineup comprising largely the same core players who carried them to a second-place finish in the previous campaign.

Coming off a sixth-place finish and finding themselves in the midst of a rapid decline after winning the pennant in 1945, the Cubs under manager Charlie Grimm sent left-hander Cliff Chambers to the hill in his major-league debut. The 28,862 spectators enjoyed an abnormally warm spring afternoon at Wrigley Field.

Despite fielding an inexperienced and "allegedly light-hitting" lineup, the Cubs opened the scoring in the bottom of the first inning on All-Star Andy Pafko's "terrific 400-foot smash."[9] The three-run home run fell into the street "behind the left-field catwalk" and scored rookie Hank Schenz and Eddie Waitkus, who had led things off with back-to-back singles.[10] The score remained 3-0 through the next two frames.

Ralph LaPointe, who had earlier been "dazed" when accidentally beaned in pregame batting practice, reached base on a bunt single to lead off the top of the fourth for the Cardinals.[11] Entering the game with 999 career hits but failing in his bid to reach 1,000 after fanning in the first inning, Musial this time was successful when he "jarred the brick wall in center" with a triple that scored the "fast Frenchman" (LaPointe).[12] All-Star Whitey Kurowski followed with a groundout to second that brought Musial home with St. Louis's second and final run of the game.

All the remaining scoring came on a continued "home run cannonade" by the Cubs to the delight of the "giddy gallery."[13] Veteran slugger Bill Nicholson belted a solo homer "into Sheffield [Avenue]" that ultimately resulted in Brazle getting sent to the showers after only four innings of work.[14] Three frames later in the bottom of the seventh, Cliff Aberson homered on a "shotput delivery" from St. Louis reliever Ken Burkhart with the bases empty to increase the lead to three runs.[15] Finally, rookie Hal Jeffcoat capped the home run "barrage" with yet another solo shot in the bottom of the eighth – the first round-tripper of his major-league career – off "Texas League terror" Al Papai, who was making his big-league debut.[16] Upon the conclusion of the offensive "laughing stock" improbably "belting souvenirs over one wall or another," Chicago came away with a 6-2 victory.[17]

Though he narrowly avoided trouble on two "tremendous drives" by Kurowski caught for outs at the center-field fence, Chambers did a "neat batch of southpawing" in his first big-

Stan Musial enjoyed his best season in 1948 and recorded his 1,000th career hit on April 24 at Wrigley Field.

league appearance after leading the Triple-A Pacific Coast League with 24 wins a year earlier for the Los Angeles Angels.[18] The rookie went the distance for the Cubs while striking out four, walking one, and scattering eight hits. Two of the hits belonged to Musial, who also picked up career hit number 1,001 with a single in the sixth after reaching his historic milestone earlier in the tilt.

The 1,000-hit milestone at first "meant little" to Musial, until he was urged by St. Louis sportswriter Bob Broeg to use it as motivation for an even higher goal.[19] "Look, Banj [short for 'Banjo,' a nickname used to describe a light hitter], if you're going to talk about hits, what about trying for 3,000?" Broeg playfully asked him after the game in the clubhouse.[20] "To get 3,000, I'd have to average 200 a year for 10 more seasons," Musial recalled thinking to himself. "To maintain that incredible pace, I'd have to be good and lucky – lucky to escape serious injury, lucky to last that long. I'd be 37 or 38 years old!"[21] But once he learned that only seven major leaguers belonged to the exclusive 3,000-hit club at the time, Musial "couldn't shrug off the challenge" – despite the daunting mathematics.[22] "Keep reminding me [of the milestone]," he told Broeg. "This is a team game and I play to win, but a fella has to have little extra incentives. They keep him going when he's tired. They keep him from getting careless when the club is way ahead or far ahead. It'll help my concentration."[23]

Whatever the motivation, Musial went on to lead all major leaguers in hits with 230 in 1948. He also produced not only the best season of his career but arguably one of the greatest offensive seasons of all time. The All-Star just missed winning the Triple Crown by one home run (he hit 39) while leading the league in numerous other categories including RBIs (131), runs, doubles, triples, and OPS en route to winning the 1948 NL MVP award. And Musial "virtually carried a ball club that might have otherwise finished near the bottom of the standings" to a second-place finish.[24]

Ten years later, Stan the Man did indeed reach the 3,000-hit plateau: on May 13, 1958, with an extra-base hit in Wrigley Field – just as he did for his 1,000th. He concluded his major-league career in 1963 with 3,630 hits. Undoubtedly, Musial would have greatly exceeded this mark and achieved his hit milestones much earlier had he not missed the entire 1945 season while serving in the US Navy during World War II.

SOURCES

The author accessed Baseball-Reference.com (https://www.baseball-reference.com/boxes/CHN/CHN194804240.shtml) for box scores/play-by-play information and other data, as well as Retrosheet (https://www.retrosheet.org/boxesetc/1948/B04240CHN1948.htm).

In addition to the sources cited in the Notes, the author also accessed GenealogyBank.com, NewspaperArchive.com, Newspapers.com, Paper of Record, Stathead.com, and Weather Underground.

NOTES

1. Some medical professionals of the day expressed skepticism regarding the efficacy of appendix freezing. In his 1946 book *The New Science of Surgery*, physician and novelist Frank Gill Slaughter wrote this of the procedure: "A customary remedy for appendicitis has long been the application of ice caps to the abdomen, in the mistaken assumption that the appendix could be 'frozen.' Surgeons in general deplore this treatment." And in their 1947 book *Surgical Treatment of the Abdomen*, surgeons Frederic Wolcott Bancroft and Preston Allen Wade echoed a similar opinion, stating that the use of ice bags as a treatment "has done untold harm by masking symptoms through its anesthetic effect." See David L. Farquhar's 2011 article, "Stan Musial and His Frozen Appendix," on the Silicon Underground website for more investigative research on this topic (https://dfarq.homeip.net/stan-musial-and-his-frozen-appendix, accessed April 2, 2024).

2. Stan Musial and Robert Broeg, *Stan Musial: "The Man's" Own Story, as Told to Bob Broeg* (Garden City, New York: Doubleday & Company, 1964), 108.

3. Derrick Goold, "Musial and His Frozen Appendix," *St. Louis Post-Dispatch*, April 4, 2011, https://www.stltoday.com/sports/professional/mlb/cardinals/musial-and-his-frozen-appendix/article_119865c-5ebc-11e0-a399-0019bb30f31a.html, accessed November 20, 2023.

4. Musial and Broeg, 109.

5. Musial and Broeg, 110.

6   Musial and Broeg, 110.
7   George Vecsey, *Stan Musial: An American Life* (New York: Random House, 2011), 200.
8   James N. Giglio, *Musial: From Stash to Stan the Man* (Columbia, Missouri: University of Missouri Press, 2001), 163.
9   Bob Broeg, "Cub Homers Beat Cards, 6-2; Brazle Lasts Only 4 Innings," *St. Louis Post-Dispatch*, April 25, 1948: 1D; Edgar Munzel, "Cub Homers Rip Cards 6-2," *Chicago Sun-Times*, April 25, 1948: 70.
10 Irving Vaughan, "Sox Lose; 4 Cub Homers Beat Cards, 6-2," *Chicago Tribune*, April 25, 1948: Part 2-1.
11 "National League," *The Sporting News*, May 5, 1948: 16.
12 Vaughan; Broeg.
13 Munzel.
14 Vaughan.
15 Broeg.
16 Associated Press, "Cubs' Homers Spill Cards, 6-2," *Springfield (Missouri) News and Leader*, April 25, 1948: C-1; Broeg.
17 Broeg.
18 Broeg; Vaughan.
19 Musial and Broeg, 111.
20 Musial and Broeg, 111.
21 Musial and Broeg, 111–112.
22 Musial and Broeg, 112.
23 Musial and Broeg, 112.
24 Giglio, 164.

STAN MUSIAL SOLIDIFIES "THE MAN" MONIKER WITH SECOND FIVE-HIT GAME OF SEASON

May 19, 1948: St. Louis Cardinals 14, Brooklyn Dodgers 7, at Ebbets Field, Brooklyn

BY MIKE EISENBATH

The night of May 19, 1948, Stan Musial strolled six times to home plate at Ebbets Field in Brooklyn. Most of those among the announced crowd of 32,888 fans in the ballpark loved their Dodgers.

Likely all of them respected The Man.

They probably collectively launched a sigh of relief when he simply drew a walk in the fourth inning. The five other trips, Dodgers pitchers managed to get to two strikes against Musial. Each time, Musial prevailed – three singles, a double, and a triple.

"I have one philosophy," Musial once said in an interview. "I expect to get a hit every time I go to the plate."[1]

Some years later, writers including Bob Broeg of the St. Louis Post-Dispatch, Ray Gillespie of The Sporting News, and Joe Reichler in Sport magazine identified Ebbets Field as the site that launched Musial's nickname – probably sometime in 1946.

Every time he came to bat, Reichler wrote in 1954, the fans nearby would say: "Oooh, oooh, here comes the man again. Here comes the man."[2]

Dodgers fans had ample reason to summon special respect for Musial early in his career. He faced them for the first time on May 3, 1942, in a doubleheader in St. Louis. The 21-year-old tattooed them with four hits, including two doubles, and swiped two bases in five at-bats.

By the time the 1948 season began, Musial owned Brooklyn pitching with a .348 batting average in 110 games. In addition to his 140 hits – 58 for extra bases – Musial had drawn 79 walks against the Dodgers and had compiled a 1.048 OPS.

That success included a .324 batting average for Musial at Ebbets Field – and that's where he and the Cardinals headed in the middle of May 1948.

Three days esrlier the Cardinals had completed a tremendously successful 12-game homestand before embarking for New York. They won nine of those games, including a three-game sweep of the Pittsburgh Pirates to close the stretch at Sportsman's Park that actually crossed 16 days off the calendar.

One of those triumphs was a 5-4 squeaker over the Dodgers on May 4 that featured a sixth-inning homer from Musial off Ralph Branca and a solo homer in the eighth inning by Enos Slaughter. Alas, the next two scheduled games against Brooklyn were rained out.

Musial didn't have a bad homestand – .311 batting average, with a couple of triples and a couple of homers while driving in six runs – but he had managed only five hits in his past 20 at-bats as he prepared to head east.

Overall, the team was riding a wave of momentum. A .500 club at the end of April, the Cardinals now sported a 13-7 record and topped the National League standings, 1½ games ahead of the second-place New York Giants and 3½ in front of the sixth-place Dodgers.

That gap increased to 4½ games after the series opener on May 18. Branca went the distance for the home squad and yielded eight hits, with three walks. Musial had a single and double in four at-bats and scored twice, including in the sixth inning on Slaughter's two-run homer. That put the Cardinals ahead 4-2, and Red Munger kept the lead en route to a 4-3 complete-game victory.

So the Cardinals had won 10 of their 13 previous games and carried a four-game winning streak into the second game of the Brooklyn series. The home team tried to play some mind games with the Cardinals before the actual game began; St. Louis had to take pregame batting practice in twilight because the Dodgers refused to turn on the ballpark lights until just before the teams took the field. Turns out that didn't affect the Cardinals – other than to get their competitive juices flowing.[3]

The Dodgers' starting lineup featured six players who appeared in the 1947 World Series, which Brooklyn dropped in seven games. That included starting pitcher Rex Barney, a mere 23-year-old who had made eight big-league starts at the age of 18 during the World War II season of 1943.

Six players in the Cardinals' starting lineup had appeared in at least 100 regular-season games in 1946, when they knocked off the Boston Red Sox in a seven-game World Series. Onto the mound against Brooklyn stepped 34-year-old lefty Al Brazle, who hadn't reached the big leagues until the age of 29. He had worked almost seven innings of ineffective relief of an even-less-effective Howie Pollet in Game Five of the 1946 Series but was a vital part of the staff in 1947 as a combo reliever-starter and again in 1948.

Alas, the youngster Barney and the more senior Brazle combined to get a total of nine outs in this matchup.

In the top of the first, Erv Dusak reached on a one-out bunt single and went to second when Musial pulled a single into right field. Slaughter's double to right brought Dusak home, and Musial was safe at the plate when Brooklyn catcher Bruce Edwards muffed the relay throw. The Dodgers eventually got out of the inning trailing only 2-0 when Edwards tagged out Slaughter trying to steal home.

The lead didn't live long. Brazle got Eddie Miksis to line out to center to open the bottom of the first, then gave up a single to Pee Wee Reese, a walk, a bases-loading single, and Edwards' two-run double. Manager Eddie Dyer pulled Brazle and called in reliever Jim Hearn. Pinch-hitter Dick Whitman greeted him with an RBI base hit. Hearn walked Spider Jorgensen to load the bases, then walked Preston Ward to put the Dodgers ahead 4-2.

They made it 5-2 when Carl Furillo's double scored Pete Reiser in the second inning.

The Cardinals knocked out Barney with a pair of runs in the third. They loaded the bases on back-to-back singles from Dusak and Musial and a walk to Slaughter. Whitey Kurowski's fly out sent Dusak home. Musial scored his second run on Nippy Jones's fielder's choice groundball. Reliever Clyde King got the third out of the inning.

King retired only one more Cardinals batsman. He issued consecutive one-out walks to Dusak, Musial, and Slaughter in the fourth inning. Reliever Hugh Casey took over and the Cardinals treated him rudely: A walk to Kurowski forced in one run, Jones's double chased home three runs, and Ralph LaPointe's double scored Jones. Suddenly, the flying-high Cardinals were back on top, 9-5.

Musial's biggest stroke of the day came in the fifth. After Red Schoendienst and Dusak drew inning-opening walks, Musial lined an opposite-field triple to left field against reliever Erv Palica. He eventually scored for the fourth time in the game, and by inning's end the Cardinals enjoyed a 13-5 lead.

Three Musial hits and a walk against three different pitchers in only five innings. His two closing hits on the historic night came against Brooklyn's fourth reliever – Preacher Roe, in the first of his seven seasons with the ballclub.

Once explaining how he approached pitching to Musial, Roe said: "I throw him four wide ones and try to pick him off first base."[4]

Musial and Roe faced each other in 184 plate appearances during their careers. As that day indicates, The Man generally came out ahead of the Preacher with his career .372 batting mark and .437 on-base percentage against him.

In this particular meeting, Musial pulled a single to right in the sixth inning off Roe, then he yanked a double into right in the eighth. Cleanup man Kurowski soon singled Musial home to put the Cardinals ahead 14-7.

With his five runs scored and two RBIs, Musial had accounted for half his club's runs. That was Musial's second five-hit game of the season. He would have two more before it ended.

"I'll never get over the way those Brooklyn fans cheered me," Musial said. "I thought for a moment I was back at Sportsman's Park."[5]

SOURCES

The author accessed Retrosheet.org and Baseball-Reference.com for pertinent information, including box scores, play-by-play, and other statistical data.

https://www.retrosheet.org/boxesetc/1948/B05190BRO1948.htm

https://www.baseball-reference.com/boxes/BRO/BRO194805190.shtml

NOTES

1   Author interview with Stan Musial in July 1992, as the author conducted interviews and research for a series of stories in the *St. Louis Post-Dispatch* commemorating the team's 100 years in the National League.

2   Joe Reichler, "Stan Musial's Ten Greatest Days," *Sport*, November 1954: 12.

3   Ray Gillespie, "Two Birds Hit, One Spilled at Ebbets Field," *The Sporting News*, May 26, 1948: 7, 14.

4   Joe Blogs, "Musial," MLB.com/Blogs, November 21, 2012. https://medium.com/joeblogs/musial-637c8d9fee2f#:~:text=He%20had%20that%20quirky%20and,pick%20him%20off%20first%20base.%E2%80%9D.

5   Ray Gillespie, "Hats Off," *The Sporting News*, May 26, 1948: 17.

STAN MUSIAL DOMINATES THE DODGERS AGAIN AS CARDINALS COMPLETE SWEEP

May 20, 1948: St. Louis Cardinals 13, Brooklyn Dodgers 4, at Ebbets Field, Brooklyn

BY ANDREW HECKROTH

The Man continued to damage Brooklyn's pitching. The day after he collected five hits in five at-bats, Stan Musial went 4-for-6 as the Cardinals romped over the Dodgers in a contentious 13-4 win that saw two Cardinals hit by pitches. It was the Cardinals' sixth win in a row.[1] Musial entered the game batting .393 and pushed his average to .411. It was the first time he reached the .400 percentage since the Cardinals' 13-7 win on April 30 at Cincinnati.[2]

These two teams had built up quite a rivalry. St. Louis held off Brooklyn in 1946 by two games to capture the National League pennant, and went on to win the World Series over Ted Williams's Boston Red Sox thanks to Enos Slaughter's mad dash in Game Seven. In 1947 Brooklyn captured the pennant with a record of 94-60 but lost in seven games to the New York Yankees in the World Series. Before the 1948 season, the Cardinals were listed as the betting favorites to capture another pennant.[3]

Third-year left-handed pitcher Joe Hatten got the start for Brooklyn on two days' rest. Hatten entered this game with a 2-1 record in his six games. In his previous appearance, on May 17 against Boston, Hatten came on in relief and pitched three shutout innings in a 12-3 Braves win.

Opposing Hatten was another southpaw, Howie Pollet. Pollet had two complete-game wins under his belt in 1948. He got the start for the Cardinals on three days' rest after he was called upon to stop a Pittsburgh Pirates rally on May 16 to secure the win in 10 innings.[4]

The game was scoreless when Erv Dusak singled to bring up Musial with two outs in the third. Musial laced a double along the right-field line to bring in the first run of the game and earn his 21st RBI in 1948.[5]

After the Dodgers equalized in the fourth on a Dick Whitman two-out single to bring in Bruce Edwards at third, the Cardinals responded with six runs in the next half-inning. Ralph LaPointe, playing in place of an injured Red Schoendienst, began the St. Louis rally with a leadoff walk. Musial stepped in with one out and crushed a 1-and-2 pitch off the right-field scoreboard for a double that sent LaPointe to third.[6]

With a base open, manager Leo Durocher opted to intentionally walk Whitey Kurowski and pitch to Slaughter. The strategy backfired, as Slaughter hit a line-drive single into center field to score LaPointe and Musial. It was the 13th straight game in which Slaughter recorded a base hit after being mired in a 1-for-35 slump earlier in the season.[7]

Nippy Jones walked, and the bases were loaded once again. With Marty Marion batting, Hatten uncorked a wild pitch that scored Kurowski and moved Slaughter to third and Jones to second. Despite Hatten's working the count full on Marion, Durocher called for his second intentional pass to load the bases again. Del Rice cleared the bases with a double into the left-field corner for the final runs of the inning.[8]

Righty Hugh Casey came on in relief of Hatten in the top of the sixth. Kurowski reached first when a Casey pitch hit him in the back. He reached third on Slaughter's double to right field. Jones singled up the middle to score both baserunners. Rice smacked a 2-and-1 pitch off the fence in left-center field that scored the 10th run for the Cardinals.[9]

Musial stepped back into the batter's box in the top of the seventh inning. He worked the count full and connected on his fifth home run of the season, the ball sailing over the wall in right field to make the score 11-1, Cardinals.[10]

Tensions reached a climax in the top of the eighth. This time, Casey drilled Rice in the head. Manager Eddie Dyer implored umpire Artie Gore to eject Casey immediately. Not only had Casey struck two Cardinal batters, he sailed pitches close to the heads of Slaughter and Rice.[11] Umpire Gore ejected Dyer for his continued argument. When Casey walked to check on the injured Rice, Dyer turned to Casey and said, "You're a better pitcher than that, Hugh."[12]

Schoendienst ran for Rice at first. In the bottom of the inning, Joe Garagiola took over catcher duties for the Cardinals.[13]

Despite being down by 10 runs, the Dodgers refused to mail it in. Don Lund led off the bottom of the eighth with a double to left field and Carl Furillo walked. Tommy Brown smacked a two-out single to right field that scored Lund from second and moved Furillo to third, and reached second on Slaughter's throw home. Whitman hit a double to left-center field that scored the Dodgers' final two runs of the game.[14]

For an encore, Musial singled off the right-field wall in the top of the ninth off righty Clyde King for his 11th and final hit of the series.[15] After reaching second on Don Lang's walk, Musial scored on Slaughter's single to right, which moved Lang to third base. Nippy Jones's fly ball to center field brought in Lang for the 13th and final run of the game. Pollet allowed a double to Lund in the bottom of the ninth but finished off the Dodgers for the complete game and his fourth win in a row.[16]

While Musial received praise for his masterful performances the last two days, the beaned batters were also the talk of the series. After the game, Casey visited Rice in the Cardinals' clubhouse and told the Brooklyn Daily Eagle writers that he did not intend to hit Rice on purpose. "I was trying to pitch him close to the letters," he said. "The ball wasn't more than an inch or so inside. Rice must have turned his head or was looking for a curve."[17]

Umpire Gore also said there seemed to be no intent on the part of Casey: "Not being a mind reader, I didn't see anything wrong. I'm not a magician, either."[18] The Cardinals remained angered after the game. as the team claimed the Dodgers tried to "low-bridge" or throw pitches with intent at the batters' heads.[19]

When he reminisced over his 10 greatest days with the Cardinals in November 1954, Musial included May 19 and May 20 in his top five. Wrote Joe Reichler in *Sport* magazine, "Many of Musial's greatest days have been against the Dodgers in Brooklyn. Stan can't explain it except that he thinks he unconsciously plays harder against the Dodgers because of the fierce competition they always provide."[20]

Perhaps the *Brooklyn Daily Eagle* said it best regarding the Cardinals-Dodgers rivalry: "It looks like a long summer."[21]

SOURCES

The author accessed Retrosheet.org and Baseball-Reference.com for pertinent information, including box scores, play-by-play, and other statistical data.

https://www.baseball-reference.com/boxes/BRO/BRO194805200.shtml

https://www.retrosheet.org/boxesetc/1948/B05200BRO1948.htm

NOTES

1. Martin J. Haley, "Red Birds Clip Brooks, 13-4, Slowly Pull Ahead of Pack," *St. Louis Globe-Democrat*, May 21, 1948: 3C.
2. The highest Musial's batting average reached in his 1948 MVP season was .415 on July 7. Musial finished his season with a career-high slash line of .376/.450/.702.
3. "Yanks, Sox A.L. Picks, Cards in N.L.," *The Sporting News*, April 7, 1948: 1.
4. Martin J. Haley, "Cards Edge Bucs in Tenth, 6-5, on Fluke Hit," *St. Louis Globe-Democrat*, May 17, 1948: 3C.
5. Bob Broeg, "Runs Come Cheap for Cards in Brooklyn; Musial Keeps Up Hot Spurt," *St. Louis Post-Dispatch*, May 20, 1948: 5B.
6. Broeg.
7. Haley.
8. Broeg.
9. Broeg.
10. Broeg.
11. Dick Young, "Cards Hand Flock 5th Straight Defeat, 13-4," *New York Daily News*, May 21, 1948: 78.
12. "Cards Rekindle Feud on Bean-Ball Charge," *Brooklyn Daily Eagle*, May 21, 1948: 16.
13. Broeg.
14. Broeg.
15. In the three-game series at Ebbets Field, Musial went 11-for-15 with 20 total bases; Young, *New York Daily News*.
16. Haley.
17. "Cards Rekindle Feud on Bean-Ball Charge."
18. "Cards Rekindle Feud on Bean-Ball Charge."
19. "Cards Rekindle Feud on Bean-Ball Charge."
20. Joe Reichler, "Stan Musial's Ten Greatest Days," *Sport*, November 1954: 15. From 1940 to 1954, Brooklyn won five pennants while the Cardinals captured four. In five of those seasons (1941, 1942, 1946, 1947, 1949), the Cardinals and the Dodgers both finished as the top two teams in the National League. St. Louis went 172-160 against Brooklyn during this time.
21. "Cards Rekindle Feud on Bean-Ball Charge."

STAN MUSIAL WOWS ST. LOUIS CROWD WITH HOME RUN IN ALL-STAR GAME

July 13, 1948: American League 5, National League 2, at Sportsman's Park, St. Louis

BY C. PAUL ROGERS III

Baseball's 15th All-Star Game took place in Sportsman's Park on July 13, 1948, before a capacity crowd of 34,009. It was the second time St. Louis had hosted the summer classic. The first time, in 1940, the host team was the St. Louis Browns. That game resulted in a 4-0 National League win behind a three-run first-inning home run by Max West of the Boston Bees. It was the first shutout in All-Star Game history. This time the American League prevailed, 5-2, in 2 hours 27 minutes behind stellar pitching by Vic Raschi of the New York Yankees and Joe Coleman of the Philadelphia A's, each of whom threw three shutout innings at the Nationals.

The National League had lost five of the last six All-Star Games and 10 of 14 overall, but it appeared to have the advantage coming into this one. The pitching staff selected by manager Leo Durocher of the Brooklyn Dodgers was well rested and the 25-man team was mostly healthy. In contrast, four of the top stars of the American League were limited because of injury and six of their pitchers had worked just two days earlier. One was Hal Newhouser, who came into the All-Star break with a 13-6 record on his way to a 21-win season. He had thrown 7⅔ innings on Sunday and asked not to be used. In addition, Joe DiMaggio was afflicted with sore heels and a swollen knee, Ted Williams was battling torn rib cartilage, and George Kell had a bum ankle. As a result, all three would-be starters were limited to pinch-hitting duties.[1]

The American Leaguers were also without Bob Feller, who had withdrawn from the game.[2] Feller was only 9-10 at the break, but his withdrawal drew a firestorm of criticism, particularly from American League manager Bucky Harris, who said that if he had his way, Feller would never be asked to another All-Star Game.[3] St. Louis Cardinals shortstop Marty Marion also drew criticism for his last-minute withdrawal from the game, all of which prompted a letter from the Cincinnati Reds, signed by veteran pitcher Bucky Walters, urging a fine equal to three days' pay for any player selected who skipped the game. That prompted Commissioner Happy Chandler to issue a statement expressing his concern "over the failure of club owners and players to take seriously the All-Star Game" and promising to take whatever steps were necessary in the future to assure participation by those selected.[4]

Although major-league baseball was integrated the previous year, no African-American players were selected for the All-Star Game until 1949. In 1948 Jackie Robinson was passed over at second base even though he was hitting a hard .295 at the break. Larry Doby was similarly bypassed in the American League despite hitting .288 for a team in the thick of the pennant race.

With his choices limited, Harris named Washington Senators right-hander Walt Masterson to start the game, even though he had only a 6-6 record and had also pitched on Sunday.[5] Durocher, who had broken convention by picking only six pitchers instead of the usual eight, started Ralph Branca, his ace from the Dodgers, who was 10-6 at the break and well rested.[6]

The game began under a blistering sun in hot, muggy conditions. Center fielder Richie Ashburn, the only rookie on either squad, led off for the National League. Ashburn had taken the National League by storm, hitting .351 to earn the starting spot.[7] He swung at the first pitch of the game and legged out a groundball to Joe Gordon at second for an infield single.[8] Ashburn stole second and advanced to third on a groundout before hometown hero Stan Musial thrilled the St. Louis fans by homering to the top of the right-field pavilion to put the National League into the lead, 2-0.[9] Although the NL threatened in the third and sixth innings with men in scoring position, they were unable to score again.

Branca sailed through the bottom of the first against the American Leaguers, striking out the first two batters. But in the second, Detroit's Hoot Evers, DiMaggio's replacement in center field, belted a one-out home run into the left-field bleachers to bring the score to 2-1. Evers thus became the second player in history to homer in his first All-Star at-bat.[10]

The National League put together singles by Musial and Slaughter in the top of the third but were unable to score as Andy Pafko hit into a force out at second to end the inning. In the American League third, Branca lost command and walked the first two batters, Mickey Vernon and Pat Mullin. He recovered to strike out Tommy Henrich looking, but Vernon and Mullin surprised by executing a double steal, aided by the fact that third baseman Pafko was playing deep and had to take Walker Cooper's throw on the run.[11] Lou Boudreau followed with a fly ball to deep right to bring in Vernon easily with the tying run.

After Johnny Schmitz relieved Branca to start the fourth inning, the American League quickly took control of the game. With one out Ken Keltner singled to left, George McQuinn singled to center, and Birdie Tebbetts walked to load the bases. Vic Raschi, a .243 hitter who had relieved Masterson on the mound in the top of the inning, got behind in the count on a couple of wild swings before lining a single to left to drive in two runs and knock Schmitz from the game.[12] Durocher brought in Johnny Sain to face Joe DiMaggio, pinch-hitting for Mullin. On the first pitch DiMaggio lined out to Musial in left, deep enough to bring in Tebbetts from third and put the American League ahead 5-2. Despite its best efforts, the National League would not be able to recover from that big inning.[13]

After five hot, muggy innings, dark thunderclouds moved in during the sixth inning accompanied by lightning bolts around the ballpark.[14] With spitting rain falling, the National League mounted a serious rally in the top of the sixth on one-out singles by Bob Elliott and Phil Masi off Raschi, who was pitching his third and final inning. Buddy Kerr then grounded out to Keltner at third, advancing both runners. With two outs, pinch-hitter Eddie Waitkus followed by working a walk to load the bases. Raschi next faced Ashburn, who already had two hits. With the count at 2-and-2 Ashburn backed away from an inside fastball that caught the corner for a called third strike.[15] It ended the uprising and was the last serious National League challenge.

In the bottom of the sixth the American League threatened against Ewell Blackwell of the Reds, who relieved Sain to start the inning. With one out McQuinn singled to left and then stole second as Tebbetts was called out on strikes. Bucky Harris surprised everyone by sending up Ted Williams, who was not expected to play, to pinch-hit for Raschi. Williams drew a walk and Newhouser, who was also not expected to participate, pinch-ran. Blackwell quickly quelled the threat by getting Al Zarilla to ground to Red Schoendienst at second for a force out.

Light rain fell intermittently through the seventh and eighth innings but it didn't bother Joe Coleman of the A's, who relieved Raschi and set the National Leaguers down in both frames, giving up only a walk to Musial in the seventh. For the Nationals, Sain pitched 1⅔ innings of scoreless baseball, while Blackwell finished with three scoreless innings, although he walked three.

The drama in the ninth was largely whether the thunderstorms would hold off long enough for the game to finish. The National League cooperated, however, and, with rain falling, could muster only a two-out walk by Bill Rigney off Coleman before Musial grounded out to second baseman Bobby Doerr to end the game on the short end of a 5-2 score.

If an All-Star MVP award had existed, it surely would have gone to Raschi, the winning pitcher, whose fourth-inning single drove in the winning run. As for the National League, its frustration would continue in 1949 with an 11-7 loss in Ebbets Field in Brooklyn before it finally broke through with a 5-4 win in 1950 in a 14-inning thriller in Chicago's Comiskey Park.

SOURCES

This article also appears in *Sportsman's Park in St. Louis: Home of the Browns and Cardinals at Grand and Dodier* (SABR, 2017), edited by Gregory H. Wolf.

NOTES

1   David Vincent, Lyle Spatz, and David W. Smith, *The Midsummer Classic – The Complete History of Baseball's All-Star* Game (Lincoln: University of Nebraska Press, 2001), 90.

2   Feller had controversially skipped the 1947 All-Star Game due to a back injury suffered in his last start before the game. He recovered well enough, however, to pitch two days after the game. In 1948 Indians owner Bill Veeck allegedly told Feller to fake an injury because, in the midst of a pennant race, he did not want to send both Bob Lemon and Feller to the game and risk injury. John Sickels, *Bob Feller – Ace of the Greatest Generation* (Washington: Brassey's, 2004), 193-94; Bob Feller with Bill Gilbert, *Now Pitching – A Baseball Memoir* (New York: Birch Lane Press, 1990), 152-53.

Stan Musial hit a two-run homer in the second inning of the 1948 All-Star Game held at Sportsman's Park in St. Louis. He signed this copy of the game program.

3. Frank Graham, *Baseball Extra* (New York: A.S. Barnes, 1954), 143-44. Harris selected Boston's Joe Dobson to replace Feller. Vincent, et al., 90.
4. Vincent et al., 90-91.
5. Masterson was on his way to an 8-15 record for the seventh-place Senators, who won only 56 games.
6. Durocher picked two sluggers instead, Sid Gordon of the Giants and Bob Elliot of the Braves. Vincent et al., 91.
7. Vincent et al., 91.
8. John Debringer, "American League Beats National 11th Time in 15 Games With Three Runs in 4th," *New York Times*, July 14, 1948: 28; Gordon's throw was wide but the official scorer ruled it an infield hit. Vincent et al., 91.
9. Debringer.
10. Max West's three-run homer off Red Ruffing in the first inning of the 1940 game, also in Sportsman's Park, was in his first All-Star at-bat.
11. Cooper was starting his sixth consecutive All-Star Game for the National League.
12. "American Leaguers Humble Nationals, 5-2," *Los Angeles Times*, July 14, 1948: 9.
13. Donald Honig, *The All-Star Game – A Pictorial History, 1933 to Present* (St. Louis: The Sporting News, 1987), 70.
14. *Los Angeles Times*, July 14, 1948: 9.
15. *Los Angeles Times*, July 14, 1948: 11.

STAN THE MAN SWINGS FIVE TIMES, GETS FIVE HITS

September 22, 1948: St. Louis Cardinals 8. Boston Braves 2, at Braves Field, Boston

BY GLEN SPARKS

Stan Musial's wrist ached from injuries. The St. Louis Cardinals' star outfielder did not want to waste even one swing on September 22, 1948, against the Boston Braves at Braves Field. Indeed, he offered at just five pitches in five at-bats.

That was enough. Stan the Man, nearing the end of a glorious season, went 5-for-5. The seven-year veteran even smacked a home run in leading his team to an 8-2 victory. It was Musial's fourth five-hit game of the season, tying the major-league record set by Detroit Tigers great Ty Cobb in 1922.[1] At the end of the day, Musial's batting average stood at .378. He had 38 homers and 122 RBIs.

By Musial's standards, this was something of a comeback year. After leading the NL in 1946 with a .365 batting average, .587 slugging percentage, 228 hits, 50 doubles, and 124 runs scored, and winning a second MVP, in 1947 he hit what was then a career-low .312. He did not top the league in any important offensive category.

Health problems plagued Musial throughout that campaign. He complained of abdominal pain during spring training and batted just .146 in April. Doctors recommended in early May that he undergo emergency surgery for appendicitis. That might have sidelined him for a month, though. Instead, doctors froze the appendix and agreed to delay any operation until the offseason. Musial, who also was battling tonsillitis, started to hit again. He batted .379 over a 58-game stretch.[2]

Fully recovered by the spring of 1948, Musial began knocking line drives at ballparks across the country. As late as the All-Star break, on July 11, he ended the day with a batting average of .403. Musial enjoyed his first five-hit game of the year on April 30. He reached that mark again on May 19 and for a third time on June 22. In the May 19 game, against the Brooklyn Dodgers at Ebbets Field, every hit came with two strikes against him.[3]

The 27-year-old also helped the Cardinals by playing outstanding defense. At Ebbets Field on September 17, he made a somersaulting catch to rob the Dodgers' Jackie Robinson of a hit in the third inning. Later, he tumbled and grabbed a short fly ball hit by Tommy Brown. The Cardinals won, 4-2. In making that catch to retire Brown, Musial jammed his left wrist.

The next afternoon Dodgers starter Carl Erskine smacked Musial in the right wrist with a pitch. Even so, Musial hit a home run later in the game. The Cardinals still lost, 3-2; worse, both of Musial's wrists were now hurt.

After playing a doubleheader against the New York Giants on September 19 at the Polo Grounds, the Cardinals traveled to Boston for a three-game series, including a doubleheader on September 21. St. Louis lost the first game, 11-3, and the second, 4-0. Musial went a combined 2-for-8 against Braves pitching.

Usually, the breeze blew into Braves Field from the nearby Charles River, making the ballpark a good one for pitchers. A hard wind, though, rushed toward the bleachers in the series finale. It seemed like a day just made for high scoring. Bob Broeg, the Cardinals beat writer for the *St. Louis Post-Dispatch*, knew it. Musial's injured wrists still bothered him.

"A great day for the hitters, Banj," Broeg said, calling Musial by another one of his nicknames.[4]

"Yeah, but I can't hit like this," Musial retorted, referring to his stiff, taped-up wrists.[5]

Angry, he tore off the bandages.

St. Louis manager Eddie Dyer wrote Musial's name in the customary third spot in the team's batting order. The Cardinals boasted a 78-66 won-lost record on this date, good for third place. They trailed the second-place Dodgers (79-66) by a half-game and the first-place Braves (86-58) by 7½ games.

Journeyman left-hander Al Brazle, 7-6, started for St. Louis. Talented left-hander Warren Spahn, 15-10, took the ball for Boston. Spahn, 27, won 21 games for Boston in 1947 and led the NL with a 2.33 ERA and seven shutouts. A crowd of 10,937 watched the action.

Musial, a "handicapped slugger,"[6] began the day by rapping a two-out single in the opening inning. Enos Slaughter, though, followed with a fly ball out to end the frame. The next inning, St. Louis scored the game's first run. Nippy Jones and Terry Moore led off with hits. With one out, Del Rice singled Jones home.

The Cardinals added two more runs in the third inning to go ahead 3-0. This time, Musial started the rally. He ripped a one-out double, his 44th two-bagger of the year, and scored on Slaughter's single. Slaughter, in turn, sprinted to third base on right fielder Tommy Holmes's error and raced home on Jones's sacrifice fly.

Boston pushed across a run in the bottom of the third. Bobby Sturgeon, pinch-hitting for Spahn, led off by hitting a triple and scoring on Alvin Dark's groundout. St. Louis answered with a big inning in the top of fourth against new Braves pitcher Red

Barrett. Don Lang greeted the 10-year veteran with a double to left field. After Rice struck out, Brazle roped an RBI single to center. Red Schoendienst doubled to right, putting runners on second and third. Marty Marion lifted a fly ball to score Brazle.

That brought up Musial for a third time. Bad wrists and all, he pulled a Barrett pitch over the right-field fence to give St. Louis a commanding 7-1 lead. "Stan almost seemed to jump into good-time Charley's pitch," wrote Broeg.[7]

Slaughter drew a walk, ending Barrett's afternoon. In came Bobby Hogue to pitch for Boston with two out and Nippy Jones up to bat. The inning ended in unusual fashion for the Cardinals and in a painful way for Slaughter. Jones hit a line drive through the middle after Slaughter had taken off for second base on an attempted steal. The ball crashed into Slaughter's face, giving him a broken nose and black eye. He was taken off the field on a stretcher. And because the ball struck him, he was out. Musial moved from right field to left field in the bottom of the fourth, and Ron Northey went in to play right.

In the sixth inning, Musial grounded a two-out single and scored on Northey's double. Boston answered in the seventh with a lone run. Clint Conatser banged a double off Brazle to start the frame and came home on Phil Masi's two-base hit. Brazle stopped the rally by getting two strikeouts and a fly out.

Musial batted for the final time with one out in the eighth. He expanded the strike zone and punched a base hit through the infield on a 2-and-0 pitch from Al Lyons, the Braves' fifth hurler of the game. "When the first two pitches were balls, I was afraid he was going to walk me, and I really wanted that last chance," Musial said.[8]

Northey and Jones flied out to end the inning. Boston failed to mount a threat the rest of the way. Brazle threw a complete game and upped his record to 8-6. Losing pitcher Spahn dropped to 15-11. The *Boston Globe* reasoned, "While everyone was disappointed with the Braves' performance, they at least had the opportunity to see Stan Musial."[9]

The Braves went on to finish 91-62 and win their first pennant since 1914. They could not, however, bring home a World Series championship. The Cleveland Indians knocked off Boston in six games. The Cardinals, meanwhile, leapt ahead of the Dodgers to finish in second place with an 85-69 mark despite Slaughter's missing the remainder of the campaign after his injuries. Slaughter ended the season with 11 home runs, 90 RBIs, and a .321 batting average.

Musial won his third of three MVP awards in 1948, the first player in the National League to achieve that milestone. He topped the NL in batting average (.376), on-base percentage (.450), runs scored (135), hits (230), doubles (46), triples (18), RBIs (131), and total bases (429).

Most satisfying to Musial, he also led the league with a .702 slugging percentage, the highest figure since Hack Wilson's .723 for the 1930 Chicago Cubs. Also, Musial's 103 extra-base hits fell just four short of matching Chuck Klein's NL record, set in 1930 with the Philadelphia Phillies, and came within 21 total bases of tying former Cardinal Rogers Hornsby's league mark of .450 in 1922.[10] "I'd actually had a piece of several great hitters' best seasons," Musial wrote.[11]

The Donora, Pennsylvania, native hit 39 homers. Both the Giants' Johnny Mize and the Pittsburgh Pirates' Ralph Kiner finished atop the NL with 40 apiece. Musial wrote that 1948 "was a once-in-a-lifetime season."[12] On September 22, 1948, he enjoyed a once-in-a-lifetime game.

SOURCES

In addition to the sources cited in the Notes, the author consulted Baseball-Reference.com and Retrosheet.org for pertinent information, including the box score and play-by-play.

https://www.baseball-reference.com/boxes/BSN/BSN194809220.shtml

https://www.retrosheet.org/boxesetc/1948/B09220BSN1948.htm

NOTES

1. Tony Gwynn and Ichiro Suzuki later tied Cobb and Musial with four five-hit games in one season. Gwynn had his four in 1993, and Suzuki in 2004.
2. James N. Giglio, *Musial: From Stash to Stan the Man* (Columbia, Missouri: University of Missouri Press, 2001), 159.
3. Bob Broeg, *Musial: The Man's Own Story* (New York: Doubleday, 1964), 116.
4. Broeg, *Musial*, 116.
5. Broeg, *Musial*, 116.
6. Bob Broeg, "Loss of Slaughter Puts Second-Place Burden on 'Five-for-Five' Musial," *St. Louis Post-Dispatch*, September 23, 1948: 16.
7. Broeg, "Loss of Slaughter Puts Second-Place Burden on 'Five-for-Five' Musial."
8. Broeg, "Loss of Slaughter Puts Second-Place Burden on 'Five-for-Five' Musial,"
9. Clif Keane, "Musial Gets Five Hits to Set League Record," *Boston Globe*, September 23, 1948: 24.
10. Broeg, *Musial*, 118.
11. Broeg, *Musial*, 118.
12. Broeg, *Musial*, 118.

MUSIAL DRIVES IN BOTH CARDINALS' RUNS AND ENDS GAME WITH THROW TO PLATE

July 5, 1949: St. Louis Cardinals 2, Chicago Cubs 1 (10 innings), at Wrigley Field, Chicago

BY RICK ZUCKER

The Cardinals and Chicago Cubs staged a 10-inning pitchers' duel on July 5, 1949, at Wrigley Field. Bob Rush threw all 10 innings for Chicago. Left-handers Harry "The Cat" Brecheen and Howard Pollet handled the pitching for St. Louis. In the Cardinals' 2-1 victory, Stan Musial drove in both of the Cardinals' runs and threw out the tying run at the plate in the bottom of the 10th inning to end the game.

In 1949 Musial was the defending National League MVP following a career year in which he registered the sixth-most total bases ever in a season. Musial hit .376 and led the NL in runs, hits, doubles, triples, RBIs, batting average, on-base percentage, slugging, and total bases. His 39 home runs fell one short of the home-run title and the Triple Crown. Musial started 1949 determined to hit more homers, but swinging for the fences led to a decline in production and he spent most of May with a batting average under .270.[1] Musial abandoned his power-happy approach and appeared to right himself in June. By the end of the month, he was hitting .303.

Beginning July 1, Musial went 1-for-11 in a three-game series at home against Cincinnati as the Cardinals dropped two of three, leaving them one game behind the league-leading Dodgers. The Cardinals traveled to Chicago for a July 4 doubleheader at Wrigley followed by a single game on July 5. They split the holiday doubleheader with the last-place Cubs, who shut them out in the nightcap, dropping them two games behind Brooklyn. Musial went 1-for-9, lowering his batting average to .288.

Musial's poor start in July prompted *St. Louis Star-Times* sportswriter Sid Keener to offer hitting advice. Keener claimed that NL pitchers were getting Musial out with off-speed pitches low and away. Keener wrote that Musial was overswinging, trying to yank home runs to right field. He suggested that Musial "let up a trifle on his swing, and with a quick twist of his body, aim for left field on that outside pitch."[2] The record does not indicate whether Musial saw, understood, or followed this advice.

On Tuesday, July 5, a Ladies Day crowd of 26,802 at Wrigley Field included 10,047 women. The heat wave in Chicago broke as a front moved in at game time. The skies grew dark and threatening, and intermittent showers fell in the early innings.

Bob Rush, a 23-year-old right-hander, handcuffed the Cardinals for five innings. Brecheen, the Cardinals starter, was coming off four straight bad outings in which he yielded 21 runs in 15⅔ innings. But on this inclement day Brecheen was in good form. He faced the minimum 12 batters in the first four innings, including pitching around an error in the fourth by getting a 5-4-3 double play.

The Cubs broke through with a run in the fifth. Hank Sauer led off with the first and only Chicago hit off Brecheen, a single to left. Hank Edwards laid down a bunt. Harry the Cat pounced on it and tried for the force out, but threw wide of shortstop Marty Marion and into center field, sending Sauer to third. One out later, Sauer tagged up and scored on Mickey Owen's fly out to Musial in center.

The Cardinals evened the score in the sixth. Red Schoendienst led off with a walk. Marion sacrificed him to second. Musial, who was hitless in his previous nine at-bats, came through with a single to left that drove in Schoendienst with the Cardinals' first run in 19 innings. Brecheen retired the Cubs in order in the bottom of the sixth as the rain returned in a downpour that caused a 32-minute rain delay.

When the game resumed, Brecheen reported to Cardinals manager Eddie Dyer that his arm had stiffened. Rush returned to the mound and struggled. After Rocky Nelson's line drive was snagged by Edwards in right field, Rush walked Eddie Kazak and Joe Garagiola. Dyer then pinch-hit for Brecheen with Enos Slaughter, who was out of the lineup with a sore right elbow. Slaughter lined a shot toward second, where Cubs second baseman Gene Mauch speared it and turned an unassisted double play to end the inning. The Cardinals sent in their top starter, Howie Pollet, to finish the game. St. Louis was headed to Pittsburgh next, and Dyer did not plan to use the lefty Pollet against Ralph Kiner and the Pirates' right-handed lineup, so Pollet was available to pitch in relief.

With the score still 1-1, St. Louis almost took the lead in the ninth. Hal Rice got a leadoff triple when Cubs center fielder Andy Pafko slipped on the wet grass. Rice was stranded at third by Mauch, who first caught Nelson's liner and, after a walk to

Kazak, fielded Garagiola's bouncer, tagged Kazak and threw to first to complete another double play.

Chicago almost won the game in its half of the ninth. Left fielder Rice made a nifty running catch on a deep drive by Frankie Gustine to start the inning. Two singles were sandwiched around a popout, putting the winning run on second with two out, but Pollet got pinch-hitter Herman Reich to ground out.

The 10th inning provided the kind of excitement that had the *Star-Times* gushing that "[t]his contest will rank as one of the classics of this or any other baseball seasons."[3] Although certainly an overstatement, in truth several decades of Cardinals baseball history converged in this inning. Pollet led off by flying out. Schoendienst, a Cardinals Hall of Fame player in the 1940s, '50s and '60s, a manager in the '60s and '70s, and a coach into the twenty-first century, singled to right. Marion, the Cardinals' 1944 NL MVP and manager of the Stadium Club in Busch Stadium II until 1984, also singled to right, sending Schoendienst to third. That brought up Musial, a legendary Cardinals player from 1941 to 1963 and the club's general manager in 1967.

With runners at first and third and one out, Cubs manager Frank Frisch, a Hall of Fame Cardinals player in the 1920s and '30s, and manager of the 1934 World Series champion Cardinals, opted to play the infield back at double-play depth. This was a risky move because if the Cubs couldn't double up the fleet Musial, the lead run would score. After the game, Frisch's decision was criticized by telecaster Rogers Hornsby, yet another Cardinals Hall of Fame player (1915-26, 1933) and player-manager of the Cardinals' first modern World Series champion in 1926. "You can't play like semipros and expect to win," sneered Hornsby. "You gotta play … your infield in."[4]

Sure enough, Musial hit a grounder to Roy Smalley at shortstop, who flipped to his future brother-in-law Mauch at second, who hurried a relay to Phil Cavaretta at first, too wide and too late to get Musial. Schoendienst scored on Musial's second RBI of the day. The Cardinals led, 2-1.

The Cardinals inserted ballhawk Chuck Diering into center field in the bottom of the 10th, and shifted Musial to right field. Smalley led off the Cubs' 10th with an infield hit to deep short. Mickey Owen sacrificed him to second. Mauch struck out. Down to their last out, the Cubs sent utility infielder Bob Ramazzotti to hit for Rush. Ramazzotti, a right-handed hitter, had been to the plate only once in the prior two weeks and was batting .111.

Ramazzotti punched a single to right. Musial, a solid four-tool player, did not have a strong arm. The former pitcher had injured it playing outfield in the minors in 1940. With two out, Smalley was running from second on contact. Musial, charging fast, fielded the ball on one hop and unleashed a clothesline strike to home plate. *St. Louis Post-Dispatch* writer Bob Broeg described Musial's heave as having "unusual strength and direction." In disbelief, Broeg added that "The Man just doesn't have the kind of arm he demonstrated in that extra-inning clutch."[5] Smalley and Musial's throw arrived at the plate almost simultaneously.

As was the practice in those days, Cardinals catcher Garagiola was blocking the plate. As he caught the throw, Smalley leapt at him and planted both spikes in his midsection. Garagiola had the wind knocked out of him but held the ball, and plate umpire George Barr called Smalley out. Frisch charged out of the dugout to protest, but the umpires vacated the field, ending the game. Garagiola took several minutes to recover before walking off.

Although not at the top of his game, Musial had managed to help engineer a 2-1 victory for the Cardinals by driving in both runs and cutting down the tying run at the plate in extra innings with a clutch throw. After the July 5 win, Musial went on a tear. For the remaining 84 games, he recaptured the magic of 1948, hitting .381 and slugging .726. He finished the 1949 season at .338 with 36 homers and 123 RBIs.

SOURCES

In addition to the sources cited in the Notes, the author consulted Baseball-Reference.com, the *Chicago Tribune*, and the *St. Louis Globe-Democrat*.

https://www.baseball-reference.com/boxes/CHN/CHN194907050.shtml

https://www.retrosheet.org/boxesetc/1949/B07050CHN1949.htm

NOTES

1 James N. Giglio, *Musial – From Stash to Stan the Man* (Columbia: University of Missouri Press, 2001), 174.

2 Sid Keener, "Tip to Stan Musial, Now in Slump, on 'How to Bat,'" *St. Louis Star-Times,* July 6, 1949: 23.

3 W. Vernon Tietjen, "Catcher's Sparkling Play in Tenth Stops Cubs, 2-1; Munger to Face Pirates," *St. Louis Star-Times,* July 6, 1949: 22.

4 Tietjen.

5 Bob Broeg, "Brecheen, Pollet Shine on Hill; Garagiola and Musial Get Final Out," *St. Louis Post-Dispatch*, July 6, 1949: 14.

MUSIAL HITS FOR CYCLE TO LEAD CARDINALS ROUT AT EBBETS FIELD

July 24, 1949: St. Louis Cardinals 14, Brooklyn Dodgers 1, Ebbets Field, Brooklyn

BY MIKE HUBER

By the middle of June 1949, the National League pennant race came down to two teams, the St. Louis Cardinals and the Brooklyn Dodgers. From that point on, those two battled for the top spot.[1] On July 22, the first-place Dodgers hosted a four-game series against the Cardinals. This wound up a 21-game road trip for St. Louis, who managed to lose half a game in the standings over the first 17 contests. Burt Shotton's Dodgers were completing a 15-game homestand and entered the series with a 2½-game edge over the Cardinals.

The second-place visitors won the first two games of the series, as the Cardinals "had outplayed and outgamed the beloved Bums."[2] Suddenly, Brooklyn held the slimmest of leads, a mere half game, in the senior circuit. A crowd of 34,042 fans turned out to root for the Dodgers on a hot Sunday afternoon, and, according to the *St. Louis Star and Times*, "The place had a World Series game air."[3] This was the fourth largest crowd of the season for the Flatbush faithful (and the first sellout Sunday crowd[4]), but many did not stay to see the final out, as the Cardinals won handily, 14-1. Six-time All-Star and reigning National League Most Valuable Player Stan Musial led all batters by hitting for the cycle.[5]

Howie Pollet, St. Louis' 12-game winner, faced off against Don Newcombe, who was in search of his eighth victory for Brooklyn. Newcombe was forced to wait another day for that win. In fact, he threw only 12 pitches before being lifted for reliever Paul Minner in the top of the first inning. Red Schoendienst and Lou Klein started the game for St. Louis with back-to-back singles. With runners at the corners, Newcombe uncorked a wild pitch, allowing Schoendienst to score. That brought Musial to the plate. He entered the game in a mini-slump, having gone just 8-for-35 (.229) in his last eight games. Musial swung at an offering from Newcombe and smacked a triple to deep center. Klein scored and Newcombe hit the showers. Shotton brought in left-hander Minner to face the Cardinals' clean-up hitter, Enos Slaughter. Slaughter greeted him with an RBI-single and Ron Northey followed with a double to left. Five batters had five hits and St. Louis had an early four-run lead.

Two innings later, the Cardinals sent eleven batters to the plate. Minner only faced the first three. Slaughter doubled, Northey singled, and Rocky Nelson tripled on a line drive to right. The second St. Louis triple of the game brought in the second reliever for the Dodgers, Carl Erskine. The Cardinals put up five more hits, including a single by Musial. With the score 8-0 and runners on first and second, Musial sent a ground ball to right field. Carl Furillo fielded the ball and threw home to catcher Bruce Edwards, whose error then allowed two runners to score, making it a 10-0 ballgame. The Cardinals put together six singles, a double, and a triple in the outburst.

The Dodgers had a chance in the first inning to score, putting two runners aboard, but Pollet worked his way out of the jam. In the bottom of the third, however, Pee Wee Reese and Billy Cox hit singles, and after Furillo hit into a double play, Jackie Robinson grounded a single through the infield to left field to plate Reese. That was the lone run Pollet allowed.

In the top of the fifth with two outs, Musial sent a 3-1 Erskine pitch out of the park for a solo home run. The blast "was a perhaps 440-foot smash that cleared the high center field wall toward right, bounding into Bedford [A]ve. and caroming off an automobile agency sign with a bang."[6] Two innings later, he completed the cycle with a double to left-center field, driving in Pollet and Klein. Musial then scored the fourteenth run of the game for St. Louis on a Chuck Diering single.

In his final plate appearance in the top of the ninth inning, "those patrons who remained gave Stan a mighty cheer as he came to bat."[7] With two outs, Musial drew a walk and was stranded when Slaughter grounded to first unassisted. Musial's line for the day was four hits and a walk in five at-bats (he had flied out to the gap in right-center in the second inning), three runs scored and four driven in, although he also accounted for two unearned runs in the third inning. Slaughter added three hits for the Cards, who amassed 16 safeties in the game. Catcher Joe Garagiola was the only starting player for St. Louis without a hit in the game.

Musial became the 10th St. Louis Cardinals batter to hit for the cycle. It had been nine years since Johnny Mize cycled

How good was Stan Musial? "Good enough to take your breath away," legendary broadcaster Vin Scully said.

(July 13, 1940) and it took another 11 years before Bill White accomplished this rare feat (August 14, 1960).[8]

Reese and Robinson were the offensive standouts for Brooklyn, each with a 2-for-4 performance, and they are the two players who figured in the Dodgers' lone tally. Erskine pitched seven innings for Brooklyn. He faced 34 batters and allowed seven runs (six earned) on eight hits and four walks. The Cardinals' Pollet, on the other hand, pitched superbly, scattering eight hits in a complete game. In "notching his thirteenth victory of the campaign, [he] never had to fret. Handed four runs before a Cardinal had been retired in the first, the stylish southpaw was able to coast."[9]

In the locker room, Musial remarked, "It's about time I had a good day."[10] In this game alone, Musial used all of Ebbets Field to spray four hits in collecting the hits necessary for the cycle (see photo below).[11] He raised his batting average to .299 and upped his slugging percentage 22 points, to .523. The next day, Musial went 3-for-4, a home run shy of the cycle, and his batting average rose to .304. He had broken out of the slump; in fact, his average never dipped below .300 for the rest of the season, finishing at .339.

In the four-game series with the Dodgers, Musial had 15 at-bats and connected nine times for hits, including two doubles, two triples, and two home runs. In the nine games played at Ebbets Field to this point in the season, Musial was batting .559 (19 for 34). For the season, Musial hit better against the Dodgers than any other team, going 37-for-90 (.411), with an incredible .523 in 12 games at Ebbets Field.

The Cardinals' victory extended their winning streak to five games (it soon reached nine — with two ties — before a 4-2 loss to Brooklyn in St. Louis). The *Brooklyn Daily Eagle* told its readers that "Musial and the rest of the maddened marauders from across the Mississippi knocked the Dodgers out of first place by making it three in a row over the stumbling Flock."[12] The victory with Musial's cycle put them a half-game ahead of the Dodgers in the National League pennant race. As Musial also told reporters about the St. Louis success, "Cream always comes to the top."[13] However, when the 1949 season ended, the Bums (97-57) finished one game ahead of the Redbirds (96-58), earning the chance to face the New York Yankees.

SOURCES

In addition to the sources mentioned in the Notes, the author consulted baseball-reference.com, mlb.com, and retrosheet.org.

baseball-reference.com/boxes/BRO/BRO194907240.shtml

retrosheet.org/boxesetc/1949/B07240BRO1949.htm

NOTES

1   The Boston Braves held first place in the NL until June 4, but by June 15, the Braves had fallen to third place and finished the 1949 campaign in fourth.

2   "Musial, Pollet Mop Up On Dodgers, 14-1," *St. Louis Star and Times*, July 25, 1949: 16.

3   *St. Louis Star and Times.*

4   *St. Louis Star and Times.*

5   Musial had played in the All-Star Game every year from 1943 to 1949 (except 1945, when he did not play baseball due to military service). He won the NL's Most Valuable Player Award in 1943, 1946 and 1948. Musial also placed second in the MVP voting four times, including three years in a row from 1949-1951.

6   *St. Louis Star and Times.*

7   *St. Louis Star and Times.*

8   As of 2020, there have been 19 cycles in St. Louis Cardinals franchise history, by 17 different players. Tip O'Neill hit for the cycle twice in an eight-day span in 1887, and Ken Boyer also hit for the cycle twice (in 1961 and 1964).

9   Louis Effrat, "Redbirds Defeat Brooklyn by 14-1," *New York Times*, July 25, 1949.

10 *St. Louis Star and Times.*

11 The photograph is an Associated Press wire photo, found in both the *St. Louis Star and Times* and the *St. Louis Post-Dispatch*.

12 Harold C. Burr, "Missouri Murder, Inc., Pushes Cards Into First," *Brooklyn Daily Eagle*, July 25, 1949: 13.

13 "Blasting in Best Bat Circles Again," *The Sporting News*, August 3, 1949: 1.

MUSIAL SLUGS TWO HOMERS ON FINAL DAY OF SEASON BUT JUST MISSES CAPTURING NL BATTING CROWN

October 2, 1949: St. Louis Cardinals 13, Chicago Cubs 5, at Wrigley Field, Chicago

BY MIKE HUBER

After winning the World Series in 1946, the St. Louis Cardinals had two straight second-place finishes and in 1949 were trying to capture the National League pennant once again.[1] With five games to play in the season, the first-place Cardinals held a 1½-game lead over the second-place Brooklyn Dodgers. The Cardinals had just swept a two-game series against the Chicago Cubs at Sportsman's Park.

Now they hit the road, with two games against the sixth-place Pittsburgh Pirates at Forbes Field, before finishing the season with three against the last-place Cubs at Chicago's Wrigley Field. The Cardinals' outlook to get back into the postseason was optimistic. The Dodgers had to play four games against the Boston Braves and Philadelphia Phillies, tougher opponents (both were just behind the Cardinals in the standings) than the Pirates and Cubs.

Within the pennant race between the Cardinals and Dodgers teams was another battle – St. Louis's Stan Musial and Brooklyn's Jackie Robinson were neck-and-neck to see who would win the National League's batting title and Most Valuable Player Award. As play started on October 2, Robinson was batting .342 with a .962 OPS. Musial was batting .337 with a 1.054 OPS. Musial had won the batting title in three of the six previous seasons. He had a chance to become the first National League batting champion to retain his title since Rogers Hornsby.[2] If each batter had four official at-bats and Jackie went hitless, then Musial, the 1948 NL Most Valuable Player, would need to bang out four hits to capture the crown by the slimmest of margins.[3]

Pittsburgh won both games against St. Louis, while Brooklyn swept a September 29 doubleheader against the Boston Braves, including a five-inning second game that was called due to rain. This dropped the Cardinals into second place, a half-game behind the Dodgers. St. Louis then lost the next two games against the Cubs, giving them their longest losing streak of the season. Meanwhile, the Dodgers lost once to the Philadelphia Phillies. Brooklyn held a one-game lead entering the season's final day.

A Wrigley crowd of 30,834 "watch[ed] the scoreboard as closely as it did the game on the field."[4]

St. Louis sent Howie Pollet to the mound against the Cubs. The 28-year-old left-hander, who had been named to his third All-Star squad in 1949, was in search of his 20th win of the year, which would make him only the second NL pitcher to get to 20 victories that year.[5] His last three appearances had been in relief, including both games against Pittsburgh, and his earned-run average was 2.72, which was second-best in the senior circuit.[6] Chicago gave the mound duties to another southpaw, Johnny Schmitz. He brought an 11-12 record and a 4.35 ERA to the hill.

The Cardinals "teed off early"[7] against Schmitz. In the top of the second with one out, Lou Klein hit a grounder to shortstop Roy Smalley, whose error allowed Klein to reach. Del Rice was hit by a pitch, and Schmitz walked Tommy Glaviano to load the bases. Pollet doubled, driving in the first two runs of the game. Chuck Diering was then walked, and the bases were full again. Five straight batters had reached, and Chicago skipper Frankie Frisch called right-handed reliever Doyle Lade from the bullpen. Marty Marion hit a fly ball, driving in the third run of the inning. Musial, who had grounded out in his first-inning at-bat, worked a walk, and the bases were once again loaded, but Steve Bilko flied out to end the inning. The Cardinals had batted around.

After Schmitz exited the game, Lade was the first in a "parade of Cub hurlers."[8] In the third inning, singles by Enos Slaughter and Glaviano resulted in another tally for St. Louis. In the next inning, Bob Rush took his turn to pitch for Chicago. He retired the first two St. Louis batters, but then he yielded a home run to Musial, his 35th of the season and the team's 100th. Rush then walked Bilko. Slaughter followed with an RBI double, and Rush was replaced by Warren Hacker, who retired Solly Hemus, but the Cardinals had built a 6-0 lead.

Pollet pitched out of a jam in the fourth. He had allowed just two singles through the first three innings. In the fourth, Smalley led off with a single and went to third on Andy Pafko's one-out double. Pollet struck out Bill Serena and retired Mickey Owen on a popout to first baseman Bilko, and the Cubs came away empty. Yet in the fifth, Pollet was tagged for a run. He walked leadoff batter Wayne Terwilliger and gave up a single to

Gene Mauch. Two groundouts sent Terwilliger home, breaking up the shutout.

Hacker pitched a scoreless fifth and 40-year-old Dutch Leonard blanked the Cards through the sixth and seventh. In the eighth, Monk Dubiel became the sixth Cubs hurler. With one down, Pollet singled and Diering hit his third home run of the year, "a blast clear over the screen back of the left-center seats."[9] That made the score 8-1.

In the eighth, Chicago's Hank Sauer singled with one out. Pafko reached on an error by third baseman Glaviano.[10] Serena hit a grounder to Klein at second, who stepped on the bag for the second out. Owen's single plated Sauer with the Cubs' second run.

St. Louis responded in the top of the ninth. Hemus singled and took second on Rice's sacrifice. After Glaviano flied out, Pollet singled in Hemus. It was Pollet's third hit of the game. Consecutive singles by Diering and Marion brought Pollet home. This prompted another pitching change, as Dewey Adkins relieved Dubiel. Musial greeted Adkins with his 36th home run, a three-run blast. It was the sixth time in the season that Musial had swatted two homers and the fourth time he had knocked in four runs. St. Louis had now scored 13 times.

The Cubs rallied with two outs in the bottom of the ninth. Pollet retired both Bob Scheffing and Hal Jeffcoat on popouts to Klein. Herman Reich singled, as did Smalley, bringing Sauer to the plate. In his final at-bat of the 1949 season, Sauer hit his 31st home run. Pollet retired Pafko on a comebacker to the mound to end the game.

The Cardinals won 13-5. Seven Chicago pitchers had given up 14 hits, including three home runs. However, the Dodgers beat the Phillies (in extra innings), and "a pennant that a week ago seemed earmarked for delivery [for St. Louis] had gone to Brooklyn instead."[11] The Cardinals had finished in either first or second place in nine straight seasons. To exaggerate their disappointment, the *St. Louis Star and Times* inserted a black box with "R.I.P." above the Cardinals-Cubs box score.[12] Pollet earned his 20th win but told reporters, "I only wish it could have been the game that won for us."[13] Even the Chicago press chimed in. The *Chicago Tribune* told its readers that Musial's home runs were "spectacular but useless because the Dodgers staggered to the wire ahead of the Phillies."[14]

On the final day of the regular season, Stan Musial had belted two homers, adding a single, a walk, two runs scored, and four RBIs. Musial's three hits in five at-bats were not enough. He finished second in the batting title race at .338 and in WAR (9.2). For the Dodgers, Robinson went 1-for-3 with two walks against the Phillies, keeping his batting average at .342. He led the majors with 37 stolen bases and had a 9.3 WAR.[15]

In 1949 Stan the Man led the majors in games played (157), hits (207), doubles (41), and total bases (382). He also paced the NL in triples (13) and on-base percentage (.438), while coming in third with 36 home runs and 123 RBIs.[16] Lastly, he hit for the cycle on July 24, in a game in which the Cardinals routed the Dodgers, 14-1.[17] Despite Musial's hitting prowess, Robinson won the MVP Award, gaining a 79 percent share of the votes (12 first-place votes) to Musial's 67 percent (five first-place votes). The next season, however, Musial led all National Leaguers in batting average with a .346 mark, and he retained the batting crown in 1951 (.355) and 1952 (.336), adding his name to Hornsby's.[18]

SOURCES

In addition to the sources mentioned in the Notes, the author consulted baseball-reference.com, mlb.com, and retrosheet.org.

https://www.baseball-reference.com/boxes/CHN/CHN194910020.shtml

https://www.retrosheet.org/boxesetc/1949/B10020CHN1949.htm

NOTES

1   The Cardinals had won the NL pennant in 1942, 1943, and 1944 as well, winning the World Series in 1942 and 1944. They placed second in 1945.

2   Hornsby won the NL batting title six years in a row, from 1920 through 1925, meaning he successfully retained his title five times.

Stan Musial made the cover of *Time* magazine on September 5, 1949.

3   Coming into the final game of the season, Robinson had 202 hits in 590 at-bats (.3424). Musial had 204 hits in 607 at-bats (.3361). With four hits, Musial's average would climb to .3404, and with no hits, Robinson's average would drop to .3401. Note: Both Baseball-Reference and Retrosheet have an at-bat discrepancy for Musial in the second game on August 23, 1949, which leads his game logs to sum to 611 AB versus his official total of 612. The author used 612 (the official total) for this potential scenario.

4   Bob Broeg, "Paradise Lost – and Yankee Dollars; Cardinals Didn't Choke, Says Dyer," *St. Louis Post-Dispatch*, October 3, 1949: 4B, 6B.

5   In 1949 (and also in 1950) Milwaukee's Warren Spahn led the National League with 21 wins.

6   Pollet's teammate Gerry Staley finished the season with a 2.73 ERA. Pollet's four earned runs in this game caused his ERA to rise to 2.77, placing Staley in second place, behind New York Giants starter-reliever Dave Koslo (2.50).

7   Broeg.

8   Martin J. Haley, "Defenseless Birds Jar Cubs, 13-5, See Last Hopes Fade With Philadelphia Story," *St. Louis Globe-Democrat*, October 3, 1949: 21.

9   Haley.

10 It was Glaviano's 20th error of the season.

11 Broeg.

12 W. Vernon Tietjen, "Birds Lost Six of Their Last 8 Games," *St. Louis Star and Times*, October 3, 1949: 20.

13 Tietjen.

14 Robert Cromie, "Cards Defeat Cubs, 13-5, but Finish in 2d," *Chicago Tribune*, October 3, 1949: 39.

15 Wins Above Replacement (WAR) did not become a statistical measure to compare players until more than 60 years after the 1949 season, but the values are included here for comparison.

16 Ralph Kiner led the league with 54 homers and 127 RBIs. He batted .310 for the season.

17 Robinson hit for a reverse natural cycle on August 29, 1948, against the Cardinals.

18 Musial also led the NL in 1957 with a .351 mark.

MUSIAL RETURNS TO MOUND, CLINCHES SIXTH BATTING TITLE

September 28, 1952: Chicago Cubs 3, St. Louis Cardinals 0, at Sportsman's Park, St. Louis

BY BILL PRUDEN

With the 1952 season drawing to a disappointing close and the St. Louis Cardinals mired in third place, the team's front office, looking for a way to draw fans to an otherwise meaningless game, decided to have its star Stan Musial hark back to the earliest days of his career.[1] That meant having the one-time minor-league pitcher take the mound for the first time in a major-league game. To add some drama to the event, the left-handed Musial, who on September 20, as the plan was being hatched, was leading the league in hitting with a .333 average, would pitch to Chicago Cubs right fielder Frank Baumholtz, whose .332 average had him nipping at the heels of the Cardinals superstar.[2] Musial later wrote that he was not happy about the plan, both because he thought it little more than a "contrived show" and because he did not want to be seen as showing up Baumholtz.[3] But Musial's concerns were ignored by the Cardinals' decision makers.

Ironically, the intervening week had seen Musial's and Baumholtz's batting averages go in opposite directions. Consequently, by game time on September 28, with Musial hitting .336 and Baumoltz at .326 the head-to-head confrontation had been reduced to little more than "a gag," although it was still technically possible for Baumholtz to catch Musial.[4]

Events unfolded quickly when, after the Cardinals starter, rookie left-hander Harvey Haddix, walked Cubs leadoff batter Tommy Brown, Cardinals manager Eddie Stanky emerged from the dugout and, walking toward Haddix, called for Musial to take his place on the mound. Haddix headed to the outfield, replacing Hal Rice in right while Rice took Musial's spot in center. While this was happening, Cubs manager Phil Cavarretta told Baumholtz that the Cardinals were trying to make a fool of him, but Baumholtz understood what was happening and told his manager, "I don't think so. I think it's just a gimmick to get a lot of people in the stands to watch two also-rans on the last day of the season."[5]

The 31-year-old Musial, seemingly anxious to complete his task, took fewer than the allotted number of warm-up pitches as he prepared for his first professional pitching effort since 1940. But as he peered toward home plate, Musial got a surprise of his own, for the left-handed-hitting Baumholtz, who could "go along with a gag as well as anyone," had stepped into the right-handed batter's box to face his Cardinals adversary.[6] Baumholtz reportedly made the decision to bat right-handed as a gesture of sportsmanship, not wanting "to try for a cheap hit" against the pitching impostor or "to get something for nothing."[7] The whole episode was over in no time. Musial threw exactly one pitch. He later said he "flipped the ball," while the *St. Louis Post Dispatch* reported it was a "fast ball."[8] Either way, Baumholtz hit "the ball squarely," sending a "sizzling grounder" to third baseman Solly Hemus, but the potential double-play ball "bounced on a big hop" and Hemus, unable to handle it, was charged with an error.[9] A hustling Brown made his way to third.

That single pitch was the sum total of Stan Musial's major-league pitching career and while "the Cubs peered toward the pressbox, begging for a basehit," the argument seemed superfluous given Musial and Baumholtz's averages at game time.[10] In the end, none of that impacted the game. In short order, Musial returned to center field, Rice to right, and Haddix to the mound, and things proceeded as expected for two teams whose offseasons were right around the corner.

Indeed, unfazed by the shenanigans, Haddix induced Cubs second baseman Bill Serena to ground into a 6-4-3 double play with Brown scoring. He then struck out left fielder Hank Sauer, who was battling Pirates slugger Ralph Kiner for the National League home-run crown.[11]

In the bottom half of the first, Cubs southpaw Paul Minner retired the first three Cardinals he faced.

In the top of the second, with two outs, Harry Chiti reached Haddix for his fifth home run of the season to put the Cubs on top 2-0. But Haddix struck out Hal Jeffcoat to end the inning. Minner gave up a single to Rice with one out in the bottom of the second but got Virgil Stallcup to line to first baseman Dee Fondy for an unassisted double play that ended the inning.

After striking our Minner to open the third, Haddix gave up a single to Tommy Brown. However, he got out of the inning, inducing Baumholtz to pop up to catcher Bill Sarni and getting Serena to fly to right.

In the bottom of the third, the Cardinals mounted a threat when Neal Hertweck's popup to first was followed by singles

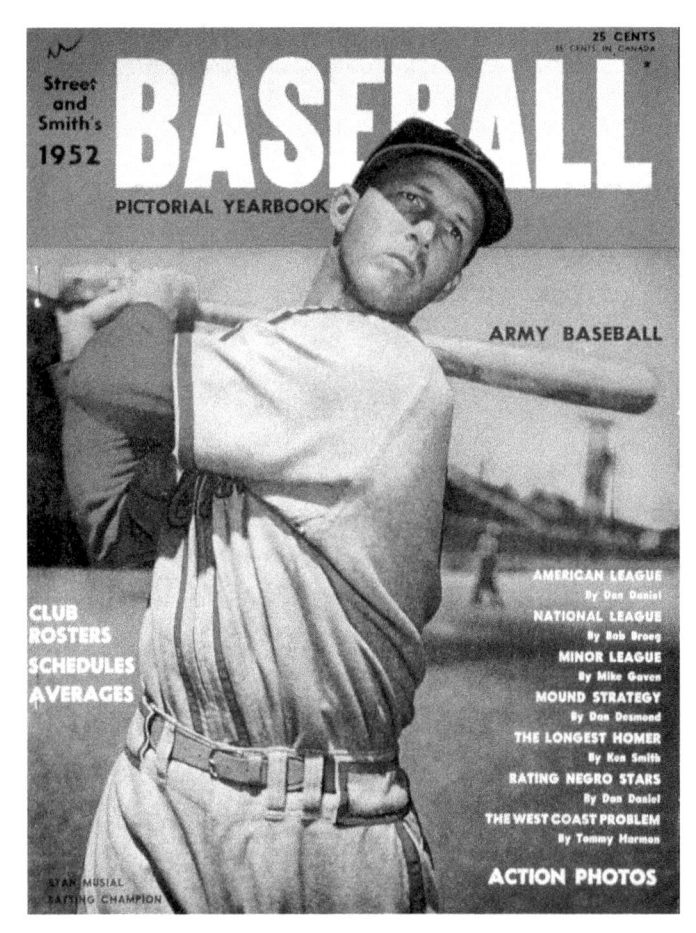

Musial finished fifth in NL MVP voting in 1952.

from Sarni and Haddix. But Minner escaped trouble, getting Hemus to fly to left and Red Schoendienst on a groundball to first baseman Fondy, who flipped to Minner covering first to end the inning.

Haddix made quick work of the Cubs in the top of the fourth, while Minner retired the Cardinals in order in their half of the inning. Both pitchers set down the side in order in the fifth.

The Cubs threatened in the top of the sixth as Baumholtz and Serena led off with a pair of singles. But with runners on first and second, Haddix got Sauer to pop to first, Randy Jackson to fly to center, and Fondy to ground out to second, ending the threat.

Haddix got his second hit of the day to start the bottom of the sixth but Hemus popped out to first and Tommy Glaviano, who had replaced Schoendienst in the fourth inning, hit into a 6-4-3 double play to end the inning.

The Cubs scored again in the top of the seventh. Chiti led off with a double, and after Haddix struck out Jeffcoat and Minner, Brown doubled, driving in Chiti and increasing the Cubs' lead to 3-0. Haddix struck out Baumholtz to end the inning.

Minner cruised through the seventh, while Haddix made quick work of the Cubs in the eighth.

The Cardinals threatened in the bottom of the eighth. With one out, Minner walked Hertweck. After Peanuts Lowrey, pinch-hitting for Sarni, singled, Minner got Del Rice, pinch-hitting for Haddix, to fly out to left. Minner then walked Hemus to load the bases. But with the game on the line, Minner notched his only strikeout of the contest, fanning Glaviano to end the threat.

Mike Clark, a 30-year-old, 6-foot-4 right-hander who made his major-league debut on July 27, replaced Haddix on the mound in the ninth. He got Fondy to pop up to third, but Chiti doubled for his third hit of the game. After Jeffcoat flied to right, Minner singled, sending Chiti to third base. But Clark got Brown to ground into a force out to end the inning.

After Musial led off the bottom of the ninth with his league-leading 194th base hit, Minner retired the next three batters in order to complete the shutout, his second of the season.

The loss left the third-place Cardinals at 88-66 while the Cubs finished fifth with a record of 77-77. Minner's win gave him a season record of 14-9 with an ERA of 3.74, while the 26-year-old Haddix finished 2-2 with a 2.79 ERA.

Musial's 1-for-3 performance left him at .336, clinching his third consecutive National League batting crown and the sixth of seven he won over his storied career. Runner-up Baumholtz finished with a career-best .325. And while they only saw Musial throw one pitch, the reported crowd of 17,422 was 5,500 more than the team's average attendance during the 1952 season.

SOURCES

In addition to the sources cited in the Notes, the author accessed Baseball-Reference.com.

https://www.baseball-reference.com/boxes/SLN/SLN195209280.shtml

https://www.retrosheet.org/boxesetc/1952/B09280SLN1952.htm

NOTES

1. Stan Musial and Bob Broeg, *Stan Musial: "The Man's" Own Story as Told to Bob Broeg* (Garden City, New York: Doubleday & Company, 1964), 153.

2. Tom Larwin, "September 20, 1952: Musial, Baumholtz Compete for National League Batting Title." Society for American Baseball Research Games Project. https://sabr.org/gamesproj/game/september-20-1952-musial-baumholtz-compete-for-national-league-batting-title/.

3. Musial and Broeg, 153.

4. "Musial Wins 6th Batting Title, Does a Little Pitching on Side; Haddix Fans 11 Cubs, but Loses." *St. Louis Post-Dispatch*, September 29, 1952: 16; "Attention, Now Pitching for the Cardinals – Stan Musial," RetroSimba: Cardinals history beyond the box score, September 20, 2022; https://retrosimba.com/2022/09/20/attention-now-pitching-for-the-cardinals-_-stan-musial/. Accessed September 26, 2023.

5. "Attention, Now Pitching for the Cardinals – Stan Musial."

6. "Musial Wins 6th Batting Title, Does a Little Pitching on Side; Haddix Fans 11 Cubs, but Loses."

7. "Attention, Now Pitching for the Cardinals – Stan Musial"; Harry Mitauer, "Stan Wraps Up Bat Crown; Cubs Grab Finale, 3-0." *St. Louis Globe Democrat*, September 29, 1952: 20.

8. "Attention, Now Pitching for the Cardinals – Stan Musial"; "Musial Wins 6th Batting Title, Does a Little Pitching on Side; Haddix Fans 11 Cubs, but Loses."

9. "Attention, Now Pitching for the Cardinals – Stan Musial"; Wayne Stewart, *Stan the Man: The Life and Times of Stan Musial* (Chicago: Triumph Books, 2014), 135.

10. "Musial Wins 6th Batting Title, Does a Little Pitching on Side; Haddix Fans 11 Cubs, but Loses."

11. "Cubs Triumph Over Cardinals 3-0." *New York Times*, September 29, 1952: 18. Sauer and Kiner ended up tied for the NL home-run lead with 37.

STAN MUSIAL SETS MAJOR-LEAGUE RECORD WITH FIVE HOME RUNS IN DOUBLEHEADER

May 2, 1954: St. Louis Cardinals 10, New York Giants 6; New York Giants 9, St. Louis Cardinals 7, at Busch Stadium, St. Louis

BY RUSSELL LAKE

Early on Sunday morning, May 2, 1954, a group of 37 people from Chillicothe, Missouri, boarded a chartered bus for the first leg of a round trip to Busch Stadium[1] in St. Louis to see a doubleheader between the Cardinals and New York Giants. The Midwestern town's depot agent, J.E. Brotherton, had arranged the excursion, which would be trailed by several carloads of locals.[2] The 235-mile route to the big riverfront city would proceed east via US 36 to Hannibal, and then southeast on US 61 before intersecting with US 40 eastward until a north turn onto Grand Boulevard.

Jack Buck arrived at the ballpark long before the 1:30 P.M. start of the first game to go over the between-innings copy he would read for D'Arcy Advertising Agency during the radio broadcast of the twin bill. A couple of months before, the 29-year-old Buck had packed his family and belongings into a 1950 Plymouth and driven from Rochester, New York, to join the Cardinals' announcing team of Harry Caray and Milo Hamilton.[3]

Horace Stoneham, president of the Giants; his son, Pete; and other representatives from the New York ballclub were attending the doubleheader. They were much impressed with the recent improvements to Busch Stadium.[4] A persistent morning rain fell long enough to cancel batting practice. Thirty minutes before game time, St. Louis skipper Eddie Stanky was on the steps of the third-base dugout when he was approached by a reporter. Arch Murray, an enterprising scribe for the *New York Post*, was working on a magazine story when he posed a carefully phrased question. "Who," Murray inquired, "is the best player in baseball? Stan Musial?" Stanky wasted little time with his reply, "You," said manager to writer, "have just asked and answered your own question." Murray nodded and explained that all other managers had agreed.[5]

Game One — The 33-year-old left-handed Musial, limping slightly with a charley horse, was batting .346, and starting in right field for St. Louis.[6] The Giants, managed by former Gas House Gang shortstop Leo "The Lip" Durocher, were in fifth place at 8-7, while the Redbirds, at 8-6, found themselves in a virtual tie for second with the Philadelphia Phillies and Brooklyn Dodgers in the early-season bottleneck of the National League standings. Johnny Antonelli (2-1, 1.12), a 6-foot-1 southpaw, would make his fourth start of the season for New York. The Cardinals' starter, 6-foot right-handed veteran Gerry Staley (2-1, 5.59), had struggled a bit during five appearances, which included three starts.

This would be the season's only scheduled Sunday doubleheader in St. Louis.[7] Staley benefited from a groundball double play to end a scoreless top half of the first. Antonelli, who had been obtained from the Milwaukee Braves in February, had not allowed a home run this season, but that changed quickly when the Cardinals' leadoff hitter Wally Moon, hammered his third homer of the year. After that blast Antonelli immediately found himself in an early jam after allowing consecutive walks to Red Schoendienst and Musial. A force play and a strikeout followed, but with two outs rookie first baseman Tom Alston, who a few weeks earlier had become the Cardinals' first African American player, singled home Schoendienst to put the Cardinals up 2-0.

Antonelli had retired five consecutive batters when he faced Musial with one out in the third. Musial parked a slow curveball onto the right-field pavilion roof for his fourth round-tripper of the season and a 3-0 St. Louis lead. Staley set down seven straight Giants until second baseman Davey Williams, who entered the day batting .137, singled to open the fourth. With one away, back-to-back doubles by Hank Thompson and Monte Irvin, followed by Don Mueller's single, produced three quick runs to tie the score. Staley escaped further trouble when Willie Mays bounced into an around-the-horn double play.

Mays, who would turn 23 in four days, had not regained his admirable major-league skill set since returning to the Giants in March from nearly two years in the US Army. In the bottom of the fourth, the left-handed-swinging, 6-foot-5 Alston launched a high "wind-blown" drive to the deep center that the "Say Hey Kid" lunged for and missed. It then bounced away toward left field while Alston circled the bases for an inside-the-park home run to give the lead back to St. Louis.[8] But the tide turned quickly when Whitey Lockman and Wes Westrum popped back-to-back home runs to begin the top of the fifth and put New York up, 5-4.

The Cardinals once again struck back quickly in the bottom half as Schoendienst reached first on shortstop Al Dark's error. Musial stepped to the dish and crouched in his trademark stance. Antonelli fired a low, inside fastball out of the strike zone, but Musial uncoiled to send another shot up and away to the right-field roof as St. Louis moved in front, 6-5.[9] Ray Jablonski singled to end Antonelli's appearance, with Durocher bringing in right-hander Jim Hearn, an ex-Cardinal who had not pitched in nine days and was rumored to be in Durocher's doghouse.[10] Burdened with an early-season ERA of 8.31, Hearn seemed to bring a gasoline can with him to put out the fire after Rip Repulski doubled Jablonski to third and Alston walked to load the bases with no outs. The veteran Hearn, though, reached back to notch a groundball force at home and followed with successive strikeouts to keep it a one-run game.

With Staley out of the game, lefty Al Brazle took the mound in the sixth for St. Louis and looked good when he fanned Thompson. That "look" certainly proved deceiving when Irvin pounded his fourth homer of the season to tie the back-and-forth affair at 6-6. Hearn, who certainly displayed some moxie a couple of innings earlier, was still toeing the rubber for the Giants in the bottom of the eighth. Moon singled, Schoendienst walked, and up strode Musial who was 3-for-3 with a pair of runs scored and three RBIs. The fans, who had been watching dark clouds move in, turned their attention back to the playing field, and the stands echoed with the rhythmic staccato clapping that traditionally accompanied Redbird rallies. Hearn pondered before he went into his stretch and fed Musial a slider. Musial ripped into it and pulled a shot down the line to right toward the 37-foot-high screen attached to the roof in front of the pavilion seating area. This drive looked too low to clear the screen, but it just made it onto the roof for Musial's third home run of the contest.[11] Hearn hung his head, and the home crowd went wild as the Cardinals took a 9-6 lead. St. Louis added another run on a pair of singles followed by a Giants fielding miscue to increase its margin to 10-6.

With threatening clouds moving closer, the stadium lights were now on as the 40-year-old Brazle had some room to work with in the top of the ninth. After the first two Giants went down easily, St. Louis native son Bobby Hofman was tabbed as a pinch-hitter. The side-armer Brazle, who was the NL's oldest player in 1954, struck out Hofman to end the lid-lifter at 2 hours and 48 minutes.

Both teams retreated quickly via the Cardinals' dugout to their respective clubhouses to rest and relax a bit before the second contest got underway. The line score for the opener showed St. Louis with 10 runs, 14 hits, and no errors. New York plated six runs on nine hits and two errors. The winning pitcher was Brazle (1-0) while the loser was Hearn (0-2). Brazle, pleased to be credited with a win, offered Musial a bonus for the upcoming game: "Hit three more, kid, and I'll buy you a beer."[12]

Musial removed his spikes and uniform number 6, draped a towel over his shoulders, and sat stoically in front of his locker while munching on a ham sandwich and drinking a glass of milk. His wife, Lil, could not attend today's action because their daughter, Jan, was sick. Lil called Stan to teasingly remind him that this was the second time she had missed seeing her husband hit three home runs in a game during his professional baseball career. At age 20, playing for Springfield (Missouri) of the Class C Western Association in 1941, Musial had swatted three round-trippers against Topeka. Lil was at this game, but not sitting in the stands during any of her husband's homers because of a trio of "under-the-stands diaper-duty trips" for their infant son, Dickie.[13]

Game Two — Before returning to the diamond, a teammate kiddingly asked Musial, "Going to change uniforms, Stosh?" Musial grinned and replied, "Heck, no."[14] Stanky also appeared superstitious when he posted the same starting lineup and batting order from the first game with the exception of the batteries. Each starting pitcher in the nightcap was making his initial start of the season. Durocher selected 5-foot-10 lefty Don Liddle (0-1 with a 9.00 ERA), while Stanky went with 5-foot-9 right-hander Joe Presko, who sported a pair of relief wins.

Presko performed admirably for the first three innings while holding the Giants scoreless on one hit. After Schoendienst's one-out double, Liddle tried to pitch around trouble in the first and walked Musial to a chorus of boos from the faithful. That strategy failed after he issued another free pass to Repulski, and Alston doubled to clear the bases for a 3-0 St. Louis lead. Leading off the third, Musial faced the southpaw again. The crack of the bat and the trajectory of the ball brought the fans to their feet once more as it appeared to be another home run. However, Mays was able to get under this 410-foot blast on the gravel warning track in dead center for an out.[15] The Cardinals threatened to score again in the frame, but left two runners on base.

During three of their previous six losses, the St. Louis pitching staff had displayed the inability to stave off a "crooked number" inning. That achilles heel flared up in the top of the fourth when New York tallied eight runs on as many hits while facing a trio of Cardinals hurlers. Three of the Giants' safeties went for extra bases with the big blow being Hofman's three-run pinch-hit home run against left-handed reliever Royce Lint. Right-hander Mel Wright entered to suppress the uprising, but he allowed both inherited runners to score on a single by Mays. Musial spared the manual scoreboard operator some grief when he nailed catcher Ebba St. Claire trying to stretch his hit into a double for the third out.

Rain had started to fall and it was enough to cause an 18-minute delay before knuckleball specialist Hoyt Wilhelm came in and retired the Cardinals in order. St. Louis was looking at an 8-3 deficit, and some in the crowd were considering departure. Wright got three quick outs from New York in the fifth, and suddenly the Redbirds' bats fired up in their half. Schoendienst tripled and Musial followed by knocking a slow curve from Wilhelm over the right-field roof onto Grand Avenue.[16] Jablonski immediately trailed "The Man's" act with a blast of his own into the left-field bleachers, and it was now 8-6.

Anticipation grew in the bottom of the sixth with a runner on second, but Wilhelm struck out Moon and got Schoendienst on a groundball to second to end the inning with Musial on deck. Right-hander Tom Poholsky dispatched the Giants in order in the seventh, and the fans eagerly waited for Musial to come to the plate. Wilhelm disdained his curveball and floated in a knuckler, but it never made it to his catcher's mitt. Musial's timing this day was impeccable as he unleashed a swing that tattooed another baseball. The crowd knew it was gone, and roared with delight as the sphere grew tinier, cleared the roof in right-center, and struck a taxi beyond the ballpark on Grand Avenue. The driver, who had been listening intently to the game on KXOK, pulled over and exited his vehicle to retrieve the baseball.[17]

Musial had just become the first major leaguer ever to hit five home runs in a doubleheader. The All-Star from Donora, Pennsylvania, smiled broadly as he started yet another trot around the Busch Stadium bases. The usually reserved Musial could not contain himself, and actually laughed for joy as he rounded third with the large crowd and his teammates cheering loudly for him.[18] Folks in the stands had to set aside their applause to realize that New York was still in front, 8-7, but that fact did not seem to matter. Jablonski stroked a single, and that was all for Wilhelm as Durocher called for veteran right-hander Larry Jansen to quell the uprising.

The 33-year-old Jansen certainly performed yeoman service for his team. He coaxed Repulski to hit into a 5-4-3 double play, then issued a pair of walks before retiring Solly Hemus on a comebacker to end the seventh. In the eighth Jansen allowed a one-out single before stabbing Schoendienst's hard grounder and starting a 1-6-3 twin killing. This defensive play occurred with the all-too-familiar uniform number 6 kneeling in the circle. Later, Jansen, batting for himself with two outs in the ninth, singled home an important insurance run to increase the Giants' slim spread to two runs. Jansen's clutch hit was struck off right-hander Cot Deal, who was Stanky's fifth hurler of the nightcap.

Nearing 8:00 P.M., Jansen strode to the mound for the last of the ninth. As Musial trekked to the plate, the crowd of 26,662 was buzzing while preparing themselves to erupt one more time for another long one. Jansen got the sign, wound up, and fired. Musial swung heartily and watched the flight of another baseball take shape. However, this one traveled a mere 90 feet and fell harmlessly into the glove of first baseman Whitey Lockman. The St. Louis fans then stood and gave Musial a thunderous ovation, and then, as if an evacuation alarm had just sounded, whisked themselves toward the nearest exit of the ballpark. Many folks had their backs to the action when Jablonski grounded out and Repulski fanned.[19] The 2-hour and 58-minute contest officially ended when Westrum picked up the dropped third strike and pegged it to first to preserve New York's 9-7 triumph.

The line score in the second game for New York read 9 runs, 13 hits, and 1 error, with the Cardinals notching 7 runs on 10 hits and no errors. The winning pitcher, with three innings of one-hit relief, was Jansen (1-0), and the loser was Lint (1-1). With the doubleheader split, the Cardinals (tied for second) and Giants (in fifth place) remained where they had started the day in the NL standings. For the two games the teams combined for 12 home runs, eight by St. Louis.

Despite Musial's setting the record for home runs hit by a player in a doubleheader, there was little celebration in the clubhouse as Stan forced a grin posing for numerous photographs. He lamented, "You can't smile too much when you lose a ballgame."[20] Musial also had his name next to a new mark for total bases (21) in a twin bill. His offensive numbers for the two games were six hits in eight official at-bats, nine RBIs, and six runs scored. His batting average jumped 54 points to .400, and his slugging percentage soared from .654 to .917. For his fast start to the season, Musial credited Stanky for playing him more during spring training, but offered, "I've never had a day like this one."[21]

The weary outfielder dutifully answered questions about the pitches he hit and the last at-bat. "Jansen got me out on a bad pitch — a high fastball, inside." He admitted, "Yeah, I was going for one that time."[22] Cab driver Joe Capraro, who had recovered the record-setting ball, returned it to the Cardinals' dressing room, and Peanuts Lowrey gave him another one to replace it.[23] Baseball Hall of Fame director Sid Keener phoned Musial from Cooperstown to request the history-making bat after he was through with it. "I'll send it right away," Stan said without delay. "I got a lot of bats."[24] The more he thought about it, the more amazed Musial was by his feat. "I still can't believe it. You mean real sluggers like Babe Ruth, Lou Gehrig, Ralph Kiner — men like them — never hit five homers in a doubleheader?"[25]

Lost in all the record-setting clamor were three other players with big days. For New York, it was Bobby Hofman[26] and Don Mueller, both natives of St. Louis. Hofman, who had starred at nearby Beaumont High School,[27] hit the big round-tripper in the nightcap to highlight the eight-run fourth inning, while Mueller went 6-for-9. The Cardinals' Tom Alston enjoyed a 5-for-6, 5-RBI total, and joked with reporters in comparing himself to Musial, "Man, every time I watch Stan hit, I'm ashamed to take a bat up to the plate."[28]

Musial was last player to get dressed and leave the clubhouse. He was beaming when he finally arrived home to his family. However, the feeling of accomplishment was tempered after he was greeted by his 13-year-old son, Dick, who inquired, "They must have been giving you fat pitches, eh, Dad?"[29]

Jack Buck just had fun being at Busch Stadium for the historic day. He was not concerned that Harry Caray was at the microphone for all five of Musial's home runs. It was just as well, since Buck already knew that it bothered Caray if something really big happened when he was not calling the game.[30]

The chartered bus finally returned to Chillicothe, Missouri, past midnight. The tired passengers smiled as they thought about the baseball history they had witnessed, courtesy of Stan "The Man" Musial.[31]

SOURCES

In addition to the sources noted in these two game accounts, the author also accessed Retrosheet.org, Baseball-Reference.com, SABR.org/bioproject, and *The Sporting News* archive via Paper of Record. Additional websites accessed were newspapers.com, mapquest.com, and modot.org.

This article also appears in *Sportsman's Park in St. Louis: Home of the Browns and Cardinals at Grand and Dodier (*SABR, 2017), edited by Gregory H. Wolf.

NOTES

1 Ray Gillespie, "Busch Buys Sportsman's Park From Browns, $400,000 Improvement Program Started," *The Sporting News*, April 15, 1953: 8.

2 "Chartered Bus Takes 37 to St. Louis Ballgame," *Chillicothe Constitution-Tribune*, May 3, 1954: 1.

3 Jack Buck with Rob Rains and Bob Broeg, *Jack Buck, That's a Winner!* (Champaign, Illinois: Sagamore Publishing, 1997), 81, 83-84.

4 Bob Broeg, "Raschi to Pitch Tonight," *St. Louis Post-Dispatch*, May 3, 1954: 4C.

5 Bob Broeg, "Musial's Five Homers in Doubleheader a New Major League Mark," *St. Louis Post-Dispatch*, May 3, 1954: 4C.

6 Jerry Lansche, *The Man Musial, Born to Be a Ballplayer* (Dallas: Taylor Publishing, 1994), 130.

7 *St. Louis Post-Dispatch*, February 5, 1954, 22. Three additional Sunday doubleheaders were played at Busch Stadium to make up weather postponements.

8 Robert L. Tiemann, *Cardinal Classics, Outstanding Games From Each of the St. Louis Baseball Club's 100 Seasons, 1882-1981* (St. Louis: Baseball Histories, Inc., 1982), 194.

9 Broeg, "Musial's Five Homers."

10 Stan Baumgartner, "Ragged Start Gives Phillies 'Job Jitters,'" *The Sporting News*, May 5, 1954: 8.

11 Tiemann.

12 Associated Press, "Loss of Game More Important to Musial Than Batting Feat," *Kansas City Times*, May 3, 1954: 22.

13 Stan Musial as told to Bob Broeg, *The Man Stan: Musial, Then and Now* (St. Louis: Bethany Press, 1977), 24, 61.

14 *Kansas City Times*, May 3, 1954: 22.

15 Broeg, "Musial's Five Homers."

16 Broeg, "Musial's Five Homers."

17 *Kansas City Times*, May 3, 1954: 22.

18 Broeg, "Musial's Five Homers."

19 Broeg, "Musial's Five Homers."

20 *Kansas City Times*, May 3, 1954: 22.

21 *Kansas City Times*, May 3, 1954: 22.

22 Broeg, "Musial's Five Homers."

23 *Kansas City Times*, May 3, 1954: 22.

24 Bob Broeg, "Stan Sends Five-Homer Bat to Museum at Cooperstown," *The Sporting News*, May 12, 1954: 6.

25 Broeg, "Musial's Five Homers."

26 Hofman was the nephew of Arthur Frederick "Circus Solly" Hofman, who played in all three major leagues from 1903 to 1916.

27 Beaumont High School (opened in 1926 and closed in 2014), located at 3836 Natural Bridge Avenue, St. Louis, was built on the same grounds that housed League Park/Cardinal Field/Robison Field (home of National League baseball in St. Louis from 1893 to 1920). Joan M. Thomas, SABR BioProject, sabr.org/bioproj/park/88929e79.

28 Bob Broeg, "Alston Knows How Gehrig Felt Hitting Behind Ruth," *The Sporting News*, May 12, 1954: 6.

29 Bob Broeg, "'Fat Pitches?' Asks Dickie After Dad Stan's Big Day," *The Sporting News*, May 12, 1954: 6.

30 Buck, 85.

31 "Chartered Bus Takes 37 to St. Louis Ballgame."

STAN MUSIAL POWERS CARDINALS TO WIN WHERE HE WAS KNOWN AS "STAN THE MAN"

August 5, 1954: St. Louis Cardinals 13, Brooklyn Dodgers 4, at Ebbets Field, Brooklyn

BY ALAN COHEN

"I'm expected to do it here anyway."
Stan Musial, August 5, 1954[1]

Stan Musial had many great games at Ebbets Field, and this one was one of the greatest. He had two homers and a sacrifice fly as the Cardinals, hitting safely in every inning, defeated the Dodgers 13-4 to snap a four-game slump.

The attendance was 10,026 as the Cardinals and Dodgers played the finale of a three-game series at the Dodgers' ballpark. Pitching for the Cardinals was Brooks Lawrence, who originally signed with Bill Veeck's Cleveland Indians in 1949 and began his career at Zanesville in the Class-D Ohio-Indiana League, breaking the color line in that circuit. He joined the Cardinals in 1954. When he made his debut on June 24, he became the third Black man to play for the Cardinals. He came into the August 5 game with an 8-3 record.

Starting for the Dodgers was Preacher Roe. The 38-year-old lefty came into the game with a 3-3 record in what was to be his last big-league season. He had not lost to the Cardinals at Ebbets Field since July 25, 1950. In the interim, he had made 12 starts with seven wins and five no-decisions in Flatbush.

Brooklyn took the early lead as a one-out walk to Pee Wee Reese was followed by Duke Snider's 27th home run of the season, a 457-foot blast. The lead held until the Cardinals attacked in the third inning. Alex Grammas led off with a single and moved to second on a sacrifice by Lawrence. Rip Repulski singled Grammas home, and a single by rookie Wally Moon set the table for "The Man." Musial's three-run homer off Roe gave the Cardinals a 4-2 lead and they had plenty left in the tank. Roe, however, had seen his last batter. Manager Walter Alston called on Erv Palica to cool the Cardinals down.

"There was no luck in that glove. He could've kept it as far as I was concerned."
Preacher Roe[2]

As Roe departed, he hurled his glove into the stands and once he got to the dugout, he tossed his jacket to the dugout roof.[3] An unidentified soldier quickly returned the jacket. The glove was retrieved by a youngster, Jimmy Reed from Babylon, Long Island, who was attending the game with his father, Don. When the father, after some prodding, returned the glove, the Dodgers gave Jimmy a new mitt, autographed by Roe.[4]

Sportswriter Roger Kahn, after noting that "it was inspiring to see Stan the Superman in form," speculated, "Perhaps Roe should have thrown his glove directly to Stan. It would have saved a lot of trouble and there's a chance Musial's weakness may be a high inside glove."[5]

Palica had been around for a while. He first appeared in New York, at the Polo Grounds, in the Esquire's All-American Boys Baseball Game in 1944.[6] He signed with Brooklyn in 1945 and appeared in a couple of games as a pinch-runner before being sent to the minors. He made his pitching debut in the National League in 1947. His best season was 1950, when he went 13-8. The Cardinals continued their assault. Red Schoendienst doubled and scored on a single by Bill Sarni, giving St. Louis five third-inning runs and a lead that they would not relinquish.

After Lawrence held the Dodgers scoreless in the bottom of the third, the Cardinals resumed their hit parade in the fourth, and once again Musial was at the center of things. With one out, Lawrence and Repulski singled and, after Palica retired Moon, up stepped the pride of Donora, Pennsylvania. Two on and two out quickly became an 8-2 Cardinals advantage as Musial hit his second three-run homer in as many innings. The home run was his 30th of the season and gave him 100 RBIs for the campaign. He was the first player in the league to reach that threshold in 1954.[7] Palica retired Ray Jablonski to end the inning. After Lawrence pitched a scoreless fourth, the Dodgers brought in an untried rookie to pitch the top of the fifth.

"This is what Bobo Milliken was sent down for?"
– Dick Young, *New York Daily News*[8]

Musial appeared on this cover of *The Saturday Evening Post* on May 1, 1954.

Bob Milliken is little remembered seven decades later, but he went 13-6 in two seasons for the Dodgers before being sent to St. Paul in early August of 1954. His replacement, brought up from Montreal, entered the game for the Dodgers in the top of the fifth and, in his first major-league inning, Thomas Charles Lasorda, after allowing singles to Schoendienst and Sarni, struck out Joe Cunningham and induced Grammas to hit into an inning-ending double play. Lawrence got the side in order in the fifth, getting Lasorda to fly out to center field after registering his fourth strikeout of the game (Rube Walker). Junior Gilliam grounded out to end the inning.

The Cardinals next scored in the sixth inning. Lasorda returned to the mound for Brooklyn. Lawrence led off with a walk and scored on Moon's one-out double. Moon advanced to third on the throw home, and Musial came to bat for the fourth time. And for the third time, he delivered. His sacrifice fly scored Moon with the Cardinals' 10th run.

Hopelessly behind, 10-2, the Dodgers had a modest rally in the sixth inning against Lawrence. With one out, Snider singled and Gil Hodges walked. A double by Sandy Amoros scored Snider, and Jackie Robinson brought Hodges home with a fly ball to Moon in center field. That was it for the Dodgers scoring.

The Cardinals added a run as Lasorda yielded a homer to Sarni leading off the seventh. There was no further scoring against Lasorda, who pitched three innings and allowed three runs in his debut before leaving for a pinch-hitter, Johnny Podres, in the seventh inning. Podres, after striking out, returned to the dugout. The Dodgers were not about to waste his arm on this Thursday afternoon.

Ben Wade finished the game for the Dodgers. The Cardinals just kept churning out the hits and scored their last two runs in the eighth inning. After Moon grounded out, Musial came up for the fifth time. Wade walked him on four pitches. Jablonski doubled, his third hit of the game, advancing Musial to third. Jablonski was given the rest of the game off as Harvey Haddix ran for him. A fielder's choice scored Musial, and Haddix came home on a single by Cunningham.

The complete-game win, his fourth, took Lawrence's record to 9-3. His ERA stood at 3.17. For the season, he wound up at 15-6 but received no Rookie of the Year consideration. That honor went to teammate Moon, who had contributed to the win on August 5 with two hits, including an RBI double.

The quartet of Dodger pitchers – Roe, Palica, Lasorda, and Wade – had collectively yielded 21 hits, and none of the pitchers figured in the Dodger plans. After the season Roe was sent to Baltimore in a trade but chose to retire. Palica was also traded to Baltimore and spent two years with the Orioles. Lasorda appeared in a total of eight games with the Dodgers, without a win, before being sold to Kansas City prior to the 1956 season. He later managed the Dodgers for more than 20 seasons, winning the World Series in 1981 and 1988. Wade, after finishing the game, was placed on waivers and immediately claimed by the Cardinals.

The Dodgers remained five games behind the Giants, who would go on to win the NL pennant. The Giants lost to the Chicago Cubs, 6-4, on this day at the Polo Grounds. The Cardinals, with the win, pulled into a fourth-place tie with Philadelphia, but they were still below .500 (51-53) and 16½ games out of first place.

For Musial, it was just another day at one of his favorite stops. His 2-for-4 afternoon lifted his batting average for the season at Ebbets Field to .417. His overall batting average stood at .343. His two homers gave him 30 for the season, and his seven RBIs put him at 101. It was his seventh season with 100 or more RBIs. By the end of his career, Musial had recorded 100 or more RBIs in a season 10 times, eclipsing the NL mark of nine that had been set by Mel Ott.[9] Musial wound up with 37 career homers at Ebbets Field, his second favorite road ballpark for homers behind the Polo Grounds (49). His third-inning homer off Roe gave him 12 off the lefty, his second favorite pitching target in the National League (behind Warren Spahn's 17). Yes, just another day.

Milton Richman in his article for the United Press made the assertion that "Stan (The Man) Musial is bound to slow down sometime."[10] By the time Musial played his last game in New York in 1963, Ebbets Field had been torn down.

Musial did come to the plate for a sixth time on August 5. (That's what happens when you bat third and your team gets 21 hits.) With runners at first and second and one out, Musial hit into a double play – Nobody's Perfect!

SOURCES

In addition to the sources shown in the Notes, the author used Retrosheet.org and Baseball-Reference.com.

https://www.baseball-reference.com/boxes/BRO/BRO195408050.shtml

https://www.retrosheet.org/boxesetc/1954/B08050BRO1954.htm

NOTES

1   Jack Rice, "Musial Hits 2 Homers, Cards Ride Over Bums, 13-4," *St. Louis Globe-Democrat*, August 6, 1954: 2B.

2   Dave Anderson, "Roe Nears End of Long Flock Trail," *Brooklyn Eagle*, August 6, 1954: 11.

3   Roscoe McGowen, "Cards Trounce Brooks by 13-4 as Musial Paces 21-Hit Attack," *New York Times*, August 6, 1954: 12.

4   Bob Broeg, "Musial Cracks Two Homers, Cards Wallop Dodgers," *St. Louis Post-Dispatch*, August 5, 1954: 14C.

5   Roger Kahn, "Cardinals Belt 21 Hits, Jar Dodgers' Roe, 13-4," *New York Herald Tribune*, August 6, 1954: 15.

6   Alan Cohen, "The Boys of the Polo Grounds: Youth Baseball, 1944-1958," in Stew Thornley, ed., *The Polo Grounds: Essays and Memories of New York City's Historic Ballpark, 1880-1963* (Jefferson, North Carolina: McFarland and Company, 2019), 115.

7   Milton Richman (United Press), "Stan's Bound to Slow Down, but Vital Question Is When," *Austin* (Texas) *American Statesman*, August 6, 1954: 18.

8   Dick Young, "Cardinals Wham Dodgers, 13-4," *New York Daily News*, August 6, 1954: 46.

9   The record has since been broken by Hank Aaron (11) and Barry Bonds (12).

10 "Stan's Bound to Slow Down, But Vital Question Is When."

STAN MUSIAL SEALS MILWAUKEE'S FIRST BASEBALL ALL-STAR CELEBRATION

July 12, 1955: National League 6, American League 5 (12 innings), at County Stadium, Milwaukee

BY NELSON "CHIP" GREENE

From the day in 1953 when the National League's Braves arrived in Milwaukee and took up residence in County Stadium, until the early 1960s, there was never a shortage of crowds. Indeed, for six consecutive seasons the Braves led the league in attendance. So when in the summer of 1954 baseball awarded the 1955 All-Star Game to Milwaukee, there was little doubt that the fans would turn out in droves for Milwaukee's first experience with the national pastime's annual spectacle.

As the day of the game arrived, excitement in Milwaukee was palpable. The following day, one reporter vividly recounted the city's festive atmosphere, writing, "All-Star fever settled on downtown shoppers. ... Traffic dwindled at game time and pedestrians settled in front of TV sets in department stores, shops, hotel lobbies and bars."[1] So caught up in the event were some Milwaukeeans that newspapers reported of an elderly shopper, standing at a bus stop and listening to the game on her portable radio. "After a long wait at the bus stop, she became engrossed in the game and, when the bus arrived, she missed it."[2] A highly anticipated exhibition, the All-Star Game was "a new high in Milwaukee's short but fabulous big league history."[3]

Game day, July 12, dawned bright and clear, and it remained that way throughout the afternoon, creating a perfect day for baseball: warm sun, low humidity, and clear skies. On the field, the pregame gathering resembled little more than a mob scene, as "[n]ewspapermen, photographers and baseball dignitaries by the hundreds, plus the inevitable gate crashers, swarm[ed] over the premises."[4] In the stands, not a seat was empty. The previous year, the stadium's seating capacity had been increased from 36,011 to 43,091;[5] yet somehow, on this day a crowd announced at 45,314 jammed into every nook and cranny of the sparkling, two-year-old facility.

In the crowd on the field, Brooklyn Dodgers owner Walter O'Malley, standing with Braves president Lou Perini, gazed at the packed stands and inquired, "How do you explain the phenomenal attendance of this town? What's the secret?"[6]

To which Perini responded, "There's no secret formula. It's just terrific enthusiasm. All the people here have something in common in the team. The priest talks about the Braves to the rabbi; the mechanic to the industrialist, the housekeeper to the butcher."[7]

It was undoubtedly that sentiment that compelled 75-year-old Calvin Smith, from Stevens Point, Wisconsin, to stick around after he collapsed in the grandstand before the game. As medical personnel sought to place Smith in an ambulance and take him to the hospital, he refused to go, insisting simply, "I don't want to leave."[8] In the end, Smith stayed.

Such was the enthusiasm that afternoon in Milwaukee.

As was customary, the two managers, Al Lopez for the American League and the National League's Leo Durocher, joined the umpires at home plate for a pregame conference, and then called their respective teams from the dugouts to stand at attention along the first- and third-base lines. This was the 22nd meeting of the two leagues' stars, but this edition was especially poignant. Twenty-two years before, *Chicago Tribune* sports editor Arch Ward had launched the first All-Star Game, in Chicago. Three days before this game, Ward had died, so everyone in attendance observed a moment of silence in his memory. When the respectful silence was ended, home-plate umpire Al Barlick hollered, "Play ball!"

Perhaps there was some degree of foreshadowing when before the game the scoreboard on the upper third-base stands displayed "American 7, National 6." For a while, it seemed that the hint of an American League victory in this National League ballpark might prove prescient. Robin Roberts took the mound as starter for the senior circuit, and the American League offense immediately struck. After singles by the game's first two batters, Harvey Kuenn and Nellie Fox, a wild pitch by Roberts allowed Kuenn to score from third. Ted Williams walked and cleanup hitter Mickey Mantle blasted a home run to straightaway center field. The American League led, 4-0. Roberts stiffened over the next two innings and escaped any further damage. He left the game after the third inning.

Meanwhile, American League starter Billy Pierce was brilliant. After the White Sox' star surrendered a leadoff single to Red Schoendienst in the bottom of the first, Schoendienst was thrown out trying to steal, and Pierce set down the next eight batters he faced, including three on strikeouts. When he, too, left the game after three innings, the American League's 4-0 lead remained intact.

Over the next two innings, Early Wynn of the American League and the National League's Harvey Haddix matched zeroes. In the top of the sixth, however, the AL struck again. After Wynn stranded runners at the corners in the bottom of the fifth to preserve the 4-0 lead, Haddix got the first out in the sixth and then allowed a single to Yogi Berra and a double to Al Kaline (whose drive caromed off third baseman Eddie Mathews' wrist), with Berra stopping at third on Kaline's hit. When the next batter, Mickey Vernon, pulled a sharp grounder to first, Berra trotted home with the AL's fifth run. Haddix struck out the next batter, Jim Finigan, to end the inning and bring his afternoon to a close.

If a 5-0 deficit with nine outs remaining was daunting for the NL, it certainly wasn't insurmountable given their explosive offense. As things turned out, though, Willie Mays' defense may have played the most pivotal role in the game's outcome. In the top of the seventh, Don Newcombe took over on the mound for the NL. With two outs and a runner on first, Ted Williams blistered a drive deep to the wall in right-center field. With impeccable timing, Mays leaped, caught the ball over the wall, and brought it back in for the final out. The two runs he saved would be crucial to the final score.

As luck would have it, Mays led off the bottom of the seventh inning; the appreciative fans gave him a round of applause for his defensive gem. Whitey Ford now took the mound for the AL. With just four hits over six innings off Pierce and Wynn, the NL was undoubtedly glad to face a new hurler, and Ford took the brunt of their renewed attack. After Mays singled, Ford retired the next two batters, but then walked Henry Aaron. When Milwaukee's own Johnny Logan singled, Mays scored the NL's first run, and then Stan Lopata reached on a throwing error by shortstop Chico Carrasquel, which scored Aaron. After seven, the score was 5-2.

In the top of the eighth, the AL loaded the bases with two outs against new hurler Sam Jones, who walked two and hit a man, but Joe Nuxhall struck out Ford to end the threat.

The bottom of the eighth brought more of the same against Ford. After the first two men grounded out, Mays, Ted Kluszewski, and Randy Jackson each singled to pull the NL within 5-3. So with Aaron due up and runners at first and second, Frank Sullivan was summoned in relief. Yet, the onslaught continued.

When Aaron singled to right field, Kluszewski scored. However, as Jackson ran to third, Kaline's throw nicked him, and the ball caromed past third baseman Al Rosen. When Jackson scored, the game was tied, 5-5. It stayed that way until the bottom of the 12th inning.

Nuxhall had been fabulous in relief for the NL. After bailing out Jones in the eighth, he pitched the next three innings, allowing just two hits and striking out five. In the top of the 12th the Reds' left-hander gave way to the Braves' Gene Conley, who entered to a raucous greeting from the home crowd. Conley

Stan Musial trots home after hitting the game-winning homer in the bottom of the 12th inning of the 1955 All-Star Game at County Stadium in Milwaukee.

struck out Kaline, Vernon, and Rosen in succession. So the game went to the bottom of the 12th.

For the AL, Sullivan returned to the mound. Despite allowing the NL's tying runs in the eighth, which had been charged to Ford, the 6-foot-7 Sullivan had pitched well, stranding baserunners in the 9th and 10th and setting the side down in order in the 11th. Now, Stan Musial led off for the NL. As he arrived in the batter's box, Musial told catcher Berra, "Boy, that ball is tough to see out there. You can't pick it up in all those shadows." Also, he said, "I'm tired."[9]

"You're tired!" responded Berra, who'd caught the whole game. "What about me? We're all tired."[10]

On Sullivan's first offering, which he later recalled as "a lousy pitch, a fastball, high and a little inside,"[11] (Musial said the pitch was belt-high.) Musial swung and drove the ball into the right-field bleachers. Immediately, the NL players erupted on their bench, yelling and dancing in celebration of the NL's fifth win in six years.

Here in Milwaukee, it was probably appropriate that Conley, the Braves pitcher, got the win.

SOURCES

In addition to the sources cited in the Notes, the author consulted Baseball-Reference.com and Retrosheet.org.

This article appears in From the Braves to the Brewers: Great Games and Exciting History at Milwaukee's County Stadium *(SABR, 2016), edited by Gregory H. Wolf. To read more stories from this book at the SABR Games Project, click here.*

NOTES

1 "Shoppers Hug TV Sets During All-Star Game," *Milwaukee Sentinel*, July 13, 1955: part 1: 2.

2. "Shoppers Hug TV Sets During All-Star Game."
3. Lloyd Larson, "Every Second Brings Thrill as All-Star Story Unfolds," *Milwaukee Sentinel*, July 13, 1955: part 2; 4.
4. Larson.
5. Philip J. Lowry, *Green Cathedrals: The Ultimate Celebration of Major League and Negro League Ballparks* (New York: Walker Publishing, 2006), 131.
6. Lou Chapman and Tony Ingrassia, "Scoreboard Was No Prophet," *Milwaukee Sentinel*, July 13, 1955: part 2: 6.
7. Chapman and Ingrassia, "Scoreboard Was No Prophet."
8. "Refuses to Miss Game," *Milwaukee Sentinel*, July 13, 1955: part 2: 6.
9. Lou Chapman, "Stan the (Old) Man Tired – So Ends game With Homer," *Milwaukee Sentinel*, July 13, 1955: part 2: 4.
10. Chapman.
11. Tony Ingrassia, "'Lousy' Pitch Beat AL," *Milwaukee Sentinel*, July 13, 1955: part 2: 4.

MUSIAL'S PERFECT OPENING DAY

April 16, 1957: St. Louis Cardinals 13, Cincinnati Redlegs 4, at Crosley Field, Cincinnati

BY DANNY SPEWAK

Stan Musial entered the 1957 season with something to prove. Although the three-time National League MVP and six-time batting champion had already cemented his case for the Hall of Fame, Musial began his 16th big-league campaign fighting the perception that his best years were behind him. The 36-year-old had not won an MVP award since 1948 or a batting title since 1952, as sportswriter George Bugbee noted in an April 15, 1957, column. "There is little grounds for hope," Bugbee wrote, "that he can erase the handwriting—that he can ever recapture in full the magic that was in his days of an enchanted youth."[1]

Musial put that narrative to rest pretty quickly on Opening Day.

With a vintage 4-for-4 performance on April 16, 1957, Musial powered the Cardinals to a 13-4 victory over the Cincinnati Redlegs and set the tone for the last truly great season of his career, one in which he would capture his seventh and final NL batting title and finish as the runner-up to Hank Aaron for MVP. In front of an opposing crowd of more than 32,000 fans at Crosley Field, he doubled twice to tie Charlie Gehringer for seventh in two-base hits on the all-time major-league list. Also, by appearing in his 775th consecutive game, Musial inched even closer to the NL record of 822 set by Gus Suhr two decades earlier – a mark he passed later in the season.

The 1957 opener carried much broader implications beyond Musial. Both St. Louis and Cincinnati entered the season with legitimate pennant aspirations, even though neither franchise had appeared in a World Series since the previous decade. The Cardinals, led by fiery manager Fred Hutchinson, had finished just shy of .500 in 1956 but beefed up their lineup during the off-season with the addition of power-hitting outfielder Del Ennis. Twenty-five-year-old Ken Boyer, a reigning NL All-Star, also returned as the team's starting third baseman. "With the line-up we have, we might go as high as second place – if the pitching steps up," Musial said before the season. "I think our [overall] hitting balance is probably the best since the time of Cooper, Kurowski and Slaughter."[2]

Cincinnati had even higher hopes. After suffering through 11 consecutive losing seasons, the Redlegs (the team's official nickname from 1953 to 1958 during the "Red Scare") took the National League by storm in 1956 with a 91-63 record. Fueled by NL Manager of the Year Birdie Tebbetts and Rookie of the Year outfielder Frank Robinson, Cincinnati finished just two games out of first place in '56 and clearly had the talent to compete for a pennant in '57.

Before Opening Day, the *Cincinnati Enquirer* summed up the city's collective optimism with the following poem:

Twas the day before opening and all over town
The fans' hopes were up, not soon to come down.
Well known were the problems, yet heard was the brag
That this year the Redlegs would capture the flag ...
THEN BRING ON THE YANKS.[3]

As first pitch approached on the afternoon of April 16, the crowd brought similar energy to Crosley Field. After a morning rainfall and lavish pregame ceremonies, as many as 3,000 fans jammed a set of temporary bleachers extending from the left-field foul line all the way past center. "The boisterous burghers," Bob Broeg of the *St. Louis Post Dispatch* observed, were practically "spilling onto the left and centerfield lawn."[4] The special accommodation for the fans intruded the playing surface by nearly 50 feet, a welcome move for the hitters on both teams though not so much for the pitchers.[5]

On the mound, the Redlegs started Johnny Klippstein against the Cardinals' Herm Wehmeier – an unremarkable Opening Day pitching matchup with few exciting storylines other than the fact that Wehmeier was a Cincinnati native competing against his hometown team. The serviceable 30-year-old righty, a former star athlete at Cincinnati's Western Hills High School, had previously played parts of nine seasons for the Reds from 1945 to 1954 before joining the Phillies in midseason in 1954 and then the Cardinals in 1956. Despite having a huge contingent of family and friends rooting for him in the Crosley Field bleachers, Wehmeier downplayed the matchup. "Merely another game," he said. "That's what it was."[6]

In the top of the first, Klippstein retired Cardinals leadoff hitter Don Blasingame but yielded a double to Alvin Dark, bringing Musial to the plate with a runner in scoring position. As he strolled to the batter's box for his first at-bat of the 1957 season, Musial loosened his trademark crouched batting stance a bit – a technique he experimented with during spring training when he hit at nearly a .400 clip. "I believe I am concentrating a little more than last year," Musial had said in March. "I certainly do feel good at the plate this year."[7]

It showed.

Facing Klippstein with a runner on second, Musial whacked a double off the fence in right field to score Dark for the season's first run. After putting the Cardinals on the board with a 1-0 lead, Musial drew a walk in the third inning and raced to third on an RBI double by cleanup hitter Del Ennis, although he did not advance any farther. In the bottom of the fourth, Redlegs catcher Ed Bailey's two-run single tied the score at 2-2 before the Cardinals sent up the top of their lineup in the fifth. With one out and a runner on first, Musial smoked another double to right, tying Gehringer's all-time doubles mark at 574[8] and setting up an RBI groundout by Ennis in the next at-bat. Given a 3-2 lead to protect, Wehmeier proceeded to pitch a fifth scoreless inning in the bottom of the frame.

The Cardinals broke open the game in the top of the sixth by exploding for five runs on six hits. After catcher Hal Smith knocked Klippstein out of the contest with an RBI single, rookie center fielder Bobby Gene Smith blasted a two-run homer to center for the first hit of his career. Four batters later, Musial came to bat again and pulled the ball to right for a single – his third hit of the day – scoring Blasingame to extend the lead to five runs. Another RBI groundout by Ennis made the score 8-2 in favor of St. Louis.

Wehmeier helped himself at the plate with a sacrifice fly in the seventh, before the Cardinals added four more runs in the top of the eighth. In his final at-bat of the afternoon, Musial completed his perfect 4-for-4 day by singling and scoring on a homer by outfielder Wally Moon. For his part, Wehmeier pitched a complete game, yielding four runs and eight hits to pick up the victory against his hometown team.

With a 13-4 win, the Cardinals dealt the Redlegs their worst Opening Day loss since 1911.[9] "We got the hell knocked out of us," manager Birdie Tebbetts said. "That's right, the hell knocked out of us. H-e-l-l."[10] Over in the St. Louis clubhouse, Musial celebrated his 4-for-4 performance with teammates by sipping a cold bottle of beer. "I can't recall," Musial said, "when I've had a better Opening Day."[11] The 13-time All-Star had put the rest of the National League on notice. "I'm going to bear down on that batting title," Musial vowed after the game.[12]

After his stellar 1957 debut in Cincinnati, Musial batted an astounding .476 throughout the rest of April and never looked back. By the end of the season, he led the much-improved Cardinals to a second-place finish and captured the final batting title of his career with a mark of .351 – 18 points higher than runner-up Willie Mays and nearly 30 points higher than Cincinnati's Frank Robinson.

So much for Stan Musial losing his magic.

SOURCES

In addition to the sources cited in the Notes, the author used Baseball Reference for more information on the April 16, 1957, contest as well as Musial's career as a whole.

https://www.baseball-reference.com/boxes/CIN/CIN195704160.shtml

https://www.retrosheet.org/boxesetc/1957/B04160CIN1957.htm

NOTES

1. George Bugbee, "Lane Takes Critical Look at Musial, Sees an All-Time Titan," *Memphis Press-Scimitar,* April 15, 1957: 18.
2. Jack Herman, "Cards Vets Report, Musial in High Spirits," *St. Louis Globe-Democrat,* March 1, 1957: 1C.
3. Richard Emerson Macke, "Twas the Day Before Opening," *Cincinnati Enquirer,* April 15, 1957: 46.
4. Bob Broeg, "Boy Named Smith and The Man Pace Cards' Romp," *St. Louis Post-Dispatch,* April 17, 1957: 1C.
5. Broeg.
6. Dick Forbes, "Hermie Relaxed, Musial Content After Inaugural," *Cincinnati Enquirer,* April 17, 1957: 25.

Rawlings recognized Musial for his consistent play as one of the game's great stars.

7 J. Roy Stockton, "Cheney's Curve and the New Musial Give Cards Spring Lilt," *St. Louis Post-Dispatch*, March 29, 1957: 4B.

8 With 725 doubles by the end of his career, Musial as of 2024 ranked third on the all-time list. https://www.baseball-reference.com/leaders/2B_career.shtml.

9 Jack Herman, "Musial Gets 4-4 in 13-4 Cards' Romp," *St. Louis Globe-Democrat*, April 17, 1957: 1C.

10 Bill Ford, "Klippstein Clouted as Control Lacks," *Cincinnati Enquirer*, April 17, 1957: 27.

11 Forbes.

12 Bob Pille, "At 36, Stan Rolls On," *Cincinnati Post*, April 17, 1957: 33.

STAN MUSIAL'S EIGHTH CAREER GRAND SLAM NOT GOOD ENOUGH

May 26, 1957: St. Louis Cardinals 6, Cincinnati Redlegs 7, at Crosley Field, Cincinnati

BY BRUCE DUNCAN

"How good was Stan Musial? He was good enough to take your breath away."

Vin Scully, on-air radio broadcast (1989)[1]

Early in the 1957 season, the St. Louis Cardinals were off to a sluggish start. But their star first baseman, Stan Musial, at 36 years old and playing in his 16th season, was on his way to breaking the National League record for consecutive games played and winning his seventh and final NL batting title. His average never dipped below .329 the entire season as he finished with a .351 mark. He also might have won his fourth Most Valuable Player Award if not for a 23-year-old Milwaukee Braves outfielder named Henry Aaron.

The attendance was 17,782 on a Sunday afternoon in late May as the Cardinals and Redlegs played the final game of a four-game series at Crosley Field. Cincinnati entered the contest leading the National League with a 23-12 record, while the Cardinals were 15-17, 6½ games back in fifth place. This was the seventh meeting of the season between the teams. They split the first six games.

Looking for their third win in a row and a chance to take the four-game series, the Cardinals sent Murry Dickson to the mound. The 40-year-old, battling a sore arm, came into the game with a 0-2 record and a 7.43 ERA. Before the season he had slipped and fallen on an icy sidewalk, straining his right shoulder. He tried to pitch through the injury but eventually went on the disabled list near the end of July and stayed there in what would turn out to be his last season with St. Louis.[2]

Starting for Cincinnati was Hal Jeffcoat. The 32-year-old former outfielder entered the game with a 2-2 record and a 2.89 ERA. Jeffcoat, who debuted with the Chicago Cubs in 1948, spent the first six years of his career as an everyday center fielder. The Cubs converted him to a pitcher in 1954. Jeffcoat appeared in 93 games as a reliever for Chicago before being traded to the Redlegs for Hobie Landrith, before the start of the 1956 season.

St. Louis took the early lead when Ken Boyer led off the second inning with a double and was chased home on a two-out single off the bat of Eddie Kasko. Musial's solo home run in the top of the third, his seventh of the season, made it 2-0, Cardinals. Musial's 359th career homer tied him with Johnny Mize for eighth place on the all-time list.[3] Dickson, who escaped a bases-loaded jam in the first inning, was holding up until Cincinnati's George Crowe belted a three-run home run in the bottom of the third that gave the Redlegs a 3-2 lead.

In the fourth inning, Cincinnati made it 4-2 when Roy McMillan lined a double to right and Johnny Temple doubled him home one out later. Dickson settled down, retiring five in a row before Don Hoak led off the Redlegs' sixth inning with a double and later scored on a sacrifice fly off the bat of Temple for a 5-2 lead. Before a game earlier in the series, Temple was looking for a batting tip and asked Musial to "take a look at me at the plate." When Temple reached first after a walk, Musial looked at him and said, "There's nothing wrong with you. You're batting .299. Who do you think you are – Stan Musial?"[4]

The Redlegs chased Dickson from the game in the bottom of the seventh inning after Gus Bell led off with a single and Frank Robinson reached safely on a throwing error by Cardinals second baseman Don Blasingame. Cardinals manager Fred Hutchinson brought in Lloyd Merritt to replace Dickson. Merritt was making his 10th relief appearance. He would go on to lead the Cardinals' staff with 44 relief appearances in his only season at the major-league level.[5] Merritt got Crowe to hit into a 3-6 fielder's choice with Bell advancing to third. Ed Bailey followed with a sacrifice fly that scored Bell, giving the Redlegs a 6-2 lead. Merritt walked Hoak before getting McMillan on a foul pop to Musial at first to end the inning.

In the top of the eighth inning, Jeffcoat – who had allowed only one hit since Musial's home run in the third inning – seemed to be in total control with a comfortable four-run lead. He got Kasko on a fly out to right field to open the inning. Del Ennis pinch-hit for Merritt and doubled to center field. Blasingame then reached safely on a fielding error by Cincinnati second baseman Temple. Jeffcoat, maybe a bit rattled for the first time in the game, hit the next batter, Al Dark, to load the bases and set the stage for The Man. Musial did not disappoint as he took Jeffcoat deep to right for his eighth career grand slam and a 6-6 tie. Musial's home run, number 360 for his career, broke the tie with Mize and moved him all alone into eighth place, just one back of Joe DiMaggio.[6]

Hutchinson called on Herm Wehmeier to pitch the bottom of the eighth. Wehmeier who was the Opening Day starter for St. Louis, threw a brilliant game earlier in the month at Ebbets Field in Brooklyn where he started and completed 12 innings, getting a no-decision in a game the Cardinals went on to win in 16 innings. But he faltered in his next three starts, allowing 25 hits, 22 runs (17 earned), 10 walks, and 5 home runs in 16⅔ innings pitched and was now being used primarily as a reliever.

According to legendary St. Louis sportswriter Bob Broeg, "Wehmeier immediately served a low let-up to rival Hal Jeffcoat, who was converted from the outfield because he couldn't hit high fastballs."[7] Jeffcoat deposited the ball deep over Crosley Field's center-field wall for the winning run in a 7-6 win for Cincinnati. Jeffcoat became the first major-league pitcher in the modern era to allow a grand slam and then hit a go-ahead home run in the same inning. Through the 2024 season, Madison Bumgarner was the only other pitcher to match that feat when he did it in 2016 with the San Francisco Giants.[8]

Jeffcoat retired the Cardinals in order in the top of the ninth inning to earn the complete-game win and improve his record to 3-2. When Jeffcoat learned he was being traded from the Cubs to Cincinnati in November 1955 for Hobie Landrith, he seriously considered retiring from baseball. A few days later he changed his mind and the deal was finalized.[9] It was only fitting that Jeffcoat retired Landrith for the final out.

Despite the disappointing loss, Musial once again showed why he was one of the greatest hitters of all time. It was the 30th time in his career that he hit multiple home runs in a game. He smashed his eighth career grand slam, and he drove in five of the Cardinals' six runs.

Stan the Man's performance wasn't good enough on this day, but he was still "good enough to take your breath away."

SOURCES

In addition to the sources shown in the Notes, the author used Retrosheet.org and Baseball-Reference.com.

https://www.baseball-reference.com/boxes/CIN/CIN195705260.shtml

https://www.retrosheet.org/boxesetc/1957/B05260CIN1957.htm

NOTES

1. "Vin Scully Quotes," Baseball Almanac, https://www.baseball-almanac.com/quotes/vin_scully_quotes.shtml, accessed December 17, 2024.
2. Warren Corbett, "Murry Dickson," SABR BioProject, https://sabr.org/bioproj/person/murry-dickson/, accessed December 17, 2024.
3. "Stan Ties DiMag for No. 7 Spot on All-Time HR Table," *The Sporting News*, June 5, 1957: 8.
4. "Who Do You Think You Are – Musial? Stan Told Temple," *The Sporting News*, June 5, 1957: 24.
5. Gregory H. Wolf, "Lloyd Merritt," SABR BioProject, https://sabr.org/bioproj/person/lloyd-merritt/, accessed December 17, 2024.
6. "Stan Ties DiMag for No. 7 Spot on All-Time HR Table."
7. Bob Broeg, "Cards Collect Quick Dividend on Hutch's 'Shakewell' System," *The Sporting News*, June 5, 1957: 8.
8. Michael Wagaman (Associated Press), "Giants Finally Get Some Offense in 10-7 Win Over Mets," August 18, 2016, https://apnews.com/7f5582a0e7534c6a88ff5e552cec64aa, accessed December 17, 2024.
9. Tom Swope, "Hal Jeffcoat Balks at Trade, Then Decides to Join Reds," *The Sporting News*, December 7, 1955: 21.

MUSIAL DELIVERS IN THE PINCH FOR NUMBER 3,000

May 13, 1958: St. Louis Cardinals 5, Chicago Cubs 3, at Wrigley Field, Chicago

BY GREGORY H. WOLF

Stan Musial didn't expect to play when his St. Louis Cardinals took on the Chicago Cubs on the North Side of the Windy City. The 37-year-old future Hall of Famer was in perfect health; he was also sitting on 2,999 hits, and with the Redbirds back in the Gateway City the next day, skipper Fred Hutchinson had every intention of letting Stan the Man join an exclusive fraternity in front of his hometown fans. Only an emergency could derail Hutchinson's plan.

In his 17th season, Musial showed no sign of slowing down. He was coming off a spectacular season in 1957, having led the NL in batting average (.351) for the seventh time and in on-base percentage (.422) for the sixth time; he also belted 29 round-trippers and knocked in 100-plus runs for the 10th time. Musial was the big leagues' hottest hitter thus far in '58. He was leading both leagues with a .483 batting average (42-for-87) and a .553 on-base percentage through 22 games, and paced the senior circuit with a .782 slugging percentage. Since he debuted as a mid-September call-up in 1941, one aspect of his hitting had remained constant: his unorthodox stance. "He stands far back from the plate," wrote the *New York Times* about the converted pitcher, "his feet close together, right shoulder pointed toward the pitcher, the bat posed motionless and out farther than any player holds it. His head is bent slightly and turned toward the pitcher."[1] You can't argue with success.

Musial played on Redbird pennant winners in his first four full seasons (1942-1944; 1946; he was in the military in 1945), but the glory years of three World Series championships must have seemed far off in '58. The Cardinals (8-14) had floundered in last place most of the season, but their current five-game winning streak pulled them into sixth, tied with the Philadelphia Phillies, seven games behind the Milwaukee Braves. Skipper Bob Scheffing's fourth-place Cubs (13-13) had dropped their last six to fall out of the top spot. The pitching matchup featured a pair of struggling right-handers. The Redbirds' Sam Jones's 1-3 record (5.28 ERA) dropped his career slate to 38-50 while the Cubs' Moe Drabowksy (1-2, 5.40 ERA) was 16-21 in parts of three seasons.

The first half of the game was a Lee Walls highlight reel. He got the Cubs rolling in the first by doubling and subsequently scoring on Ernie Banks's sacrifice. After a walk, two errors and Irv Noren's single tied the game for the Cardinals in the third, Walls smacked a deep home run, his 10th, over the "wide screen in left," according to sportswriter Edward Prell of the *Chicago Tribune*, to give the Cubs a 2-1 lead.[2] With the bases loaded and one out in the fifth, Walls's sacrifice fly drove in Bobby Thomson for another run.

The Cardinals trailed, 3-1, when Gene Green led off the top of the sixth with a double. After Hal Smith grounded out, Hutchinson motioned to Musial to grab a bat and pinch-hit for Jones. Musial wasn't sitting on the dugout bench; rather, he had been "sunning himself in a green folding chair in the Cardinals' bullpen" along the first-base line, according to the *Tribune*.[3] His afternoon leisure rudely interrupted, Musial sauntered to the plate. After fouling off three pitches to the left and taking two balls, Musial took a cut at the sixth offering and sent a liner into the left-field corner for an RBI double.

Musial's hit brought the modest crowd of 5,692 at Wrigley Field on a Tuesday afternoon to its feet for a rousing standing ovation. The following few minutes were, according to St. Louis sportswriter Bob Broeg, like a scene from "Mack Sennett's old Keystone Kops" routine.[4] Photographers, normally barred from field, poured onto the diamond to record the feat for posterity. While play was interrupted, Musial walked to the pitcher's mound, where he was met by Hutchinson and third-base umpire Frank Dascoli, who gave him the historic ball. After a few ceremonial waves to the crowd, Musial walked back to the dugout, savoring the moment, and was replaced by pinch-runner Frank Barnes.

The Cardinals tied the score, 3-3, two batters later when Don Blasingame, hitless in his last 16 at-bats, singled. After Drabowsky intentionally walked Joe Cunningham to load the bases with one out, Noren's groundout force at second plated Dick Schofield to give the Cardinals the lead. Wally Moon's double to right drove in Blasingame, but Noren was out at home on second baseman Tony Taylor's relay strike to catcher Sammy Taylor.

The final 3½ frames were anticlimactic. Jones was relieved by Billy Muffett, who tossed four scoreless innings, yielding two hits and walking one. He fanned Chuck Tanner to end the game in 2 hours and 27 minutes. The victory went to Jones, whose five-hit, three-run outing was less than stellar. Tagged with the loss, Drabowsky surrendered eight hits and five runs (four earned) in seven innings.

Immediately after the game, Cubs announcer Jack Brickhouse of WGN interviewed Musial on the field. "I was pressing a little the last few games," said Musial in his Western Pennsylvanian accent. "I was mighty anxious to get this 3000th hit and get it over with."[5] True to his approach to hitting, Musial said he was just trying to make contact and not blast one out of the park. "I went for a base hit. It was a curveball going away, I swung and the next thing I knew I was on second with a double."[6]

Musial became the first major leaguer to reach 3,000 hits since the Boston Braves' Paul Waner in 1942 (though most of his hits were as a Pittsburgh Pirate). Cap Anson (1897), Honus Wager (1914), Nap Lajoie (1914), Ty Cobb (1921), Tris Speaker (1925), and Eddie Collins (1925) preceded them.

The celebration for Musial's accomplishment began in earnest that evening when he and his teammates boarded an Illinois Central Railroad train at Union Station and headed home to St. Louis. He was in a car with close friends from Pennsylvania and Missouri, as well as his wife, Lil. According to the *St. Loui Post-Dispatch*, Musial was presented with a cake with the number 3,000. A team of St. Louis broadcasters gave him a pair of commemorative cufflinks.[7] When the train pulled into Union Station in the Mound City later that evening, about a thousand fans enthusiastically greeted Musial.

Musial continued to pelt the pill the rest of the season, finishing with a .337 batting average (third highest in the league), though his power numbers dropped. For the first time since 1947, he failed to hit at least 20 home runs, finishing with 17, and his 62 runs batted in were a career low. Musial retired after the 1963 season with an NL record 3,630 hits.

SOURCES

In addition to the sources cited in the Notes, the author accessed Retrosheet.org, Baseball-Reference.com, and SABR.org.

NOTES

1   "Safeties in Numbers: Stanley Frank Musial," *New York Times*, May 14, 1958: 39.
2   Edward Prell, "Musial's 3000th Is Pinch Hit," *Chicago Tribune*, May 14, 1958: C1.
3   Prell.
4   Bob Broeg, "Musial Eyes .400 Average After Getting 3000 Hits," *St. Louis Post-Dispatch*, May 14, 1958: 4D.
5   "Musial Relaxes, Now That Pressure's Off," *Chicago Tribune*, May 14, 1958: C1.
6   "Musial Relaxes, Now That Pressure's Off."
7   The *St. Louis Post-Dispatch* did not mention the names of the broadcasters; however, at the time they were Jack Buck, Harry Caray, and Joe Garagiola. See Broeg.

STAN MUSIAL KNOCKS IN SEVEN RUNS

June 23, 1961: St. Louis Cardinals 10, San Francisco Giants 5, at Busch Stadium, St. Louis

BY TOM HAWTHORN

The turnstiles at Busch Stadium, the renamed Sportsman's Park in St. Louis, counted 15,444 customers for a game played on June 23, 1961, a Friday evening in early summer. The San Francisco Giants were in town, trying to halt a three-game losing streak against a hometown club not yet playing .500 ball.

The Giants starter was Billy "Digger" O'Dell (3-3), a left-hander who, as a member of the Baltimore Orioles, had been named the Most Valuable Player of the 1958 All-Star Game after retiring the nine National League batters he faced. Behind him on this night was a lineup that included future Hall of Famers Orlando Cepeda and Willie Mays. Willie McCovey, another future inductee, pinch-hit later in the game.

Veteran lefty Curt Simmons (2-6), the one-time schoolboy phenom from Egypt, Pennsylvania, who made his major-league debut at age 18 in 1947, took to the mound for the hometown side. The Cardinals had some offensive stars of their own, including Ken Boyer at third base and Bill White at first base. Tim McCarver, a chatty rookie, was behind the plate, though he would spend most of the season in the minors. The lineup included Stan Musial – Stan the Man, the Donora Greyhound (after his Pennsylvania birthplace), the surefire future Hall of Famer whose name had been on the roster for nearly two decades. The left fielder had marked his 40th birthday seven months earlier and his numbers, while solid, were no longer spectacular. He went into the game hitting .305 with 7 home runs and 27 runs batted in.

Musial was nursing the lingering effects of a head cold, as well as the nuisance of a sore heel. He was also approaching the 20th anniversary of his major-league debut, on September 17, 1941. The newspapers were already speculating whether this season would be his last. In the end, he did not retire until the end of the 1963 campaign, missing out on the Cardinals' pennant and World Series championship the season after that.

The third-place Giants (36-27) were starting to slip in pursuit of the Cincinnati Reds, whom they now trailed by four games. The Cardinals were already a disappointing 11 games back with a 28-33 record in sixth place, ahead of only the Chicago Cubs and Philadelphia Phillies.

Both teams went out in order in the first. Mays got things going for the Giants in the second with a single and a stolen base, only to be picked off by Simmons. The putout went 1-4-5, Simmons to second baseman Bob Lillis to Boyer at third. The Cardinals sandwiched two singles around a Musial fly out to right to open their half of the second inning, but the rally ended without damage when Simmons struck out with the bases loaded.

The game remained scoreless until the bottom of the third, when Musial stepped to the plate with two outs, White on third and Boyer on second, both getting on base via walks and advancing on a groundout to first. Musial promptly sent an O'Dell pitch over the screen and onto the roof of the pavilion in right field to give his club a 3-0 lead.

The Giants got on the board in the fourth when Mays reached on a single and scored on Cepeda's two-out double to left in the fourth. The Cardinals responded in the fifth by pushing across a run on four singles in an inning in which Musial popped out to shortstop.

The Giants chased Cardinals starter Simmons in the sixth by bunching two singles, a Harvey Kuenn double, and a Cepeda triple, which tied the game, 4-4. Ernie Broglio coaxed a flyout, with Cepeda tagging up and scoring the go-ahead run, before he issued a walk to Ed Bailey. Manager Solly Hemus pulled Broglio for Craig Anderson, a 6-foot-2 reliever called up from Portland of the Pacific Coast League the previous day. The 22-year-old right-hander was making his major-league debut. With one out, Bailey was caught stealing second before Anderson ended the inning by striking out O'Dell. But the Giants led 5-4.

The Cardinals tied the game in the bottom of the inning, with Boyer scoring on a double by Charlie James. Stu Miller came in to walk Musial intentionally. He then walked Curt Flood before ending the inning by inducing McCarver to pop out to Cepeda at first.

In the seventh, the Cardinals retook the lead on back-to-back doubles by Anderson, in his first major-league at-bat, and Julio Gotay. A single by White chased Miller, who was replaced by righty Bobby Bolin. The new reliever intentionally walked Boyer before fanning James.

Next, Musial came to the plate with the bases loaded and two outs. A *St. Louis Post-Dispatch* photographer captured the veteran completing his swing, an image that appeared in the paper the next day. It showed Musial erect, the result of a fluid swing whose grace belied the power behind it, his left foot pivoting on the toes, his right foot bent slightly to the outside from the torque, his upper hand leaving the bat in the follow-through, his mouth open as his 40-year-old eyes followed the trajectory of the ball over the head of right fielder Kuenn toward the fence and, beyond that, the stands. "I didn't hit the second one real good, and I thought it would just hit the screen," Musial said after the game.[1]

The ball landed in nearly the same spot as the first homer.[2] The grand slam was the ninth of Musial's career, giving him seven RBIs for the game. The blast also gave him 2,340 extra bases on long hits, as he surpassed Lou Gehrig on the all-time list (2,339), trailing only Babe Ruth (2,926). (Musial had once recorded seven RBIs in a spring-training game against the Philadelphia Phillies on March 23, 1954, on a homer, triple, and a single. He also recorded seven RBIs in a doubleheader sweep of the Chicago Cubs on May 27, 1956.) Carl Warwick replaced Musial in the field for the next inning, as the Cardinals won, 10-5. Anderson earned the win in his debut, while Miller suffered his first loss of the season against six wins.

After the game Musial insisted he was not considering an imminent retirement. "I don't feel any older than, say, seven years ago when I hit five homers in a doubleheader off the Giants," he told a reporter.[3] Musial recorded nine RBIs in those games on May 2, 1954.

St. Louis manager Hemus was hopeful the victory would spark the Cards. "A big win can make a turning point," he said. "It's not just that Musial hit the grand slammer. He doesn't surprise you when he does anything. People get to expect it, because he's so great. The new momentum goes to everything we did right, especially getting a relief pitcher to come in and stop them."[4]

In the Giants clubhouse, manager Alvin Dark was asked his opinion of Musial's work after the two-homer, seven-RBI performance. "He sure can hit 'em, can't he?" Dark said, echoing what managers had been saying about Stan the Man for 20 years.[5]

The outfielder got the next day off, standard practice for the veteran when a day game followed a night game. Musial posed on the infield for teenage photographers before the game as part of a Camera Day promotion.

Hemus's optimism turned out to be misplaced. The Cardinals won just three of their next 11 games and Hemus was fired on July 6, replaced by his lieutenant, Johnny Keane, a St. Louis-born career minor leaguer who days later would make an example of pitcher Mickey McDermott by releasing him after he missed a bedcheck before a doubleheader in San Francisco. (At the same time as the change in manager was announced, second baseman Red Schoendienst was made a playing coach. He'd replace Keane as manager after the Cards won the 1964 World Series.) The Cardinals improved their play considerably over the rest of the season, finishing 80-74, but managed to overtake only the Pittsburgh Pirates in the standings, finishing fifth, 13 games behind the Reds.

SOURCES

In addition to the sources listed in the Notes, the author consulted the *St. Louis Post-Dispatch*, the *Oakland Tribune*, the *Daily Capital* (Jefferson City, Missouri), the *Hayward* (California) *News*, *The Sporting News*, and Retrosheet.org.

NOTES

1 "Ailing Musial Rocks Giants With Grand Slam and 3-Run Homer," *St. Louis Post-Dispatch*, June 24, 1961: 6.
2 "Giants Losing String Hits 4," *Oakland Tribune*, June 24, 1961: 11.
3 "Cards Gain Steam," *Oakland Tribune*, June 24, 1961: 11.
4 "Cards Gain Steam."
5 "Cards Gain Steam."

MUSIAL HOMERS IN FOUR CONSECUTIVE AT-BATS VS. METS

July 8, 1962: St. Louis Cardinals 15, New York Mets 1, at Polo Grounds V, New York

BY PAUL HOFMANN

A Sunday afternoon crowd of 12,460 came to watch an aging superstar and the St. Louis Cardinals take on the New York Mets in the final game of a four-game series at the Polo Grounds. The Mets had taken the first two games of the series and the Cardinals won the third.

The temperature reached 93 degrees, 10 degrees warmer than the average temperature for July 8. The wind was out of the south-southwest blowing at 10-15 MPH.[1]

The Cardinals entered play in fifth place with a record of 46-38, 9½ games behind the front-running San Francisco Giants. The Mets were in the middle of the franchise's dismal inaugural season and started play in last place, 31 games off the pace with a record of 23-58.

Twenty-six-year-old right-hander Bob Gibson started for the Cardinals. The 1957 graduate of Creighton University was 9-6 with a 3.20 ERA. He was opposed by right-hander Jay Hook, who was drafted from the Cincinnati Reds in the 1961 expansion draft. He was 6-8 with a 5.70 ERA and had only lasted two-thirds of an inning in his previous start.

The game started with back-to-back comebackers to Hook by Curt Flood and Julian Javier and it seemed the Mets were going to have an easy first inning. Bill White spoiled this plan when he hit a home run to deep right field. It was White's 15th home run of the season, and the Cardinals took a 1-0 lead. That brought Stan Musial, the aging superstar, to the plate.

Musial entered the game with a .325 batting average, 9 home runs, and 37 RBIs, representing a resurgence for the seven-time batting champion, who had not hit .300 since 1958. A day earlier he hit an eighth-inning, game-winning home run in game two of a doubleheader off right-hander Craig Anderson to give the Cardinals a 3-2 victory. The solo home run to deep right field came in Musial's last at-bat of the day.

Picking up where he left off a day earlier, Musial followed White's home run with a blast of his own to right field. It was Musial's 10th home run of the season and gave the Cardinals a 2-0 lead. Hook struck out third baseman Ken Boyer to end the inning. Gibson retired the Mets in the top of the first, giving up only a walk to Gene Woodling.

Hook retired the Cardinals in order in the top of the second and Gibson navigated his way out of trouble when the Mets put runners on second and third with two outs in the bottom of the inning.

Gibson dispelled any notion that the game might be developing into a pitchers' duel when he led off the third inning with a home run to left. It was Gibson's first homer of the season and the second of his 24 career home runs.

Flood followed Gibson's blast with a single to left and proceeded to steal second base. He moved to third on Javier's fly out to center field. White struck out and Musial followed with a walk.[2] With runners on first and third, Boyer came to the plate and drove in Flood with an infield single to shortstop. Carl Sawatski grounded out to third to end the inning. The Cardinals were now leading 4-0.

Gibson walked Richie Ashburn and hit Rod Kanehl to start the bottom of the third. Woodling grounded back to the mound, moving Ashburn and Kanehl up a base. Gibson then retired Frank Thomas on a popout to first and Sammy Taylor on a liner to second to end the inning.

The Mets melted down defensively in the top of the fourth. With one out, Dal Maxvill reached when Mets shortstop Felix Mantilla threw wild to first base; Maxvill reached second. Gibson hit an infield single to third and Maxvill scored on third baseman Thomas's throwing error that allowed Gibson to reach second. Javier grounded out to third, advancing Gibson to second. Thomas made his second error of the inning (and the Mets' third) on a groundball off the bat of Javier. Gibson scored to increase the Cardinals' lead to 6-0 as Javier took second. White's double to left-center drove in Javier, and Musial followed with his second home run of the day, to deep right, to give the Cardinals a 9-0 lead. All five Cardinal runs in the inning were unearned.

Marv Throneberry led off the bottom of the fourth with a single to left field before Gibson retired the next three batters to keep the Mets scoreless.

Left-hander Willard Hunter relieved Hook in the top of the fifth. The Mets had acquired Hunter on May 25 as a player to be named later in a trade made with the Los Angeles Dodgers the previous December. Hunter, who was making his eighth appearance of the season for the Mets and was 1-4 with a gaudy 8.83 ERA, retired the Cardinals in order in the fifth.

The score remained 9-0 until the top of the seventh. Musial, who had hit a home run in each of his three previous at-bats, led off the inning with a home run to right field, his third of the day and fourth in as many at-bats over the past two days, tying a major-league record.[3] The moment was extra-special for Musial as his wife, Lil, and daughter Janet were in first-row box seats. Musial remembered the "warm glow" he felt as he stepped on home plate after the homer.[4] (Lil was not in attendance the only other time he hit three home runs in a game.[5])

Musial first hit a trio of homers in the first game of a doubleheader against the New York Giants at Busch Stadium on May 2, 1954.[6] At 41 years and 229 days old, Musial became the oldest major leaguer with a three-homer game.[7]

Boyer followed with a single to center but was stranded at first after Hunter retired the next three Cardinals. The score was now 10-0.

Gibson walked center fielder Joe Christopher and pinch-hitter Gil Hodges to lead off the bottom of the seventh. However, just as he had in previous innings, he kept the Mets off the scoreboard, this time retiring Ashburn, Kanehl, and Woodling.

Former Cardinal Bob Miller came in to pitch the eighth inning after Hunter was lifted for Hodges in the bottom of the seventh. The right-handed Miller was winless (0-7) with a 4.94 ERA. With one out, Flood singled to center, his third hit of the game. After Javier struck out for the second out, Fred Whitfield, who had replaced White at first base in the bottom of the fourth, hit a two-run homer to left that extended the Cardinals lead to 12-0. Musial came to the plate with a chance to hit his fourth home run of the game and fifth in a row. He struck out on a pitch in the dirt but reached first when the ball eluded the catcher.[8] Bobby Smith came in to run for Musial. Miller then struck out Boyer to end the inning.

In an interview after the game, Musial acknowledged that he knew had a chance at history. "I heard the public address announcer tell the crowd I had four in a row when I came up in the eighth. But I really couldn't get too worked up about it," he said.[9]

Gibson retired the Mets in order in the bottom of the eighth before the Cardinals added three more runs in the top of the ninth. With one out, Charlie James tripled to left-center and Julio Gotay, who had replaced Maxvill at short, was hit by a pitch to put runners on the corners for Gibson, who singled to center, scoring James and moving Gotay to second. Flood reached on an error by second baseman Kanehl that allowed Gotay to score the Cardinals' 14th run. Whitfield's single to left drove in Gibson to make the score 15-0. Smith ended the inning with a fly out to left.

The only question remaining was whether Gibson would shut out the Mets. Mantilla tripled to left-center to lead off the bottom of the ninth. Christopher grounded out to second to

A veteran Stan Musial gets in a few practice swings.

score the Mets' lone run. Cliff Cook pinch-hit for Miller and struck out, then Ashburn ended the game with a fly out to center.

Gibson improved his record to 10-6, lowered his ERA to 3.05, and was named to his first All-Star team. Hook took the loss and dropped to 6-9. The time of the game was 2 hours 47 minutes.

Afterward, a throng of Little Leaguers chanted, "We want Stan."[10] After obliging his young fans with autographs, Musial and his family went to Washington, where he played in his 19th All-Star Game and met President John F. Kennedy.[11]

SOURCES

In addition to the sources cited in the Notes, the author relied on Baseball-reference.com and Retrosheet.org.

https://www.baseball-reference.com/boxes/NYN/NYN196207080.shtml

https://www.retrosheet.org/boxesetc/1962/B07080NYN1962.htm

NOTES

1. "New York City, NY Weather History: July 8, 1962," retrieved on September 2, 2023, from www.wunderground.com/history/daily/KLGA/date/1962-7-8.

2. Because walks are not at-bats, Musial's streak of consecutive at-bats with a home run remained intact.

3. As of 2024 a player has hit home runs in four consecutive at-bats 36 times. Six players have accomplished the feat in one game, 27 have done it over two games, two did it over three games, and Ted Williams did it over four games. Two players have done it twice, Ralph Kiner (both times in two games) and Mike Schmidt (once in one game and once in two games). Mickey Mantle accomplished the feat two days before Musial. Reggie Jackson is the only player to do it in postseason play, in the 1977 World Series.

4. James N. Giglio. *Musial: From Stash to Stan the Man* (Columbia, Missouri: University of Missouri Press, 2001), 260-261.

5. Joseph Stanton, *Baseball's All-time Greatest Hitters: Stan Musial* (Westport, Connecticut: Greenwood Press, 2007), 100.

6. Musial hit two more in game two of the doubleheader, becoming the first player in baseball history to collect five home runs in a doubleheader. The feat has been matched only once since, in 1972 by the San Diego Padres' Nate Colbert.

7. "Stan Musial Stats." Baseball Almanac, retrieved on September 3, 2023, from www.baseball-almanac.com/players/player.php?p=musias01. As of the 2024 season, Musial was still the oldest major leaguer with a three-homer game.

8. Jack Herman, "Stan Hits 3 Homers in 15-1 Romp," *St. Louis Globe-Democrat*, July 9, 1962: 19.

9. "Mighty Musial Fans in Bid for 5 Homers in a Row," *Troy* (New York) *Times Record*, July 9, 1962: 30.

10. Herman.

11. Giglio, 261.

STAN MUSIAL'S FIVE HITS HIGHLIGHT DAY AS CARDINALS DEFEAT GIANTS

September 27, 1962: St. Louis Cardinals 7, San Francisco Giants 4, at Candlestick Park, San Francisco

BY ALAN COHEN

"It was just another one of his usual days. I got over being amazed at him 10 years ago."
– Ken Boyer, speaking of Stan Musial, September 27, 1962[1]

"I'll just have to try to stroke the ball to left field. O'Dell has good breaking stuff."
– Stan Musial, September 27, 1962[2]

A late September afternoon game on an overcast day at Candlestick Park attracted only 6,812 fans as the San Francisco Giants, looking to somehow close the gap with the front-running Los Angeles Dodgers, hosted the Cardinals. The Giants started Billy O'Dell (19-13), the former Oriole who had paid big dividends since being acquired before the season. The Cardinals countered with Ray Washburn (11-9).

Stan Musial could have taken the day off against the lefty pitcher, but he was in the lineup. At age 41, he had played in 131 of his team's games and was sporting a .325 batting average.

The Giants were showing more than a bit of nervousness. They had spent much of the first two months of the season in first place and led the league as recently as July 1, but the Dodgers had moved past them and were poised to win the pennant. As play began on September 27, the Giants were on the brink of elimination, two games back with four games to play. The magic number was three.

The game was deemed "a lousy but thrilling exhibition" by Harry Jupiter of the *San Francisco Examiner*.[3]

Giants manager Al Dark elected to go with a lineup that maximized offense and minimized defense. He had Willie McCovey in left field and Harvey Kuenn at third base.

The Cardinals did not overwhelm the Giants. They just kept pecking away, and the jabs began in the first inning. Singles by Curt Flood to left field and Musial to right field were sandwiched by a pair of outs, and Bill White came to the plate. Seeing Kuenn playing deeper than necessary at third, the lefty-hitting first baseman laid down a bunt that would do Phil Rizzuto proud for a single. Flood scored from third and Musial advanced to second. Charlie James then singled to left field, scoring Musial.

In the bottom of the second, the Giants wasted a leadoff double by McCovey. After Orlando Cepeda walked and Tom Haller flied out, José Pagán hit into a double play.

In the top of the third, after Willie Mays had robbed Flood of a hit with a sensational shoestring catch, Musial singled to left field, but he was left stranded. The Cardinals added another run in the fourth inning. Gene Oliver doubled and advanced to third when Kuenn misplayed Dal Maxvill's grounder. Washburn singled home Oliver, but Julián Javier hit into his second inning-ending double play of the game. The score was 3-0.

Musial came up with one out in the fifth inning and stroked his third consecutive single. After O'Dell retired Ken Boyer for the second out of the inning, White advanced Musial to third with a single and James got his second RBI of the game, singling Musial home. Dark decided a pitching change was in order and brought in righty Don Larsen of World Series fame. Gene Oliver hit Larsen's third pitch over the left-field fence to give the Cardinals a 7-0 lead.

Washburn was mowing down the Giants, scattering four hits through five innings. In the fifth, he had gotten Carl Boles (hitting for Larsen), Kuenn, and Chuck Hiller on successive groundouts. The sixth inning was a different story.

"I just didn't know how many were out."
– Willie Mays, September 27, 1962[4]

In the sixth inning, with the Giants trailing 7-0, Matty Alou singled and came home on a double by Mays, who had so far in the game been hitless. With McCovey and Cepeda due up, there was a chance for the Giants to close the gap further. McCovey grounded out to second, advancing Mays to third. Then, after Cepeda struck out (the second of his three strikeouts in the game), Mays, thinking there were three out, headed toward center field and was picked off as Boyer at third took the throw from Cardinals catcher Oliver and made the easy tag.[5]

In the top of the seventh, as the Giant fans were flabbergasted over Mays' poor play, Musial came up for the fourth time, leading off the inning. Once again, he stroked a single to left field, but the Cardinals did not capitalize. Giants pitcher Jim Duffalo, in his second inning of work, stranded Musial and White.

Giant fans were mumbling, "What if Mays hadn't blundered?" as the Giants reached Washburn for three quick runs in the seventh. Haller walked, Pagán singled, and Ed Bailey, batting for Duffalo, homered. The Giants trailed 7-4, but they could not close the gap further. Washburn was, at that point, out of gas. He interspaced two fly-ball outs with two walks and the Giants had the tying run at the plate. Cardinals manager Johnny Keane decided it was time for a pitching change and brought in veteran lefty Bobby Shantz. Dark countered with a pinch-hitter, calling on right-hand-hitting Felipe Alou to bat for McCovey. Alou forced Mays, who had walked, at second base, and the game moved to the eighth inning.

The concept of baseball being a contact game, bat on ball, essentially vanished at this point. Stu Miller came in to pitch for the Giants and retired the Cardinals on two strikeouts and a comebacker. Shantz struck out the side in the bottom of the eighth.

The crowd by this point had accepted that the Giants were about to fall short and be virtually eliminated from the pennant race. Their attention turned to the man in the on-deck circle as the ninth inning began. Stu Miller began his second inning of relief and promptly retired Flood. Up came Musial, the crowd fully aware that he was going for a 5-for-5 day. None of the sportswriters knew when he had last done it. Even Musial did not know. It was no wonder, as Musial had most recently gone 5-for-5 on September 22, 1948. Only once in his seven previous five-hit games had he hit five singles in a game (June 22, 1948). That was about to change.

Even against the slow-throwing Miller, Musial was determined to stroke the ball to left field (only one of his hits that day had been to right field), and when he singled for the fifth time, it was to left field. Manager Keane called for a pinch-runner, Bobby Gene Smith, and Musial left the field to a standing ovation with several fans reaching out to shake his hand.[6] Musial headed not to the clubhouse but to the Cardinals bullpen down the right-field line at the end of the dugout.[7]

Miller proceeded to retire the Cardinals without a run scoring in the ninth, and the Giants were left with three outs in which to score three runs. After Cap Peterson, batting for Miller, struck out, Kuenn doubled to left field and Hiller had an infield hit, advancing Kuenn to third. Matty Alou flied to short center field. Mays came to the plate with runners on the corners and two men out. He represented the tying run. Shantz got him to swing at an off-speed curve for strike three and the game was over.

Washburn was credited with the win and O'Dell took the loss. Shantz earned his fourth save of the season.

The Giants were 2½ games out of first and a Koufax win that night would take the magic number to one. But the Dodgers defense failed Koufax, and the Giants went into the last three games down by two in the standings. At the end of 162 games, the teams were tied as Gene Oliver, who had doubled and homered against the Giants on Musial's big day, homered against the Dodgers on the last day of the season. The Giants prevailed in the three-game playoff and advanced to the World Series.

Musial's 5-for-5 garnered the headlines and raised his batting average to .333. It was the eighth and last time he had five hits in a game. He wound up third in the batting race, trailing only Tommy Davis and Frank Robinson.

It was pointed out by Sam Balter in the *Los Angeles Herald-Examiner* that Musial, to this point, was the only player with both 3,000 hits and 400 homers.[8] Over time, he would be joined by several others, including Willie Mays.

Mays, who contributed to his team's loss by being picked off due to absent-mindedness and striking out due to misjudgment, had this to say about Musial's performance:

"If you got to lose, lose on a day when Stan Musial is going five-for-five. I was glad to see him do it, that fifth time up. It makes me feel good to see such a great athlete keep giving the fans a thrill. I just hope I'm doing half as well a few years from now."[9]

SOURCES

In addition to the sources shown in the notes, the author used Retrosheet.org and Baseball-Reference.com.

https://www.baseball-reference.com/players/gl.fcgi?id=musiast01&t=b&year=1962

https://www.retrosheet.org/boxesetc/1962/B09270SFN1962.htm

NOTES

1 Harry Jupiter, "Stan Says Long Ball Costly; No Chance for Batting Title," *San Francisco Examiner*, September 28, 1962: 62.

2 Bob Broeg, "Musial's 5-for-5 Day Cools Giant Hopes," *St. Louis Post-Dispatch*, September 28, 1962: 4C.

3 Harry Jupiter, "Musial Goes 5 for 5; Mays' 'Skull' Hurts," *San Francisco Examiner*, September 28, 1962: 61.

4 Scott Bailie (United Press International), "Musial Cards deliver Serious Loss to SF," *Barstow* (California) *Desert Dispatch*, September 28, 1962: 4.

5 Milton Richman (United Press International), "Do They Really Want to Win? SF, LA Lose," *Oroville* (California) *Mercury-Register*, September 28, 1962: 8.

6 Jack Hanley, "Musial Softens Giant Loss," *San Jose* (California) *News*, September 28, 1962: 19.

7 Bob Stevens, "S.F. Rally Short as Cards Win," *San Francisco Chronicle*, September 28, 1962: 43, 45.

8 Sam Balter, "One for the Book," *Los Angeles Herald-Examiner*, September 28, 1962: C-4.

9 George Ross, "Who's on Third," *Oakland Tribune*, September 28, 1962: 36.

NEW GRANDFATHER STAN MUSIAL MAKES HOME-RUN HISTORY WITH SURGING CARDINALS

September 10, 1963: St. Louis Cardinals 8, Chicago Cubs 0 at Busch Stadium, St. Louis

BY ANDREW HARNER

More than 70 former major-league players gathered for Old Timers' Day at Busch Stadium on September 10, 1963, giving a Tuesday night crowd plenty of grandfathers to root for. And while the 1½-inning exhibition game undoubtedly delighted fans,[1] the 13,883 patrons on hand really wanted to see the newest grandfather of them all – Stan Musial of the red-hot St. Louis Cardinals.

The weary 42-year-old – feeling exhausted, yet exuberant – had become a grandfather only about 15 hours before slugging the first pitch he saw from 27-year-old Chicago Cubs veteran Glen Hobbie onto the pavilion roof in right field, making his 474th career home run one to remember and opening the floodgates on an 8-0 victory that kept the Cardinals in the thick of the pennant chase.

"I can't ever remember a major-league grandfather hitting a home run," said 51-year-old Cardinals manager Johnny Keane, who broke into professional baseball in 1930. "What a way to celebrate a grandson."[2]

One night earlier, Musial collected a single in three at-bats as the Cardinals shut out the Cubs 6-0 in a game that ended around 10:30 P.M. Afterward, Musial and his wife of 23 years, Lil, anxiously kept each other company in their modest ranch home on Westway Road in the St. Louis Hills neighborhood. They awaited a long-distance phone call from their son, Richard, an Army lieutenant stationed at Fort Riley, Kansas. The couple knew that call would most likely let them know they had become grandparents, so going to sleep did not seem like a viable option, even for an aging ballplayer weeks away from retirement. But as the clock ticked in slow circles and the phone never rang, the Musials eventually relented and went to sleep around 1:30 A.M. A few hours later, something – a premonition, perhaps – abruptly woke them both.

"Lil and I awakened with a start at exactly the same time – 4:40 A.M. – and got up, troubled," Stan said. "As she brewed coffee, I paced the floor. Suddenly, the phone rang. Son Dick was calling from Fort Riley, Kansas. Sharon had given birth to a boy. When? Just two minutes after Lil and I woke up."[3]

The Musials eventually fell back asleep after digesting the news of a 7-pound 15½-ounce baby boy named Jeffrey Stanton, but Stan's body likely would have preferred more sleep before trotting out to first base that night to face the Cubs again. Luckily, he secured a quick nap at the ballpark, and adrenaline seemed to kick in before home-plate umpire Vinnie Smith yelled, "Play ball!" on another crucial matchup in the Cardinals' last-season pennant push.

St. Louis had fallen seven games behind the Los Angeles Dodgers in the National League standings on August 30, but with an 11-6 victory over the Philadelphia Phillies that night, the Cardinals started an incredible stretch that eventually pushed them to within a game of their West Coast rivals. With triumphs in 12 of 13 games prior to September 10, St. Louis turned to right-hander Bob Gibson, now in his fifth season, to keep their winning ways intact against the Cubs. Chicago countered with the surging Hobbie, who had pitched 18 straight scoreless innings dating back to August 30 and had allowed only a single run in his past 27⅓ innings.

Lou Brock, then a 24-year-old outfielder in his second season with Chicago, led off the game with a single, but the next three batters could not get the ball out of the infield – a sign of how much of the night would go for the Cubs. In the bottom of the first, Dick Groat slashed a one-out single to bring Musial to the plate. Musial, who hit the first home run Hobbie surrendered in the majors on April 17, 1958, had struggled against the right-hander in the years since, collecting only 8 hits in 43 at-bats between 1959 and '62. But the excitement of the pennant chase and his expanding family seemed to light up Musial's eyes, and he knocked Hobbie's first offering into right field for a home run that *Sports Illustrated* suggested was proof that Musial was "even a perfectionist in his manner of celebration."[4]

"That one," Musial recalled of the first known major-league home run ever hit by a grandfather, "was for Jeffrey Stanton Musial."[5]

In the second, the Cardinals looked to strike again as Curt Flood singled and George Altman walked before Gibson stepped to the plate with a chance to aid his own cause. Gibson drove one of Hobbie's pitches to the first row of the left-field bleachers for his second home run in eight days to open a 5-0

An older Musial could look back on an outstanding big-league career.

lead. The rally, however, would not be complete until Grandpa Stan got back into the action.

Groat, who had returned to the lineup for the first time since getting hit by a pitch in the ribs on September 6, hit a two-out double[6] and scampered home when Musial greeted reliever Jim Brewer with an RBI single. Tim McCarver scored on Altman's sacrifice in the third, and with that 7-0 lead, Keane felt comfortable removing both the grimacing Groat and the bleary-eyed Musial from the game after they batted in the fourth inning.

"I was a tired, but happy grandfather as I passed the cigars in the clubhouse that night," said Musial, who shared his postgame celebration with 25-year-old September call-up Corky Withrow.[7] That morning, Withrow's wife, Barbara, had given birth to a son in Owensboro, Kentucky.

St. Louis continued the onslaught in the fifth, as Ken Boyer led off with a double and moved to third on Bill White's single. After Flood lined into an unassisted double play to first baseman Ernie Banks, McCarver poked an RBI single to give St. Louis an 8-0 advantage. Cubs reliever Jack Warner, making his first appearance since Chicago recalled him from the Salt Lake City Bees, finally cooled the St. Louis offense, holding the Cardinals without a hit over the final three innings.

Chicago threatened in the seventh after Jimmy Stewart and Brock singled and doubled in consecutive two-out at-bats, but Gibson induced a grounder to end the inning. That marked the only time the Cubs got a runner to third base as Gibson improved his career-high win total to 17 and tallied his second shutout of the season.[8]

Gibson's effort also helped mark the second year in a row that the Cardinals had shut out the Cubs in consecutive games, after also sweeping a doubleheader on June 27, 1962. And the torment did not stop there, as Ray Sadecki and Ron Taylor combined for a shutout the next day, and the Cubs did not score in the following game until the seventh inning for a 33-inning scoreless stretch. They had not suffered three straight shutouts since July 1950, while St. Louis had not shut out an opponent in three consecutive games since 1944.[9]

The Cardinals improved to 85-61 after earning their 13th win in 14 games but could not gain any ground on the Dodgers, who picked up a 4-2 win at Pittsburgh to protect their three-game lead in the standings. St. Louis's run of success eventually resulted in 19 wins in 20 games by September 15.

"The Cardinals' streak was the most incredible of my 22 years in the majors, not for sustained play as in 1942, but for spectacular results over a three-week period," Musial recalled. "Day after day, game after game, we'd rock the opposition at the outset so that they had to try to play catch-up.... St. Louis was pennant happy, and I know I felt like a kid."[10]

As the streaking Cardinals romped to a four-game sweep of the Cubs,[11] nerves fluttered inside Dodgers fans who feared their team would lose a late-season lead for a third straight season.

"Every year, the Dodgers lead the pack quietly into September, and when they turn around, there's always somebody on the stairs with a crooked grin silently patting a coffin and pointing. 'For you,' the specter says," wrote *Los Angeles Times* columnist Jim Murray. "It was the Reds in '61, the Giants last year. This year, it might be Stan Musial, of all people."[12]

The Cardinals, however, lost eight of their final 10 games, spoiling the chances of sending Musial out in style, but he still had a remarkable finish to his career. From the date of Jeffrey's birth until the end of the season, Musial hit .341 with 2 home runs over 16 games.

SOURCES

In addition to the sources cited in the Notes, the author consulted the Baseball-Reference.com, Stathead.com, and Retrosheet.org websites for pertinent materials and box scores. He also used information obtained from news coverage by the *St. Louis Post-Dispatch*, the *St. Louis Globe-Democrat*, and the *Chicago Tribune*.

https://www.baseball-reference.com/boxes/SLN/SLN196309100.shtml

https://www.retrosheet.org/boxesetc/1963/B09100SLN1963.htm

NOTES

1. Hank Arft, a 41-year-old former St. Louis Browns first baseman, slugged a grand slam as the squad of American League players won, 4-1. Other players in action included former Cardinals Terry Moore, Ray Sanders, Joe Medwick, and Heinie Mueller – a right fielder within days of turning 64.

2. Tom Pendergast (Associated Press), "Gibson Helps With Slugging," *Springfield* (Missouri) *Leader-Press*, September 11, 1963: 22.

3. Bob Broeg, *Stan Musial: "The Man's" Own Story as Told to Bob Broeg* (Garden City, New York: Doubleday & Company, Inc., 1964), 238.

4. Theodore M. O'Leary, "Last Time Around With Stan," *Sports Illustrated*, October 7, 1963: 20.

5. Broeg, 238.

6. At the time, Groat (.330) led Milwaukee's Henry Aaron (.324) and Los Angeles' Tommy Davis (.323) in the batting race. By season's end, Groat's average settled at .319 in his first season with the Cardinals, falling shy of Davis (.326) and Pittsburgh's Roberto Clemente (.320). Groat, the runner-up to Sandy Koufax in MVP voting, led the NL with 43 doubles, a career-high total.

7. Broeg, 238.

8. Gibson finished 1963 with a career-best 18-9 record, though he exceeded that win total in six of the next seven seasons.

9. The Cardinals shut out the Boston Braves three straight times on July 8 and 9, 1944, on the way to the World Series championship.

10. Broeg, 239.

11. Those losses sent Chicago to its longest losing streak of the season – six games. The Cubs finished seventh in standings at 82-80.

12. Jim Murray, "Ghostly Echoes," *Los Angeles Times*, September 12, 1963: 47. Despite the concerns, the Dodgers never lost their lead in the standings and swept the New York Yankees to win the World Series.

MUSIAL EQUALS TY COBB; SPAHN TAKES AN EARLY SHOWER

September 13, 1963: St. Louis Cardinals 7, Milwaukee Braves 0, at Busch Stadium, St. Louis

BY JEFF FINDLEY

Stan Musial's career was winding down. It was September of his final season, and his St. Louis Cardinals were making a late run toward the National League pennant, trailing the league-leading Los Angeles Dodgers by three games entering play on September 13, 1963.

Just 16 days earlier, at the close of play on August 28, the Cardinals were in third place and trailed the Dodgers by 6½ games. But a 15-1 record since then catapulted St. Louis into striking distance with 14 games left, and the third-place Milwaukee Braves coming to town for a four-game set.

Despite their proximity in the standings, the National League race was now a two-team affair, as the Braves languished 9½ games behind the Dodgers. Still, Milwaukee was a formidable roadblock, with a lineup featuring four future Hall of Famers[1] when Curt Simmons threw the opening pitch of the series for the Cardinals.

"It should be an interesting match," Cardinals manager Johnny Keane said before the game.[2]

Simmons surrendered a leadoff single to Roy McMillan, but any hint of an early rally disappeared for the Braves when Frank Bolling was retired and Henry Aaron struck out, with McMillan caught stealing on the pitch.

As the Cardinals came to bat, Milwaukee marched 42-year-old Warren Spahn to the mound. Spahn had won his eighth straight and 20th game of the season five days earlier in a complete-game 3-2 victory over the Philadelphia Phillies. It was the 13th time in his career that he had won 20 or more games in a season, and he became the oldest player to accomplish the feat, topping Cy Young's 21-win season at age 41 in 1908. The record still stood as of 2024.

Spahn downplayed the accomplishment.

"This means I've got a job next year," he commented. "No, I'm not kidding. Say I win 12 or 13. They've got a lot of young guys on this club who can do that, and they don't have to pay me what I get for that kind of performance."[3]

This outing wouldn't resemble his season's successes.

After Spahn retired Julián Javier and Dick Groat to start the game, Musial came to the plate. The pair had a storied history, facing each other 360 previous times, and despite the lefty-vs.-lefty matchup, Musial sported a .317 batting average against Spahn.

This at-bat mirrored Musial's previous success against the Braves hurler, as he doubled, his 22nd all-time against Spahn, and more importantly, the 725th regular-season two-bagger of his career, giving him the second-most of all-time, passing Ty Cobb.[4] Only Tris Speaker, with 792, had hit more doubles than Musial, who topped the National League in this category eight times with a career-high 53 in 1953.

Ken Boyer followed Musial by blasting a pitch into the outfield bleachers, staking St. Louis to a 2-0 lead. Future National League President Bill White flied out to right to end the inning.

The Spahn/Musial matchup was noted in the *St. Louis Post-Dispatch* game recap the next day, as Musial's double was the final time the pair would face each other.

"I never appreciated having to face Stan," Spahn said. "It seemed every time I wound up, he knew what I was going to throw. I have only one regret. I didn't find out how to pitch to him before I quit. I don't really think there is a way."[5]

In the second inning, Milwaukee answered with two baserunners, one reaching on an error by second baseman Javier and the other on a walk, but they failed to score.

The bottom of the second didn't go any better for Spahn.

Curt Flood singled and went to second when right fielder Aaron booted the ball. Charlie James followed with a single, scoring Flood. After Tim McCarver's sacrifice moved James to second, Simmons aided his own cause with a double, scoring James and chasing Spahn, who surrendered five earned runs on five hits in an inning and a third.

Hank Fischer replaced Spahn and gave up a single to Javier, scoring Simmons. Javier stole second before Groat struck out, but Musial collected his second hit of the day, a single that scored Javier and pushed the St. Louis margin to 6-0.

Boyer then singled and Braves manager Bobby Bragan substituted Dan Schneider for Fischer to face White, who drove in Musial with a single before Flood popped out to first to end the inning.

The Cardinals led 7-0, and all promise of a competitive matchup evaporated.

Despite the St. Louis offensive onslaught, it was Simmons's performance on the mound that stole the headlines. The left-hander scattered five hits, and with the exception of loading the bases in the Braves' seventh, the outcome was never in question. It was Simmons's third successive shutout and pushed his season record to 15-7.

"I don't remember ever doing that before," Simmons noted about the consecutive shutouts. "I had a slow curve, and it was a good one, so I used it."[6]

Roy McMillan tallied two hits for Milwaukee, but he was the Braves' lone bright spot. Future Hall of Famers Aaron, Eddie Mathews, and Joe Torre were a combined 0-for-12 for the Braves. Spahn, the other future Cooperstown member, was knocked out before he could record a plate appearance.

The Cardinals received multi-hit games from Javier, Musial, Boyer, and Flood. Every player in the starting lineup had at least one hit except Dick Groat, who was hitless in four at-bats. (Entering the game, Groat was leading the National League with a .331 batting average. He finished the season in a tie with Aaron for third in the league, trailing Tommy Davis, the leader at .326, and Roberto Clemente.)

The Cardinals gained a half-game on the Dodgers, who split a doubleheader with Philadelphia that day. They continued their surge, winning three more against the Braves and moving to within one game of the Dodgers on September 15. But the streak ended there, as St. Louis lost eight of the next 10 games and finished a distant six games behind National League champion Los Angeles.

Spahn pitched two additional seasons for three teams, adding 13 victories before retiring after the 1965 season at age 44.

And Musial, who became a grandfather[7] two days before passing Cobb's doubles total, wrapped up his career in St. Louis playing 12 additional games, including a single off Jim Maloney of the Cincinnati Reds, almost 20 years his junior, in his final at-bat. Musial never hit another double after that one against Spahn. (Pete Rose later passed Musial on the all-time doubles list with 746.)

Despite the Cardinals' failure to win the pennant in his final season, Musial still made an appearance in the 1963 World Series. As a guest of the New York Yankees, he threw out the first pitch in the World Series opener.[8]

SOURCES

In addition to the sources credited in the Notes, the author consulted Baseball-Reference.com, Retrosheet.org, SABR.org, and Stathead.com for information on players, teams, and seasons.

https://www.baseball-reference.com/boxes/SLN/SLN196309130.shtml

https://www.retrosheet.org/boxesetc/1963/B09130SLN1963.htm

NOTES

1   Hank Aaron (1982), Eddie Mathews (1978), Joe Torre (2014), and Warren Spahn (1973) are all members of the National Baseball Hall of Fame. Stan Musial, in the St. Louis lineup this day, was elected to the Hall in 1969.

2   "Old Pro Spahn Next Hurdle for Ambitious Red Birds," *St. Louis Globe-Democrat*, September 13, 1963: 15.

3   Bob Wolf, "Hats Off …!" *The Sporting News*, September 21, 1963: 21.

4   The double by Spahn broke a career tie with Ty Cobb, moving him into second place behind Tris Speaker, who had 792 in his career. Pete Rose later passed Musial, recording 746 in his career.

5   Neal Russo, "Simmons Pitches 3rd Consecutive Shutout," *St. Louis Post-Dispatch*, September 14, 1963: 6.

6   "Simmons Is a Card – He Can Hit," *Newsday* (Long Island, New York), September 14, 1963: 52.

7   "You Can Call Stan Musial Grandpa Now," *Des Moines Tribune*, September 10, 1963: 18.

8   "Stan to 'Hurl'," *New York Daily News*, September 29, 1963: 96.

STAN MUSIAL HITS HIS FINAL HOME RUN

September 16, 1963: Los Angeles Dodgers 3, St. Louis Cardinals 1, at Busch Stadium, St. Louis

BY CHRIS BETSCH

As the 1963 season approached mid-September, St. Louis Cardinals fans were growing cautiously optimistic over the possibility that their team might finally reach the postseason for the first time since 1946. But if the team was going to win the National League pennant, it was going to have to overtake the first-place Los Angeles Dodgers, who as of September 16 were one game ahead of the Cardinals. Naturally, the Cardinals faithful hoped to see a world championship brought back to St. Louis, but they especially hoped to see their hero Stan Musial play in the World Series one last time. Television commentator and former teammate Joe Garagiola expressed the feelings of the city: "If there's such a thing as justice … he's got to wind up in the World Series, and it goes seven games and Stan wins the last one with – with a five-run homer!"[1]

During the Cardinals' team summer picnic on August 12, Musial made the official announcement that the current season would be his last as a player and that he would take a role in the St. Louis front office.[2] Musial had considered retiring after 1962, but after batting .330 with 19 home runs and finishing 10th in the league MVP voting, he decided to come back for another year. The Cardinals welcomed Musial back in 1963 for his 22nd season,[3] but at the age of 42, he was not nearly as productive. At the time of the announcement, his batting average was .260 and he had only 9 home runs.

Musial's decision could be given at least some credit for the Cardinals' surge that followed. The team went on a tear starting on August 30 and won 19 of 20 games. On September 15 the Cardinals swept a doubleheader from the Milwaukee Braves,[4] their 9th and 10th wins in a row, and moved to within one game of first place. The Dodgers' supporters could understandably be getting nervous. They had been up by seven games as late as August 30, and concerns were arising that the team would repeat its epic collapse of the previous year. In 1962 the Dodgers were in first place from July 8 until September 30, when on the last day of the season their rivals, the San Francisco Giants, caught up to them. The Dodgers lost a best-of-three tiebreaker and had to watch the World Series from home. Now they had to travel to St. Louis for a three-game series that could either help cement their lead for the National League pennant or drop them to second place.

The Dodgers had held a tribute night for Musial on August 22 when the Cardinals were in town for their last appearance of the season. Over 48,000 fans gave Musial a standing ovation, while the Dodgers greeted him with handshakes and presented him with a plaque of appreciation.[5] But it was all business when the two teams met again on Monday, September 16, at St. Louis's Busch Stadium for a night game to start the three-game set. The Cardinals aimed to win at least two games of the series and come out in first place, with a chance to send "Stan the Man" out with one more World Series appearance and ideally a championship. But there were questions about how much Musial himself might be able to contribute. Heading into that weekend, Musial had hit only three home runs since the beginning of June. Fans had to be quietly wondering if he might ever hit another round-tripper or if 474 would be his final career total.[6]

St. Louis's largest home crowd of the year, 34,442, packed into Busch Stadium for the first game of the series. Dodgers fans back in Los Angeles would be glued to their television sets at 8 P.M. CST to watch the game on KTTV, the first time that season that the station televised any games outside of a handful of matchups with the rival Giants in San Francisco.[7] The Dodgers looked to southpaw Johnny Podres to get them off to a good start in the series opener. He would oppose Cardinals righty Ernie Broglio.

Before the game started, Dodgers manager Walter Alston, along with coach Leo Durocher and pitcher Don Drysdale, approached the umpires protesting that the grounds crew had the pitcher's mound built up higher than the regulation 15 inches. They presumed such an alteration was ordered by Cardinals manager Johnny Keane to aid Broglio, who pitched with an overhead delivery. The umpires measured the height of the mound and found that it met league specifications, and the game could begin.

The Dodgers started the offense in the second inning when catcher Johnny Roseboro drove a shot off the right-field screen that he legged out for a two-out triple, or so he thought. Broglio was ready to go into his windup for the next batter when he noticed his teammates in the dugout frantically waving their arms to get his attention. They saw that Roseboro had missed second base on his way to third and were yelling for the pitcher to appeal the play. Broglio tossed the ball over to shortstop Dick Groat, who was standing ready at second. Umpire Ed Sudol had also witnessed the miscue, and he called Roseboro out on the appeal to end the inning.

Podres did not allow a single baserunner through the first five innings. Broglio likewise had a shutout in place through the fifth, but the Dodgers finally got on the board in the sixth inning when Tommy Davis singled to center field and knocked in Maury Wills with the first run of the game. Podres had a perfect game going into the sixth inning, and now had a 1-0 lead to work with. After Groat was retired on a grounder back to Podres to start the seventh, it looked as if the Cardinals could have another scoreless inning ahead. Stan Musial was 0-for-2, but the fans still buzzed with anticipation, as they did every time he stepped to the plate. Podres tossed the first pitch of the at-bat low and outside for a ball. Musial crouched into his familiar batting stance and awaited the next pitch. Podres figured Musial would be looking for another outside pitch and instead threw a fastball high and inside.[8] Musial sprang forward and turned into the pitch, sending a line drive over the fence and nearly onto the roof of the ballpark's right-field pavilion. With one swing Musial tied the game, 1-1, and sent the home crowd into a frenzy. Joyful screaming and yelling from the stands resonated throughout the ballpark as Musial rounded the bases. Musial remembered the event well in a biography that was published a year later. "I hit my last major league home run, No. 475, a line shot to the pavilion roof, tying the score, and I thought the fans would tear down the park with joy."[9]

The St. Louis fans knew that with Musial's retirement on the horizon, this might be the last time they would see him take a home-run trot. The noise from the crowd was still deafening as Musial arrived back at home plate and shook hands with Ken Boyer, and it continued into Boyer's at-bat. After Boyer popped out for the second out, Bill White reached first on an error by Wills. Center fielder Curt Flood then singled, and the Cards thought they might have their first rally of the game going. Alston made a visit to the mound that let Podres catch his breath and settle down, and the pitcher induced Charlie James to fly out, ending the threat.

Broglio left the game when fellow pitcher Bob Gibson pinch-hit for him in the eighth inning, and he was replaced on the mound by lefty Bobby Shantz. Shantz's outing was a short one; he was pulled by Keane after the Dodgers took the lead with a run on two hits and a walk in a third of an inning. (He was also charged with the Dodgers' third run.) The Cardinals didn't score again after Musial's solo shot, and Shantz took the loss. Podres struck out six and allowed one run on only three hits over eight innings to earn the win. If Keane had instructed the grounds crew to alter the mound before the game, it wound up working in Podres' favor. The home run given up to Musial was the only mistake the pitcher made during the game. "I've always had trouble getting him out so, much as I admire him, I'll be glad when he retires," Podres said.[10]

The Cardinals' 10-game win streak was over, as was their 16-game win streak at Busch Stadium. St. Louis still hoped to win the next two games and come out of the series tied for first, but the season took a downturn. They were swept by Los Angeles and lost eight of their final 10 games. They still finished in second place, but ultimately fell six games back from the pennant-winning Dodgers. Musial had seven hits over eight games after his round-tripper on September 16. But that home run, number 475 for the future Hall of Famer, would be his last. St. Louis fans did get to see the Cardinals win another World Series in 1964, but sadly it was done without the beloved Stan Musial on the field.

SOURCES

In addition to the sources cited in the Notes, the author consulted Baseball-Reference.com, Newspapers.com, and YouTube.

https://www.baseball-reference.com/boxes/SLN/SLN196309160.shtml

https://www.youtube.com/watch?v=HwHsZyF_30w

NOTES

1 Red Smith, "Garagiola: It Just Has to Be," *St. Louis Post-Dispatch*, September 17, 1963: 15.

2 Neal Russo, "'I've Had My Share of Baseball,' Says Musial," *St. Louis Post-Dispatch*, August 13, 1963: 24.

3 The 22 years do not count the 1945 season, which Musial spent in the US Navy during World War II.

4 The sweep of the Braves was hardly the most important event to occur the day before Musial's last home-run game. On the morning of September 15, a bomb exploded at a predominantly Black church in Birmingham, Alabama, killing four young girls and injuring many others. The devastating event helped draw national attention to the growing civil rights movement.

5 Bob Speck, "L.A. Stops The Man, but Not His Cards," *Los Angeles Evening Citizen News*, August 23, 1963: 20.

6 When he retired, Musial ranked behind only Mel Ott's 511 home runs for the all-time National League career lead.

7 "Drysdale Raps 'Choke' Charge," *St. Louis Post-Dispatch*, September 17, 1963: 14.

8 "L.A. Confident After Taking Series Opener at St. Louis," *Pomona (California) Progress-Bulletin*, September 17, 1963: 16.

9 Bob Broeg, *Stan Musial: The Man's Own Story* (Garden City, New York: Doubleday and Company, 1964), 239-240.

10 L.A. Confident After Taking Series Opener at St. Louis."

STAN MUSIAL'S FINAL GAME

September 29, 1963: St. Louis Cardinals 3, Cincinnati Reds 2, at Busch Stadium, St. Louis

BY JOE SCHUSTER

There was symmetry to the first weeks of Stan Musial's career in September 1941 and the last weeks 22 autumns later: Both saw the St. Louis Cardinals chasing the Dodgers for the pennant. Both saw them fall short but in each case, despite having the nucleus in place that would help them win the World Series the following season.

Even Musial's first and last games echoed one another: In both, Musial had two hits and drove in crucial runs in contests that ended in identical 3-2 Cardinal walk-off wins..

In between lay one of the finest baseball careers ever. By the time he played the last of his 3,026 games, Musial had been an All-Star in all but his first full season, 1942. He had collected a then-league-record 3,630 hits. Although his 475 home runs seem modest today, when he retired they ranked second in the National League, behind only Mel Ott's 511. All in all, when he retired as a player, Musial held 17 major-league and 29 National League records.[1]

By the time Musial made the formal announcement that he was retiring, he had been considering it for quite a while. He had publicly floated the idea in 1958, when he signed the National League's first $100,000 contract, saying that he saw himself playing "one or two more years."[2] In the offseason after 1962 – when Musial had something of a career second wind, hitting .330 after three consecutive uncharacteristic seasons of sub-.300 averages – he actually found himself in the middle of a controversy about the subject. That fall, Cardinals owner August A. Busch Jr. hired legendary baseball executive Branch Rickey as a senior consultant to general manager Bing Devine.[3] Almost immediately, Rickey – someone used to pulling the strings and not merely suggesting which strings someone else should pull – ended up in a power struggle with Devine that created "[a] schism … so deep that both seriously considered quitting."[4] One of Rickey's most drastic declarations was that Musial should retire to make way for younger players but Busch was quick to quash the notion: "Since when do you ask a .330 hitter to retire…?"[5]

Early in 1963 it became evident that Rickey may have been correct: By mid-May, Musial was hitting .215. By the All-Star break, his average was up to .279 but despite the mild offensive surge, he began to recognize this would be his final season. Selected for the National League squad as a reserve, he later said, "I knew, in my heart, that this would be my last All-Star appearance."[6]

Musial made his official announcement at the team's annual picnic at Busch's estate, Grant's Farm, on August 12, saying, "I figured on quitting, no matter what kind of year I had. … After all, I'll be 43 next season and I feel I've had more than my share from baseball."[7]

For a while it seemed to energize the team: Six games behind the Dodgers the day of the picnic, they went 27-8 over the next five weeks, pulling within one. However, a late September 1-8 stretch pushed the team seven back by the time of Musial's finale on September 29.

His departure was marked with tribute after tribute: Nationally, ABC aired a special that evening celebrating his career.[8] In St. Louis, the *Post-Dispatch* ran a five-page photographic feature in its Sunday magazine supplement; radio station KMOX, which broadcast Cardinals games, did an hour-long program about Musial before the game, while two St. Louis television channels also ran features about him.[9]

In the ballpark, before a standing-room-only crowd, a pregame ceremony included a jazz band and speeches by team officials, media figures, the presidents of the National and American Leagues, and Commissioner Ford Frick, who famously declared of Musial, "Here stands baseball's happy warrior, here stands baseball's perfect knight."[10] After the speeches, Musial toured the ballpark in a convertible while fans tossed confetti.[11]

The game itself carried little weight. Win or lose, the Cardinals were assured of second place, as they stood five games in front of third-place San Francisco; their opponents, the Cincinnati Reds, came in 13 games behind the Dodgers, tied with Philadelphia for fourth place. On the mound were future Hall of Famer Bob Gibson, 18-9 as the day began, and Jim Maloney, 23-7, whose 254 strikeouts stood second to eventual Cy Young Award winner Sandy Koufax's 306.

Both pitchers were sharp early and the game remained scoreless through five. To that point, Gibson had six strikeouts and no walks, while the only hit he had surrendered was a leadoff single by rookie Pete Rose. Maloney struck out eight Cardinals through five innings, giving up two walks and a single by Musial in the fourth that just eluded Rose at second base.[12]

The Cards finally broke through in what turned out to be an emotional sixth inning. Curt Flood led off with a double. After

Dick Groat struck out, Musial came to the plate for what would be his final at-bat. He fouled off the first pitch, took two balls, and then lined a curveball past first baseman Gordy Coleman, who dove for the ball but couldn't snag it. Musial's single drove in Flood, giving St. Louis a 1-0 lead.[13]

The crowd's cheers shifted to boos as manager Johnny Keane sent Gary Kolb to pinch-run for Musial. Before the game Keane had promised Musial would play most of it so he would "go out on a good note, not a popup," and an RBI single was that note.[14] To a resounding ovation, Musial jogged off the field for the last time as a player and went to the clubhouse to wait for the final out. There, he slipped off his iconic number-6 jersey for the last time as a player and hung it up, pausing for a moment to touch his name above the number, and said, "If I do say so myself, pal, you're all right."[15]

In a way, it was as if no one else wanted it to end. The Cards added a second run in the sixth on singles by Ken Boyer and Bill White.

The lead held in the seventh and eighth innings, though the Reds put two runners on in both innings, and the Cardinals mustered an eighth-inning single by Boyer against Jim O'Toole, who was on the mound after Bob Skinner pinch-hit for Maloney in the top of that inning. In the top of the ninth, however, Gibson finally broke. After retiring the first two hitters, he gave up consecutive singles to Coleman and Don Pavletich, threw a wild pitch, and then gave up a game-tying single to Leo Cardenas.

The Cardinals tried to win it in regulation against Al Worthington, loading the bases on two walks and a single with one out, but Flood grounded to Rose, who forced the runner at home, and then Dal Maxvill, who had replaced Groat at short, flied out to send the game into extra innings.

The Reds threatened in the top of the 10th. Rose doubled leading off and went to third on a sacrifice. After an intentional walk, Ron Taylor, who relieved Gibson after nine, struck out Frank Robinson for a huge second out. Coleman drew a walk but Taylor retired Pavletich to leave the bases full. While the Cardinals were going down quietly from the 10th through the 13th, the Reds threatened again in the 14th, when Cardenas singled and Ernie Broglio, who relieved Taylor in the 12th, threw two wild pitches, putting a runner on third with one out. Cincinnati could not push him across, though, as Joey Jay (the fifth Reds pitcher of the day) struck out and, after Rose walked, Tommy Harper popped out to first.

The game ended in the bottom of the inning. Jerry Buchek singled. Broglio tried but failed to advance him on a bunt, and Buchek was out at second. Flood singled, moving Broglio to second, and then the notoriously light-hitting Maxvill doubled, bringing Broglio in for the victory.

Not surprisingly, Musial was the "Star of the Game" on broadcaster Harry Caray's postgame show on KMOX radio.[16] There, the conversation centered on Musial's reflection on his career; among other things, he pointed to Warren Spahn as the best pitcher he had faced and Willie Mays as the best all-around player he had seen before giving way to an emotional admission: "This has been a terrific way to end my career, on a victorious note. Several times I came close to tears before the game, but I thought I had some reason.[17]

A half-hour later, Musial drove away from the ballpark. A *St. Louis Post-Dispatch* reporter wrote that kids with programs chased after him, yelling, "One more! One more!"[18]

But there weren't any more. Musial was finished.

SOURCES

In addition to the sources cited in the Notes, the author also consulted the *New York Times,* Baseball-Reference.com, and Retrosheet.org.

NOTES

1. "Musial's Record," *St. Louis Post-Dispatch,* September 30, 1963: 6B.
2. Bob Broeg, "Stan at $100,000 on First Hike in 6 Years," *The Sporting News,* February 5, 1958: 3.
3. Bob Broeg, "Rickey, 80, Hired by Redbirds as Player Personnel Consultant," *St. Louis Post-Dispatch,* October 29, 1962: 5C.
4. Bob Burnes, "B.R.'s Return Ruffles Redbird Feathers," *The Sporting News,* November 17, 1962: 7.
5. Bob Broeg, "Rickey's Proposal to Retire Musial Stirs Discord," *St. Louis Post-Dispatch,* November 6, 1962: 4C.
6. Stan Musial and Bob Broeg, *Stan Musial: The "Man's" Own Story as Told to Bob Broeg* (Garden City, New York: Doubleday & Company, 1964), 236.
7. Neal Russo, "Even in Auld Lang Syne, The Man Hits Grand Slam," *The Sporting News,* August 24, 1963: 7.

A souvenir pin commemorates Stan Musial's career with the Cardinals.

8. Don Page, "Dodger Banjo Parade vs. the Yankee Ballet," *Los Angeles Times,* September 28, 1963: 33.
9. Neal Russo, "The Last Stan Like the First: A Hero in a Cardinal Victory," *St. Louis Post-Dispatch*, September 30, 1963: 4B.
10. "The Last Stan Like the First: A Hero in a Cardinal Victory."
11. "The Last Stan Like the First: A Hero in a Cardinal Victory."
12. Ed Wilks, "Day Was Long for Stan, Not Long Enough for Fans," *St. Louis Post-Dispatch,* September 30, 1963: 4B.
13. Wilks.
14. Russo, "The Last Stan."
15. Lowell Reidenbaugh, "'A Day I Will Always Remember,'" *The Sporting News*, October 12, 1963: 19.
16. Reidenbaug.
17. Reidenbaugh.
18. Wilks.

CONTRIBUTORS

Chris Betsch has been a SABR member since 2019. He and his family reside in New Albany, Indiana, and he is a member of the Pee Wee Reese SABR Chapter (Louisville, Kentucky). Chris has written several SABR BioProject and Games Project articles, as well as articles for the newsletters of the Minor Leagues and Deadball Eras committees. He has contributed to SABR publications including *The 1939 Baltimore Elite Giants* and *When Minor League Baseball Almost Went Bust*.

A lifelong White Sox fan now living in Cedarburg, Wisconsin, **Ken Carrano** works as the business operations manager for SABR. He has been a SABR member since 1992 and has contributed to several SABR publications and the SABR Games Project. Ken and his Brewers' fan wife, Ann, share two children, two golden retrievers, and a mutual disdain for the blue side of Chicago.

Josh Chetwynd has written seven books, including *Baseball in Europe: A Country by Country History*. He is also a past recipient of a SABR Baseball Research Award. A long-time journalist and broadcaster, Chetwynd has served as an on-air analyst and host for baseball telecasts on both television and radio. As a player, Chetwynd competed at the NCAA Division I, independent minor league, and international levels. He was a member of the Great Britain National Baseball Team for a decade and was inducted into the British Baseball Hall of Fame in 2014.

Alan Cohen has been a SABR member since 2011. He chairs the BioProject fact-checking team, serves as vice president-treasurer of the Connecticut Smoky Joe Wood Chapter, and is a datacaster (MiLB stringer) with the Eastern League Hartford Yard Goats, the Double-A affiliate of the Colorado Rockies. He also works with the Retrosheet Negro Leagues project and has served on SABR's Negro League Committee. His biographies, game stories, and essays have appeared in more than 80 baseball-related publications. He has four children, nine grandchildren, and one great-grandchild, and resides in Connecticut with his wife, Frances, their cats, Zoe and Ava, and their dog, Buddy.

Everett "Ev" Cope joined SABR in 1979. From 1981 to 1986 he was chairman of the SABR Records Committee. In working with Cliff Kachline at the National Baseball Hall of Fame, and Paul MacFarlane at *The Sporting News*, Ev helped correct and add to player batting, fielding, baserunning, and pitching records. A monthly newsletter, *Roundin' Third*, was the result of unusual findings in doing records research as well as updating records of the current seasons. More recently the internet has led to creation and sharing of findings in an occasional email known as *Ev Cope's Baseball Records Digest*.

Richard Cuicchi joined SABR in 1983 and is an active member of the Schott-Pelican Chapter. Since his retirement as an information technology executive, Richard authored *Family Ties: A Comprehensive Collection of Facts and Trivia about Baseball's Relatives*. He has contributed to numerous SABR BioProject and Games Project publications. He does freelance writing and blogging about a variety of baseball topics on his website, TheTenthInning.com. Richard is a regular contributor to CrescentCitySports.com, where he writes about New Orleans baseball history. Richard lives in New Orleans with his wife, Mary.

Bruce Duncan is a retired Air Force officer who served 26 years on active duty, and an additional 14 years as Air Force Special Operations Command's deputy director for strategic plans. He is a lifelong Cardinals fan who loves anything and everything about baseball. His claim to fame is playing collegiate baseball with Hall of Famer Ozzie Smith while at Cal Poly San Luis Obispo in 1976 and playing a couple of years of semipro baseball in Santa Maria, California. Bruce became a member of SABR in 2024 and lives on Florida's Emerald Coast with his wife, Linda. He still competes as a somewhat decent shortstop for an "over-70" slow-pitch softball team in Florida.

Mike Eisenbath grew up an obsessed baseball fan in St. Charles, Missouri, still lives only one block from where he played wiffle ball in his backyard, and has passed his passion on to his four children and (most of) his six grandchildren. He went on to work more than 25 years as a professional sportswriter, with more than 10 of his 18 years at the *St. Louis Post-Dispatch* dedicated to covering the Cardinals and MLB. He is the author of *The Cardinals Encyclopedia* and has been assisting as an editor for the SABR BioProject for several years. Mike also is an avid collector of baseball cards and memorabilia, and he's a member of the SABR Baseball Cards Committee.

Jeff Findley has been a member of SABR since 2009. A native of Eastern Iowa, he did the only logical thing growing up in the heart of the Cubs-Cardinals rivalry – he embraced the 1969 Baltimore Orioles and became a lifelong fan. When he's not watching baseball, he works as an information security professional for a Fortune 50 financial services company in central

Illinois. He enjoys doing historical research and contributing to both the SABR BioProject and the Games Project.

A retired English professor, **Jan Finkel** joined SABR in 1994 and has attended every convention since 1995. He was born and grew up in Pittsburgh. Despite everything Stan did to the Pirates, he was and remains Jan's favorite player. Jan has contributed to several SABR endeavors, including the Biography Project, of which he was chief editor for over 10 years. He lives almost directly across the Allegheny River from PNC Park, and he and Judy enjoy a partial season package to Pirates games.

Jeremy Gibbs is a high-school teacher from St. Peters, Missouri, with a deep passion for baseball history. A lifelong St. Louis Cardinals fan, he enjoys catching games at Busch Stadium and competing in fantasy baseball. He lives in St. Peters with his wife, stepson, and their cat, Stanley "Musial" Gibbs, named after the Cardinals legend.

Chip Greene, a SABR member for 20 years, is the grandson of Nelson Greene, who pitched 15 games for the Brooklyn Dodgers. A frequent contributor to SABR's Biography Project, Chip lives with his wife, Elaine, in Waynesboro, Pennsylvania.

Vince Guerrieri is a journalist and author in the Cleveland area. He's the secretary-treasurer of the Jack Graney SABR Chapter, and has contributed to the SABR BioProject, the SABR Games Project, and several SABR anthologies, serving as an editor for the book on the 1945 Cleveland Buckeyes. Additionally, he's written about baseball history for a variety of publications, including *Ohio Magazine*, *Cleveland Magazine*, *Smithsonian*, and *Defector*. He can be reached at vaguerrieri@gmail.com or found on Twitter @vinceguerrieri.

Clem Hamilton began his career as a professor of horticulture and botany at the University of Washington (Seattle) and Claremont Graduate University in California, conducting fieldwork in Thailand, Panama, Chile, and Costa Rica. From 1992 through 2017 he served as chief executive officer and VP of research at botanical gardens and arboretums in Seattle, Claremont, Chicago, and Cleveland. In his retirement Clem conducts research focused primarily on Black baseball and presents at each year's SABR Jerry Malloy Conference. He also works for the St. Louis Cardinals as a part-time tour guide, museum docent, photographer, and instructor of energetic third- through sixth-graders. In 2022 he won the Jim Rygelski Research Award from SABR's Bob Broeg (St. Louis) chapter. Clem resides in St. Louis with his wife, Karen, and in close proximity to his daughter and granddaughter.

A love of baseball was instilled in **Andrew Harner** from childhood, but since he had next to no athletic skills, he instead dove into the game's history and pored over box scores as often as he could. And because baseball history wasn't offered as a college major, he settled for the next best thing – a bachelor's degree in sports journalism with a minor in history. He graduated from Bowling Green State University in 2010 and spent nearly seven years as a sports editor before leaving the newspaper industry to pursue a career in hospitality management. Andrew has since published baseball research for HowTheyPlay and spent a little over a year producing online NFL content for *Sports Illustrated*. He has been married to his wife, Elizabeth, since 2011, and they have two daughters.

Tom Hawthorn is a longtime newspaper and magazine writer. He is the author of *Play Ball!*, an anecdotal history of professional baseball in Vancouver, British Columbia, which is scheduled for publication during the 2025 season. He has also written *Deadlines*, *The Year Canadians Lost Their Minds and Found Their Country: The Centennial of 1967*, and *UVic Athletics: A Century of Excellence: The McKinnon Years*. He has served on the selection committees of two sports halls of fame and has been made an honorary member of Havana's Peña Deportivo for his writing on Cuban baseball. Born in Winnipeg and raised in Montreal and Toronto, he lives in Victoria, British Columbia, where he is a speechwriter for Premier David Eby. He is a member of Expos Nation and a proud Canadian citizen. Bats: Right. Throws: Up.

Andrew Heckroth is a professional librarian, freelance sportswriter, and lifelong St. Louis Cardinals fan. He graduated from Wartburg College with a BA in History in 2016 and from the University of Wisconsin-Madison with an MA in Library and Information Studies in 2018. He resides in Carroll, Iowa, with his cat, Harper.

Paul Hofmann has been a SABR member since 2002. He has contributed to more than 25 SABR publications and co-edited *The 1883 Philadelphia Athletics: American Association Champions*. Paul is currently the assistant vice provost for international affairs at the University of Louisville and teaches in the College of Management at National Changhua University of Education in Taiwan. A native of Detroit, Paul is an avid baseball card collector and lifelong Detroit Tigers fan. He currently resides in Lakeville, Minnesota.

Mike Huber is professor emeritus of mathematics at Muhlenberg College, where he routinely taught a course titled Reasoning With Sabermetrics. He also sponsored several undergraduate research projects involving simulating and predicting rare events in baseball, such as pitching a no-hitter or hitting for the cycle. He joined SABR in 1996 and enjoys writing and fact-checking for the Games Project.

Russ Lake lives in Champaign, Illinois, and is a retired college professor. The 1964 St. Louis Cardinals remain his favorite team. He was distressed to see Sportsman's Park (aka Busch Stadium I) being demolished not long after he had attended the last game there on May 8, 1966. His wife, Carol, deserves an MVP award for watching all of a 13-inning ballgame in Cincinnati with Russ in 1971 – during their honeymoon. In 1994 he was an editor for David Halberstam's baseball book *October 1964*.

For over 20 years, **Kevin Larkin** patrolled the highways and byways of his hometown, Great Barrington, Massachusetts. When not at work keeping the citizens of his hometown safe, inevitably Larkin was listening to a baseball game on the radio. He has been going to baseball games since he was 5 years old. His baseball life is the only thing he loves more than his children and grandchildren. He has written a number of books on baseball and the Civil War and also hosts his own radio show.

Len Levin is a longtime newspaper editor in New England, now retired. He lives in Providence with his wife, Linda, and an overachieving orange cat. He now (Len, not the cat) is the grammarian for the Rhode Island Supreme Court and copy-edits its decisions. He also copy-edits many SABR books, including this one. He is just down the interstate from Fenway Park, where he has spent many happy – and some not-so-happy – hours.

Nick Malian lives with his wife, daughter, and son in LaSalle, Ontario, where he was born and raised. Growing up in a border city, he idolized Detroit Tigers greats Cecil Fielder and Alan Trammell. However, as an impressionable 12-year-old, his allegiance shifted to the New York Yankees after their 1996 World Series victory. Nick is a pharmacist by day, an amateur chef by night, and found time to earn an Executive MBA degree at the Ivey Business School in London, Ontario, Canada.

Chad Moody is a nearly lifelong resident of the Detroit area, where he has been a fan of the Detroit Tigers from birth. An alumnus of both the University of Michigan and Michigan State University, he has spent over 30 years working in various supply-chain and finance roles within the automotive industry. Chad has contributed to numerous SABR and Professional Football Researchers Association projects. He and his wife, Lisa, live in Plymouth, Michigan, with their dog, Daisy.

Bill Nowlin has been active in SABR since the current century began and has written hundreds of articles, primarily for BioProject and the Games Project. He also finds great pleasure working with other SABR members in putting together many of SABR's books. A Boston native and lifelong Red Sox fan, he was one of founders of Rounder Records and more recently Down the Road Records. On more than one occasion, he heard Stan Musial play "Take Me Out to the Ball Game" on his harmonica.

Bill Pruden has been a teacher of American history and government for over 40 years. A SABR member for over two decades, he has contributed to SABR's BioProject and Games project as well as a number of book projects. He has also written on a range of American history subjects, an interest undoubtedly fueled by the fact that as a seven-year-old he was at Yankee Stadium to witness Roger Maris's historic 61st home run.

Carl Riechers never saw Stan Musial play. However, on a Sunday evening in 1967 he was accompanying his parents taking his aunt and uncle to the airport to catch a flight home. Who does he spot but the St. Louis Cardinals returning from a day game in Pittsburgh. And walking with the group is the team's general manager, Stan Musial, and lead broadcaster, Jack Buck. Carl frantically asks for a paper and pen so he can get an autograph. His mom said they had no time but his aunt pulled out autograph implements from her fully stocked purse and handed them over with the command, "Run!" Carl high-tailed it over and both men signed his sheet. While Buck signed, Stan politely asked Carl if he played ball and Carl bored the great man with his talk of playing catcher on his Little League team. He'll never forget Stan's manners and the fact that he actually listened to young Carl's story. Thanks for the memories, Stan and Jack. And the precious autographs? One week later, Carl's sister lost the paper with the autographs at a school show and tell.

Paul Rogers is the president of the Ernie Banks – Bobby Bragan (Dallas-Fort Worth) SABR Chapter and the co-author of four baseball books, including *The Whiz Kids and the 1950 Pennant* written with his boyhood hero Robin Roberts, and *Lucky Me: My 65 Years in Baseball*, authored with Eddie Robinson. He is also co-editor of SABR team histories of the 1951 New York Giants and the 1950 Philadelphia Phillies as well as a frequent contributor to the SABR BioProject and Games Project. His real job is as a law professor at SMU, where he was dean of the law school for nine years and has served as the university's faculty athletic representative for 38 years.

Tom Schott joined SABR in 2020 and has written for the BioProject and Games Project and contributed to several books. He got his start in sports journalism at age 12 when he co-founded his own magazine called *The Redbird Chirps*, interviewing nearly 100 major-league players, managers, coaches, and broadcasters from 1981 to 1986. A native of St. Louis, Schott has been a contributing writer for the Cardinals media guide, Hall of Fame induction program, magazine, and website (Cardinals.com). He is co-author of *The Giants Encyclopedia* and *The Giants Encyclopedia: Second Edition* – the definitive history of the New York and San Francisco Giants franchise. He also has written for the Giants website (SFGiants.com), the Atlanta Braves media guide and website (Braves.com), and the National Baseball Hall of Fame and Museum website (BaseballHall.org). Schott resides in West Lafayette, Indiana, with his wife, Jane. They have two sons, August and Sam.

Joe Schuster is the author of the baseball novel *The Might Have Been*, which was a finalist for the CASEY Award for 2012. He has published more than 500 articles, essays, and reviews in national and regional magazines as well as in metropolitan newspapers, and has contributed nearly 30 articles to several SABR publications, including *One-Win Wonders, One-Hit Wonders, 20-Game Losers,* and *Sweet 60: the 1960 Pittsburgh Pirates,* among others. He retired from Webster University in 2018 after teaching for a third of a century. Married, he is the father of five children and three grandchildren – all of whom live and breathe Cardinals baseball.

Glen Sparks has co-edited several books for SABR, including this one on Stan Musial, and others on Babe Ruth, Jackie Robinson, Roberto Clemente, Willie Mays, and Sandy Koufax. A lifelong Dodgers fan, he wrote the first full-length biography of Pee Wee Reese, published by McFarland in 2023. Sparks has a journalism degree from the University of Missouri and worked for several years in the newspaper field. He lives with his wife, Pam, and two cats, Kasper and Buster, plus a large aquarium that includes a trio of tetras known collectively as the Stooges.

Danny Spewak is a journalist and author who has written two nonfiction books on sports history. A native of the St. Louis area and a lifelong fan of the Cardinals, Spewak graduated from the University of Missouri with dual degrees in journalism and political science. He joined SABR in 2022 while working on his second book, *Cardinal Dreams: The Legacy of Charlie Peete and a Life Cut Short,* which tells the story of a top St. Louis Cardinals prospect whose promising career was cut short in a 1956 commercial plane crash. Spewak's first book, *From the Gridiron to the Battlefield,* was a finalist for the Emilie Buchwald Award for Minnesota Nonfiction.

A native New Yorker and longtime fan of the Yankees who has lived deep in enemy territory in greater Boston for nearly three decades, **Mark S. Sternman** has no particular connection to Stan Musial although Sternman would have pulled for Musial in the 1946 World Series since he played against the Red Sox.

Gregory H. Wolf was born in Pittsburgh but now resides in the Chicagoland area with his wife, Margaret. A professor of German studies and holder of the Dennis and Jean Bauman Endowed Chair in the Humanities at North Central College in Naperville, Illinois, he has edited more than a dozen books for SABR. Since January 2017 he has been co-director of SABR's BioProject, which you can follow on Facebook and X.

Rick Zucker is a retired regulatory attorney. He grew up and lives in the city where Stan Musial was, is, and always will be the gold standard. Rick played D3 baseball for Washington University in St. Louis, in the pre-NIL days. He is active in the Bob Broeg SABR Chapter and served as president from 2018 to 2022. He is proud to have won the chapter's Rygelski Research Conference award in 2017. He created a poster for the SABR 51 convention in Chicago with the help of his daughter, Samantha, a crackerjack graphic design artist.

Unveiled in 1968, this Stan Musial statue is a familiar meeting place for Cardinal fans before the game. Photograph by Glen Sparks.

SABR Books on Significant Players and Figures in Baseball

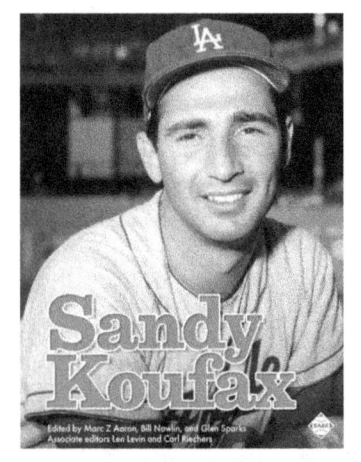

SANDY KOUFAX

SABR's book on Sandy Koufax explores what made him so special in baseball and American society through 17 insightful essays and recaps of 36 key games in his career. Touching on subjects from Koufax's potential basketball (!) career, his relationship with manager Walt Alston, celebrity culture in LA, and his effect on the hurlers who came after him, to analyses of Koufax's stats and records, SANDY KOUFAX takes a deep dive into one of baseball's true greats. Many pitchers enjoyed longer careers than Sandy Koufax. Few, however, reached the glorious heights of this Dodgers left-hander.

Edited by Marc Z Aaron, Bill Nowlin, and Glen Sparks
Associate Editors: Len Levin and Carl Riechers
ISBN (ebook): 978-1-960819-26-0, $9.99
ISBN (paperback): 978-1-960819-27-7, $24.95
8.5" x 11", 186 pages

WILLIE MAYS, FIVE TOOLS

Willie Mays thrilled baseball fans for more than two decades. He could do it all—in the outfield, at bat, and on the bases. Five Tools tells the story of arguably the greatest baseball player in the game's history, through more than 20 insightful essays and recaps of over 30 of the most significant games in his career. Some essays explore Mays' time in the Negro Leagues and minor leagues, while others examine the the relationship of Mays to his managers, the press, and his mentoring of Bobby and Barry Bonds.

Edited by Bill Nowlin and Glen Sparks
Associate editors: Len Levin and Carl Riechers
978-1-960819-02-4 (ebook) $9.99
978-1-960819-03-1 (paperback) $29.95
8.5"X11", 308 pages

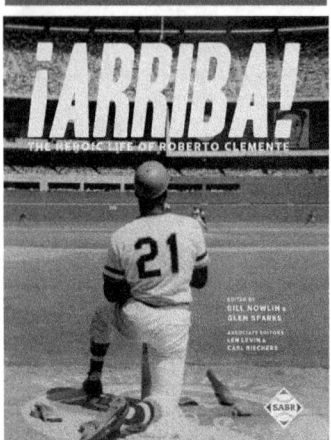

¡ARRIBA!
THE HEROIC LIFE OF ROBERTO CLEMENTE

The first universally acknowledged Latino inductee into the National Baseball Hall of Fame, Roberto Clemente played every one of his 18 seasons for the Pittsburgh Pirates. He became the 11th player to reach the 3,000-hit milestone, finishing his final season by hitting number 3000 on the season's last day. Named to 15 All-Star Game squads, Clemente also won 12 Gold Gloves, four batting titles, and was the National League's Most Valuable Player in 1966. He was twice a World Series champion, winning with the Pirates in both 1960 and 1971.

Edited by Bill Nowlin and Glen Sparks
Associate Editors: Len Levin and Carl Riechers
ISBN (ebook): 978-1-970159-87-5, $9.99
ISBN (paperback): 978-1-970159-88-2, $34.95
8.5" x 11", 338 pages

NOT AN EASY TALE TO TELL:
JACKIE ROBINSON ON THE PAGE, STAGE, AND SCREEN

Few athletes have sparked the creative imaginations of artists more than Jackie Robinson. His presence can be seen in cinema, on television and on stages, big and small; even tucked within the pages of written fiction. As we celebrate the seventy-fifth anniversary of Robinson's integration of the Dodgers, he continues to inspire, including a recent appearance in HBO's groundbreaking *Lovecraft Country*. Artists keep returning to Robinson because he is one of the most inspirational figures of the twentieth century not in spite of, but because of his complexities. He did more than change the game of baseball—he changed America.

Edited by Ralph Carhart
Associate Editors: Bill Nowlin, Carl Riechers, and Kate Nachman
ISBN (paperback): 978-1-970159-72-1, $19.95 US
ISBN (ebook): 978-1-970159-71-4, $9.99
128 pages, 8.5" x 11"

SABR has published over 100 books of baseball research, on topics ranging from championship teams to the Negro Leagues to great games in bygone stadiums to Babe Ruth. SABR members can purchase the paperbacks for half price and access the ebooks for free as a member benefit. Visit SABR.org to learn more.

More Books From SABR!
SABR Members can download all SABR publications for free, and purchase hard copies at a deep discount, usually 50% off cover price.

One-Win Wonders
ISBN 9978-1-960819-13-0 $39.95 paperback
ISBN 9978-1-960819-12-3 $9.99 ebook

Biographies of 78 players whose entire major-league pitching record consisted of just one win: from the tragic, like Nick Adenhart, an Angels rookie who was killed by a drunk driver, to the improbable, like catcher Brent Mayne, who was the last player left on the Colorado Rockies bench in an extra inning game after the final bullpen pitcher was ejected.

One-Hit Wonders
ISBN 978-1-9701-5956-1 $32.95 paperback
ISBN 978-1-9701-5957-8 $9.99 ebook

The stories of 70 players who got exactly one hit in the majors. Some, like pitcher Arthur Rhodes, were in the big leagues a long time. Rhodes appeared in 900 games but only notched one base hit. Others, like Dan Ardell, had only a cup of coffee. When asked if he thought his story wouldn't have been as interesting if he'd had TWO hits, Ardell replied, "I think that's exactly true."

Baseball's Greatest Comeback Games
ISBN 978-1-9701-5946-2, $9.99 ebook
ISBN 978-1-9701-5947-9, $29.95 paperback

What are Major League Baseball's greatest comeback games? Retrosheet ranked a master list of 630 games and we include the top 64, plus seven postseason games in this volume. In the end, every major-league team is represented. The Phillies lead the list with six comeback wins in the top 64. Tied for second for most comebacks are four American League teams: the Boston Red Sox, Cleveland Indians/Guardians, Detroit Tigers, and New York Yankees.

Baseball's Biggest Blowout Games
ISBN 978-1-9701-5943-1, $24.95 paperback
ISBN 978-1-9701-5942-4, $9.99 ebook

The most lopsided games in major-league baseball history. Since 1901, the biggest blowout game in major-league history was on August 22, 2007, when the Texas Rangers beat the Baltimore Orioles, 30-3—a 27-run difference. It eclipsed the 25 runs between the Red Sox and Browns on June 8, 1950, 29-4, a game that followed a 20-4 blowout the day before! We've included the top four games for each franchise so every fan can have a chance to read about their team winning big, plus the six biggest blowouts from the postseason.

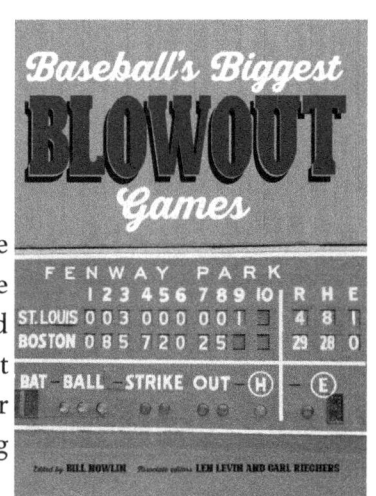